NTC's
Super-Mini
ENGLISH
IDIOMS
Dictionary

Richard A. Spears, Ph.D.
Betty Kirkpatrick

NTC Publishing Group

Library of Congress Cataloging-in-Publication Data

Spears, Richard A.
    [Essential English idioms]
    NTC's super-mini English idioms dictionary / Richard A. Spears, Betty Kirkpatrick.
        p.   cm. — (NTC's super-minis)
    Originally published as Essential English idioms—T.p. verso.
    Includes index.
    ISBN 0-8442-0108-1
    1. English language—Idioms—Dictionaries.   I. Kirkpatrick, E. M.
(Elizabeth McLaren).   II. NTC Publishing Group.   III. Title.   IV. Series.
PE1464.S64   1999
423'.1—dc21
                                                                            99-58277
                                                                                    CIP

Interior design by Terry Stone

Originally published as *Essential English Idioms*

This edition first published in 2000 by NTC Publishing Group
A division of NTC/Contemporary Publishing Group, Inc.
4255 West Touhy Avenue, Lincolnwood (Chicago), Illinois 60712-1975 U.S.A.
Copyright © 2000 by NTC/Contemporary Publishing Group, Inc.
Printed in Canada
International Standard Book Number : 978-0-8442-0108-5
        20 19 18 17 16 15 14 13 12 11 10 9 8 7 6 5

Contents

To the User

All languages have phrases or sentences that cannot be understood literally. Even if you know all the words in a phrase and understand all the grammar of the phrase completely, the meaning may still not be apparent. Many proverbs, informal phrases, and common sayings offer this kind of problem. A phrase or sentence of this type is said to be idiomatic. This dictionary is a collection of the idiomatic phrases and sentences that occur frequently in the varieties of English that follow the British standard.

The dictionary is designed for easy use by lifelong speakers of English, as well as by the new-to-English speaker or learner. Readers who are native speakers of American, Australian, Canadian, or other varieties of English will find the entries fascinating and entertaining. Special features, such as numerous full-sentence examples and a Phrase-Finder Index, make this dictionary uniquely effective for language learners.

How to Use
This Dictionary

First, try looking up the complete phrase in the dictionary. The entries are in absolute alphabetical order; that is, phrases are alphabetized letter by letter, disregarding spaces, hyphens, and punctuation. Entry phrases are never inverted or reordered. For example, **in the same boat** is listed under **in**, not as **the same boat, in**; **boat, in the same**; or **same boat, in the**. In the entry heads, the word *someone* or *one* stands for persons, and *something* stands for things.

If you do not find the phrase you want, or if you cannot decide exactly what the phrase is, look up any of its major words in the Phrase-Finder Index, which begins on page 207. There you will find listed, under the key word you have looked up, all the phrases that contain that word. Pick out the phrase you want, and look it up in the main body of the dictionary.

Terms and Symbols

☐   (a box) marks the beginning of an example.

ALSO: introduces additional forms within an entry that are related to the main entry head.

AND   indicates that an entry head has variant forms that are the same as, or similar to, the entry head in meaning. One or more variant forms may be preceded by AND.

entry head   is the first word or phrase, in boldface type, of an entry; the word or phrase that the definition explains.

see   means to turn to the entry head indicated.

see also   means to consult the entry head indicated for additional information or to find expressions similar in form or meaning to the entry head containing the "see also" instruction.

see under   means to search within the text of the entry indicated for a phrase that is in boldface type and introduced by ALSO.

A

above one's station higher than one's social class or position in society. □ *He has been educated above his station and is now ashamed of his parents' poverty.* □ *She is getting above her station since she started working in the office. She ignores her old friends in the warehouse.*

above someone's head too difficult or clever for someone to understand. □ *The children have no idea what the new teacher is talking about. Her ideas are way above their heads.* □ *She started a physics course, but it turned out to be miles above her head.*

according to one's (own) lights according to the way one believes; according to the way one's conscience or inclinations lead one. □ *People must act on this matter according to their own lights.* □ *John may have been wrong, but he did what he did according to his lights.*

act the goat deliberately to behave in a silly or eccentric way; to play the fool. (Informal.) □ *He was asked to leave the class because he was always acting the goat.* □ *No one takes him seriously. He acts the goat too much.*

advanced in years old; elderly. □ *My uncle is advanced in years and can't hear too well.* □ *Many people lose their hearing somewhat when they are advanced in years.*

afraid of one's own shadow easily frightened; always frightened, timid, or suspicious. □ *After Tom was robbed, he was afraid of his own shadow.* □ *Jane has always been a shy child. She has been afraid of her own shadow since she was three.*

aid and abet someone to help someone, especially in a crime or misdeed; to incite someone to do something which is wrong. □ *He was scolded for aiding and abetting the boys who were fighting.* □ *It's illegal to aid and abet a thief.*

air of sanctity See odour of sanctity.

1

airs and graces proud behaviour adopted by one who is trying to impress others by appearing more important than one actually is. □ *She is only a junior secretary, but from her airs and graces you would think she was managing director.* □ *Jane has a very humble background—despite her airs and graces.*

(all) at sea (about something) confused; lost and bewildered. □ *Mary is all at sea about the process of getting married.* □ *When it comes to maths, John is totally at sea.*

all ears (and eyes) listening eagerly and carefully. (Informal.) □ *Well, hurry up and tell me! I'm all ears.* □ *Be careful what you say. The children are all ears and eyes.*

(all) Greek to me unintelligible to me. (Usually with some form of *be.*) □ *I can't understand it. It's Greek to me.* □ *It's all Greek to me. Maybe Sally knows what it means.*

all hours (of the day and night) very late in the night or very early in the morning. □ *Why do you always stay out until all hours of the day and night?* □ *I like to stay out until all hours partying.*

all over bar the shouting decided and concluded; finished except for the formalities. (Informal. An elaboration of *all over,* which means "finished.") □ *The last goal was made just as the final whistle sounded. Tom said, "Well, it's all over bar the shouting."* □ *Tom has finished his exams and is waiting to graduate. It's all over bar the shouting.*

all skin and bones See nothing but skin and bones.

all thumbs very awkward and clumsy, especially with one's hands. (Informal.) □ *Poor Bob can't play the piano at all. He's all thumbs.* □ *Mary is all thumbs when it comes to gardening.*

all to the good for the best; for one's benefit. □ *He missed his train, but it was all to the good because the train had a crash.* □ *It was all to the good that he died before his wife. He couldn't have coped without her.*

any port in a storm a phrase indicating that when one is in difficulties one must accept any way out, whether one likes the solution or not. □ *I don't want to live with my parents, but it's a case of any port in a storm. I can't find a flat.* □ *He hates his job, but he can't get another. Any port in a storm, you know.*

apple of someone's eye someone's favourite person or thing. □ *Tom is the apple of Mary's eye. She thinks he's great.* □ *Jean is the apple of her father's eye.*

armed to the teeth heavily armed with weapons. □ *The bank robber was armed to the teeth when he was caught.* □ *There are too many guns around. The entire country is armed to the teeth.*

as a duck takes to water easily and naturally. (Informal.) □ *She took to singing just as a duck takes to water.* □ *The baby adapted to the feeding-bottle as a duck takes to water.*

as black as one is painted as evil or unpleasant as one is thought to be. (Usually negative.) □ *The landlord is not as black as he is painted. He seems quite generous.* □ *Young people are rarely as black as they are painted in the media.*

(as) black as pitch very black; very dark. □ *The night was as black as pitch.* □ *The rocks seemed black as pitch against the silver sand.*

(as) bold as brass brazen; very bold and impertinent. □ *She went up to her lover's wife, bold as brass.* □ *The girl arrives late every morning as bold as brass.*

(as) bright as a button very intelligent; extremely alert. □ *The little girl is as bright as a button.* □ *Her new dog is bright as a button.*

(as) calm as a millpond [for water to be] exceptionally calm. (Referring to the still water in a pond around a mill in contrast to the fast-flowing stream which supplies it.) □ *The English channel was calm as a millpond that day.* □ *Jane gets seasick even when the sea is calm as a millpond.*

(as) cold as charity 1. very cold; icy. □ *The room was as cold as charity.* □ *It was snowing and the moors were cold as charity.* **2.** very unresponsive; lacking in passion. □ *Their mother keeps them clean and fed, but she is cold as charity.* □ *John's sister is generous and welcoming, but John is as cold as charity.*

(as) fit as a fiddle healthy and physically fit. (Informal.) □ *In spite of her age, Mary is as fit as a fiddle.* □ *Tom used to be fit as a fiddle. Look at him now!*

(as) happy as a lark visibly happy and cheerful. (Note the variations in the examples.) □ *Sally walked along whistling, as happy as a lark.* □ *The children danced and sang, happy as larks.*

(as) happy as a sandboy AND **(as) happy as Larry; (as) happy as the day is long** very happy; carefree. □ *Mary's as happy as a sandboy now that she is at home all day with her children.* □ *Peter earns very little money, but he's happy as Larry in his job.* □ *The old lady has many friends and is happy as the day is long.*

(as) happy as Larry See (as) happy as a sandboy.

(as) happy as the day is long See (as) happy as a sandboy.

(as) hungry as a hunter very hungry. □ *I'm as hungry as a hunter. I could eat anything!* □ *Whenever I jog, I get hungry as a hunter.*

(as) large as life (and twice as ugly) an exaggerated way of saying that a person or a thing actually appeared in a particular place. (Informal.) □ *The little child just stood there as large as life and laughed very hard.* □ *I opened the door, and there was Tom, large as life.* □ *I came home and found this cat in my chair, as large as life and twice as ugly.*

asleep at the wheel not attending to one's assigned task; failing to do one's duty at the proper time. □ *I should have spotted the error. I must have been asleep at the wheel.* □ *The management must have been asleep at the wheel to let the firm get into such a state.*

(as) near as dammit very nearly. (Informal.) □ *He earns sixty thousand pounds a year as near as dammit.* □ *She was naked near as dammit.*

(as) plain as a pikestaff very obvious; clearly visible. (*Pikestaff* was originally *packstaff*, a stick on which a pedlar's or traveller's pack was supported. The original reference was to the smoothness of this staff, although the allusion is to another sense of plain: clear or obvious.) □ *The 'no parking' sign was as plain as a pikestaff. How did he miss it?* □ *It's plain as a pikestaff. The children are unhappy.*

(as) pleased as Punch very pleased or happy. (From the puppet-show character, who is depicted as smiling gleefully.) □ *The little girl was pleased as Punch with her new dress.* □ *Jack's as pleased as Punch with his new car.*

(as) quiet as the grave very quiet; silent. □ *The house is as quiet as the grave when the children are at school.* □ *This town is quiet as the grave now that the offices have closed.*

(as) safe as houses completely safe. □ *The children will be as safe as houses on holiday with your parents.* □ *The dog will be safe as houses in the boarding-kennels.*

(as) sound as a bell in perfect condition or health; undamaged. □ *The doctor says the old man's heart is as sound as a bell.* □ *I thought the vase was broken when it fell, but it was sound as a bell.*

(as) thick as thieves very close-knit; friendly; allied. (Informal.) □ *Mary, Tom, and Sally are as thick as thieves. They go everywhere together.* □ *Those two families are thick as thieves.*

(as) thick as two short planks very stupid. (Informal.) □ *Jim must be as thick as two short planks, not able to understand the plans.* □ *Some of the children are clever, but the rest are as thick as two short planks.*

(as) thin as a rake very thin; too thin. □ *Mary's thin as a rake since she's been ill.* □ *Jean's been on a diet and is now as thin as a rake.*

at a loose end restless and unsettled; unemployed. (Informal.) □ *Just before school starts, all the children are at a loose end.* □ *When Tom is home at the week-ends, he's always at a loose end.* □ *Jane has been at a loose end ever since she lost her job.*

at a pinch if absolutely necessary. □ *At a pinch, I could come tomorrow, but it's not really convenient.* □ *He could commute to work from home at a pinch, but it is a long way.*

at a rate of knots very fast. (Informal.) □ *They'll have to drive at a rate of knots to get there on time.* □ *They were travelling at a rate of knots when they passed us.*

at death's door near death. (Euphemistic.) □ *I was so ill that I was at death's door.* □ *The family dog was at death's door for three days, and then it finally died.*

at first glance when first examined; at an early stage. □ *At first glance, the problem appeared quite simple. Later we learned just how complex it really was.* □ *He appeared quite healthy at first glance.*

at full stretch with as much energy and strength as possible. □ *The police are working at full stretch to find the murderer.* □ *We cannot accept any more work. We are already working at full stretch.*

at half-mast half-way up or down. (Primarily referring to flags. Can be used for things other than flags as a joke.) □ *The flag was flying at half-mast because the general had died.* □ *We fly flags at half-mast when someone important dies.* □ *The little boy ran out of the house with his trousers at half-mast.*

at large free; uncaptured. (Usually said of criminals running loose.) □ *At midday the day after the robbery, the thieves were still at large.* □ *There is a murderer at large in the city.*

at liberty free; unrestrained. □ *You're at liberty to go anywhere you wish.* □ *I'm not at liberty to discuss the matter.*

at loggerheads (with someone) in opposition; at an impasse; in a quarrel. □ *Mr. and Mrs. Jones have been at loggerheads with each other for years.* □ *The two political parties were at loggerheads during the entire legislative session.*

at one's wits' end at the limits of one's mental resources. □ *I'm at my wits' end trying to solve this problem.* □ *Tom could do no more to earn money. He was at his wits' end.*

at sixes and sevens disorderly; completely disorganized. (Informal.) □ *Mrs. Smith is at sixes and sevens since the death of her husband.* □ *The house is always at sixes and sevens when Bill's home by himself.*

at someone's beck and call always ready to obey someone. □ *What makes you think I wait around here at your beck and call? I live here, too, you know!* □ *It was a fine hotel. There were dozens of maids and waiters at our beck and call.*

at the bottom of the ladder at the lowest level of pay and status. □ *Most people start work at the bottom of the ladder.* □ *When Ann was declared redundant, she had to start all over again at the bottom of the ladder.*

at the drop of a hat immediately and without urging. □ *John was always ready to go fishing at the drop of a hat.* □ *If you need help, just call on me. I can come at the drop of a hat.*

at the eleventh hour at the last possible moment. (Biblical.) □ *She always handed her term essays in at the eleventh hour.* □ *We don't worry about death until the eleventh hour.*

at the end of one's tether at the limits of one's endurance. □ *I'm at the end of my tether! I just can't go on this way!* □ *These children are driving me out of my mind. I'm at the end of my tether.*

at the expense of someone or something to the detriment of someone or something; to the harm or disadvantage of someone or something. □ *He had a good laugh at the expense of his brother.* □ *He took employment in a better place at the expense of a larger income.*

at the top of one's voice with a very loud voice. □ *Bill called to Mary at the top of his voice.* □ *How can I work when you're all talking at the top of your voices?*

avoid someone or something like the plague to avoid someone or something totally. (Informal.) □ *What's wrong with Bob? Everyone avoids him like the plague.* □ *I don't like opera. I avoid it like the plague.*

B

babe in arms an innocent or naive person. (Informal.) □ He's a babe in arms when it comes to taking girls out. □ Mary has no idea how to fight the election. Politically, she's a babe in arms.

back of beyond the most remote place; somewhere very remote. (Informal.) □ John hardly ever comes to the city. He lives at the back of beyond. □ Mary likes lively entertainment, but her husband likes to holiday in the back of beyond.

back to the drawing-board [it is] time to start over again; [it is] time to plan something over again, especially if it has gone wrong. (Also with *old* as in the examples.) □ The scheme didn't work. Back to the drawing-board. □ I failed English this term. Well, back to the old drawing-board.

bag and baggage with one's luggage; with all one's possessions. (Informal.) □ Sally showed up at our door bag and baggage one Sunday morning. □ All right, if you won't pay the rent, out with you, bag and baggage!

baptism of fire a first experience of something, usually something difficult or unpleasant. □ My son's just had his first visit to the dentist. He stood up to the baptism of fire very well. □ Mary's had her baptism of fire as a teacher. She had to take the worst class in the school.

beard the lion in his den to face an adversary on the adversary's home ground. □ I went to the solicitor's office to beard the lion in his den. □ He said he hadn't wanted to come to my home, but it was better to beard the lion in his den.

beat about the bush to avoid answering a question or discussing a subject directly; to stall; to waste time. □ Let's stop beating about the bush and discuss this matter. □ Stop beating about the bush and answer my question.

beat a (hasty) retreat to retreat or withdraw very quickly. □ *We went out into the cold weather, but beat a retreat to the warmth of our fire.* □ *The cat beat a hasty retreat to its own garden when it saw the dog.*

be a thorn in someone's side to be a constant source of annoyance to someone. □ *This problem is a thorn in my side. I wish I had a solution to it.* □ *John was a thorn in my side for years before I finally got rid of him.*

bed of roses a situation or way of life that is always happy and comfortable. □ *Living with Pat can't be a bed of roses, but her husband is always smiling.* □ *Being the boss isn't exactly a bed of roses. There are so many problems to sort out.*

before you can say Jack Robinson almost immediately. □ *And before you could say Jack Robinson, the bird flew away.* □ *I'll catch a plane and be there before you can say Jack Robinson.*

be getting on for something to be close to something; to be nearly at something, such as a time, date, age, etc. (Informal.) □ *It's getting on for midnight.* □ *He must be getting on for fifty.*

beggar description to be impossible to describe well enough to give an accurate picture; to be impossible to do justice to in words. □ *Her cruelty to her child beggars description.* □ *The soprano's voice beggars description.*

beg off to ask to be released from something; to refuse an invitation. □ *I have an important meeting, so I'll have to beg off.* □ *I wanted to go to the affair, but I had to beg off.*

believe it or not to choose to believe something or not. □ *Believe it or not, I just got home from work.* □ *I'm over fifty years old, believe it or not.*

bend someone's ear to talk to someone at length, perhaps annoyingly. (Informal.) □ *Tom is over there bending Jane's ear about something.* □ *I'm sorry. I didn't mean to bend your ear for an hour, but I'm upset.*

be old hat to be old-fashioned; to be outmoded. (Informal.) □ *That's a silly idea. It's old hat.* □ *Nobody does that any more. That's just old hat.*

be poles apart to be very different, especially in opinions or attitudes; to be far from coming to an agreement. □ *Mr. and Mrs. Jones don't get along well. They are poles apart.* □ *They'll never sign the contract because they are poles apart.*

best bib and tucker one's best clothing. (Informal.) □ *I always put on my best bib and tucker on Sundays.* □ *Put on your best bib and tucker, and let's go to the city.*

be thankful for small mercies to be grateful for any small benefits or advantages one has, especially in a generally difficult situation. □ *We have very little money, but we must be grateful for small mercies. At least we have enough food.* □ *Bob was badly injured in the accident, but at least he's still alive. Let's be grateful for small mercies.*

beyond one's ken outside the extent of one's knowledge or understanding. □ *Why she married him is beyond our ken.* □ *His attitude to others is quite beyond my ken.*

beyond the pale unacceptable; outlawed. (The Pale historically was the area of English government around Dublin. The people who lived outside this area were regarded as uncivilized.) □ *Your behaviour is simply beyond the pale.* □ *Because of Tom's rudeness, he's considered beyond the pale and is never asked to parties any more.*

beyond the shadow of a doubt AND **beyond any shadow of doubt** completely without doubt. (Said of a fact, not a person.) □ *We accepted her story as true beyond the shadow of a doubt.* □ *Please assure us that you are certain of the facts beyond any shadow of doubt.*

beyond words more than one can say. (Especially with *grateful* and *thankful*.) □ *Sally was thankful beyond words at being released.* □ *I don't know how to thank you. I'm grateful beyond words.*

bide one's time to wait patiently. □ *I've been biding my time for years, just waiting for a chance like this.* □ *He's not the type to just sit there and bide his time. He wants some action.*

bite someone's head off to speak sharply and angrily to someone. (Informal.) □ *There was no need to bite Mary's head off just because she was five minutes late.* □ *The boss has been biting everybody's head off since his wife left him.*

bite the hand that feeds one to do harm to someone who does good things for you. □ *I'm your mother! How can you bite the hand* *that feeds you?* □ *It's a real case of biting the hand that feeds her. She's reported her stepmother to the police for shop-lifting.*

bitter pill to swallow an unpleasant fact that has to be accepted. □ *It was a bitter pill for her brother to swallow when she married his enemy.* □ *We found his deception a bitter pill to swallow.*

black sheep (of the family) a member of a family or group who is unsatisfactory or not up to the standard of the rest; the worst member of the family. □ *Mary is the black sheep of the family. She's always in trouble with the police.* □ *The others are all in well-paid jobs, but John is unemployed. He's the black sheep of the family.*

blank cheque freedom or permission to act as one wishes or thinks necessary. (From a signed bank cheque with the amount left blank.) □ *He's been given a blank cheque with regard to reorganizing the work-force.* □ *The manager has been given no instructions about how to train the staff. He's just been given a blank cheque.*

blow hot and cold to be changeable or uncertain (about some-thing). (Informal.) □ *He keeps blowing hot and cold on the question of moving to the country.* □ *He blows hot and cold about this. I wish he'd make up his mind.*

blow off steam See let off steam.

blow one's own trumpet to boast; to praise oneself. □ *Tom is always blowing his own trumpet. Is he really as good as he says he is?* □ *I find it hard to blow my own trumpet, so no one takes any notice of me.*

blow the lid off (something) to reveal something, especially wrongdoing; to make wrongdoing public. (Informal.) □ *The police blew the lid off the smuggling ring.* □ *The journalists blew the lid off the group's illegal activities.*

blow up in someone's face [for something] suddenly to get ruined or destroyed while seeming to go well. □ *All my plans blew up in my face when she broke off the engagement.* □ *It is terrible for your hopes of promotion to blow up in your face.*

blue blood the blood [heredity] of a noble family; aristocratic ancestry. □ *The earl refuses to allow anyone who is not of blue blood to marry his son.* □ *Although Mary's family are poor, she has blue blood in her veins.*

bone of contention the subject or point of an argument; an unsettled point of disagreement. □ *We've fought for so long that we've forgotten what the bone of contention is.* □ *The question of a fence between the houses has become quite a bone of contention.*

born with a silver spoon in one's mouth born with many advantages; born to a wealthy family; born to have good fortune. □ *Sally was born with a silver spoon in her mouth.* □ *It never rains when he goes on holiday. He was born with a silver spoon in his mouth.*

bow and scrape to be very humble and subservient. □ *Please don't bow and scrape. We are all equal here.* □ *The shop assistant came in, bowing and scraping, and asked if he could help us.*

Box and Cox two people who keep failing to meet. (Although they both sometimes go to the same place, they are never there at the same time. From characters in a nineteenth-century play, one of whom rented a room by day, the other the same room by night.) □ *Since her husband started doing night-shifts, they are Box and Cox. She leaves for work in the morning before he gets home.* □ *The two teachers are Box and Cox. Mr. Smith takes class on Monday and Wednesday, and Mr. Brown on Tuesday and Thursday.*

break new ground to begin to do something which no one else has done; to pioneer (in an enterprise). □ *Dr. Anderson was breaking new ground in cancer research.* □ *They were breaking new ground in consumer electronics.*

break one's duck to have one's first success at something. (From a cricketing expression meaning "to begin scoring.") □ *At last Jim's broken his duck. He's got a girl to go out with him.* □ *Jane has failed all her exams up until now, but she's broken her duck by passing French.*

break one's word not to do what one said one would; not to keep one's promise. □ *Don't say you'll visit your grandmother if you can't go. She hates for people to break their word.* □ *If you break your word, she won't trust you again.*

break someone's fall to cushion a falling person; to lessen the impact of a falling person. □ *When the little boy fell out of the window, the bushes broke his fall.* □ *The old lady slipped on the ice, but a snowbank broke her fall.*

break someone's heart to cause someone emotional pain. □ *It just broke my heart when Tom ran away from home.* □ *Sally broke John's heart when she refused to marry him.*

break the ice to start social communication and conversation. □ *Tom is so outgoing. He's always the first one to break the ice at parties.* □ *It's hard to break the ice at formal events.*

break the news (to someone) to tell someone some important news, usually bad news. □ *The doctor had to break the news to Jane about her husband's cancer.* □ *I hope that the doctor broke the news gently.*

breathe down someone's neck to keep close watch on someone, causing worry and irritation; to watch someone's activities, especially to try to hurry something along. (Informal. Refers to standing very close behind a person.) □ *I can't work with you breathing down my neck all the time. Go away.* □ *I will get through my life without your help. Stop breathing down my neck.*

breathe one's last to die; to breathe one's last breath. □ *Mrs. Smith breathed her last this morning.* □ *I'll keep running every day until I breathe my last.*

bring down the curtain (on something) See ring down the curtain (on something).

bring home the bacon to earn a salary. (Informal.) □ *I've got to get to work if I'm going to bring home the bacon.* □ *Go out and get a job so you can bring home the bacon.*

bring something home to someone to cause someone to realize the truth of something. □ *Seeing the starving refugees on television really brings home the tragedy of their situation.* □ *It wasn't until she failed her exam that the importance of studying was brought home to her.*

bring something to a head to cause something to come to the point when a decision has to be made or action taken. □ *The latest disagreement between management and the union has brought matters to a head. There will be an all-out strike now.* □ *It's a relief that things have been brought to a head. The disputes have been going on for months.*

bring something to light to make something known; to discover something. □ *The scientists brought their findings to light.* □ *We must bring this new evidence to light.*

brush something under the carpet See sweep something under the carpet.

bull in a china shop a very clumsy person around breakable things; a thoughtless or tactless person. (*China* is fine crockery.) □ *Look at Bill, as awkward as a bull in a china shop.* □ *Get that big dog out of my garden. It's like a bull in a china shop.* □ *Bob is so rude, a real bull in a china shop.*

burn one's boats AND **burn one's bridges (behind one)** to go so far in a course of action that one cannot turn back; to do something which makes it impossible to return to one's former position. □ *I don't want to emigrate now, but I've rather burned my boats by giving up my job and selling my house.* □ *Mary would now like to marry Peter, but she burned her bridges behind her by breaking off the engagement.*

burn one's bridges (behind one) See burn one's boats.

burn the candle at both ends to exhaust oneself by doing too much, for example by working very hard during the day and also staying up very late at night. □ *No wonder Mary is ill. She has been burning the candle at both ends for a long time.* □ *You can't keep on burning the candle at both ends.*

burn the midnight oil to stay up working, especially studying, late at night. (Refers to working by the light of an oil-lamp.) □ *I have to go home and burn the midnight oil tonight.* □ *If you burn the midnight oil night after night, you'll probably become ill.*

bury the hatchet to stop fighting or arguing; to end old resentments. □ *All right, you two. Calm down and bury the hatchet.* □ *I wish Mr. and Mrs. Franklin would bury the hatchet. They argue all the time.*

bush telegraph the informal, usually rapid spreading of news or information by word of mouth. □ *The bush telegraph tells me that the manager is leaving.* □ *How did John know that Kate was divorced? He must have heard it on the bush telegraph.*

business end of something the part or end of something that actually does the work or carries out the procedure. □ *Keep away* *from the business end of the electric drill in case you get hurt.* □ *Don't point the business end of that gun at anyone. It might go off.*

busman's holiday leisure time spent doing something similar to what one does at work. □ *Tutoring pupils in the evening is too much of a busman's holiday for our English teacher.* □ *It's a bit of a busman's holiday to ask her to be wardrobe mistress for our amateur production in the summer. She's a professional dressmaker.*

buy a pig in a poke to purchase or accept something without having seen or examined it. (*Poke* means "bag.") □ *Buying a car without test driving it is like buying a pig in a poke.* □ *He bought a pig in a poke when he ordered a diamond ring by mail order.*

buy something for a song to buy something cheaply. □ *No one else wanted it, so I bought it for a song.* □ *I could buy this house for a song, because it's so ugly.*

by fits and starts irregularly; unevenly; with much stopping and starting. (Informal.) □ *Somehow, they got the job done, by fits and starts.* □ *By fits and starts, the old car finally got us to town.*

by leaps and bounds AND **in leaps and bounds** rapidly; by large movements forward. □ *Our garden is growing by leaps and bounds.* □ *The profits of my company are increasing in leaps and bounds.*

by no means absolutely not; certainly not. □ *I'm by no means angry with you.* □ *"Did you put this box here?" "By no means. I didn't do it, I'm sure."*

by return post by a subsequent immediate posting (back to the sender). (A phrase indicating that an answer is expected soon, by mail.) □ *Since this bill is overdue, would you kindly send us your cheque by return post?* □ *I answered your request by return post over a year ago. Please check your records.*

by the same token in the same way; reciprocally. □ *Tom must be good when he comes here, and, by the same token, I expect you to behave properly when you go to his house.* □ *The mayor votes for his friend's causes. By the same token, the friend votes for the mayor's causes.*

by the seat of one's pants by sheer luck and very little skill. (Informal. Especially with *fly*.) □ *I got through school by the seat of my pants.* □ *The jungle pilot spent most of his days flying by the seat of his pants.*

by the skin of one's teeth just barely; by an amount equal to the thickness of the (imaginary) skin on one's teeth. (Informal.) □ *I got through that exam by the skin of my teeth.* □ *I got to the airport late and caught the plane by the skin of my teeth.*

by the sweat of one's brow by one's efforts; by one's hard work. □ *Tom grew these vegetables by the sweat of his brow.* □ *Sally made her fortune by the sweat of her brow.*

by virtue of something because of something; owing to something. □ *She's permitted to vote by virtue of her age.* □ *They are members of the club by virtue of their great wealth.*

by word of mouth by speaking rather than writing. □ *I learned about it by word of mouth.* □ *I need it in writing. I don't trust things I hear about by word of mouth.*

C

call a spade a spade to call something by its right name; to speak frankly about something, even if it is unpleasant. □ *Well, I believe it's time to call a spade a spade. We are just avoiding the issue.* □ *Let's call a spade a spade. The man is a liar.*

call it a day to leave work and go home; to say that a day's work has been completed; to bring something to an end; to stop doing something. (Informal.) □ *I'm tired. Let's call it a day even though it's only three o'clock.* □ *They're not engaged any more. They called it a day.* □ *I haven't finished this essay, but I'm calling it a day.*

call of nature the need to go to the lavatory. (Humorous.) □ *Stop the car here! I have to answer the call of nature.* □ *There was no interval in the meeting to take account of the call of nature.*

can't hold a candle to someone not equal to someone; unable to measure up to someone. (Also with *cannot.*) □ *Mary can't hold a candle to Ann when it comes to playing the piano.* □ *As for singing, John can't hold a candle to Jane.*

can't make head nor tail of someone or something unable to understand someone or something. (Also with *cannot.*) □ *John is so strange. I can't make head nor tail of him.* □ *Do this report again. I can't make head nor tail of it.*

can't see beyond the end of one's nose unaware of and uncaring for the things which might happen in the future; not far-sighted. (Also with *cannot.*) □ *John is a very poor planner. He can't see beyond the end of his nose.* □ *Ann can't see beyond the end of her nose. She's taken a job without finding out if the firm is financially secure.*

can't see one's hand in front of one's face unable to see very far, usually owing to darkness or fog. (Also with *cannot.*) □ *It was so dark that I couldn't see my hand in front of my face.* □ *Bob said that the fog was so thick he couldn't see his hand in front of his face.*

carry all before one to be exceptionally successful. □ *He carried all before him on school prize day.* □ *In the sports event, Mary just carried all before her.*

carry a torch for someone to be in love with someone who does not return love; to brood over a hopeless love affair. □ *John is carrying a torch for Jane.* □ *Is John still carrying a torch for his lost love?*

carry the day See win the day.

carry the weight of the world on one's shoulders to appear to be burdened by many problems. □ *Look at Tom. He seems to be carrying the weight of the world on his shoulders.* □ *Cheer up, Tom! You don't need to carry the weight of the world on your shoulders.*

carte blanche complete freedom to act or proceed as one pleases. (Literally, a white or blank card.) □ *We were given carte blanche to choose the colour scheme.* □ *They were not instructed where to shop. It was a case of carte blanche.*

cast in the same mould very similar. □ *The two sisters are cast in the same mould—equally mean.* □ *All the members of that family are cast in the same mould, and all have ended up in prison.*

catch one's breath to resume one's normal breathing after exertion; to return to normal after being busy or very active. □ *I ran so fast that it took me ten minutes to catch my breath.* □ *I don't have time to catch my breath. I have to start work immediately.*

catch someone on the hop to find someone unprepared or defenceless. (Informal.) □ *The unexpected exam caught some of the pupils on the hop.* □ *The police caught the suspect on the hop and without an alibi.*

catch someone's eye to establish eye contact with someone; to attract someone's attention. □ *Try and catch the barman's eye.* □ *The shiny red car caught Mary's eye.*

catch the sun to become sunburnt. (Informal.) □ *The baby's face is red—she's caught the sun.* □ *Fair-skinned people catch the sun easily.*

Cat got your tongue? Why don't you speak?; Speak up and answer my question! (Informal.) □ *Answer me! What's the matter, cat got your tongue?* □ *Why don't you speak up? Cat got your tongue?*

caught over a barrel at the mercy of someone; under the control of someone. (Informal.) □ *I'm caught over a barrel, and I have to do what he says.* □ *Ann will do exactly what I say. She's caught over a barrel.*

cause tongues to wag to cause people to gossip; to give people something to gossip about. □ *The way John was looking at Mary will surely cause tongues to wag.* □ *The way Mary was dressed will also cause tongues to wag.*

champ at the bit to be ready and anxious to do something; to be impatient. (Originally said about horses.) □ *The children were champing at the bit to get into the swimming-pool.* □ *The hounds were champing at the bit to begin the hunt.*

chance one's arm to do something risky or dangerous. □ *He certainly chanced his arm when he was rude to the boss's wife.* □ *Don't chance your arm by asking for yet another day off.*

change hands [for something] to be sold. (Refers to the changing of owners.) □ *How many times has this house changed hands in the last ten years?* □ *We built this house in 1920, and it has never changed hands.*

change horses in mid-stream to make major changes in an activity which has already begun; to choose someone or something else after it is too late. □ *I'm already baking a cherry pie. I can't bake an apple pie. It's too late to change horses in mid-stream.* □ *The house is half built. It's too late to employ a different architect. You can't change horses in mid-stream.*

change someone's tune to change the manner, attitude, or behaviour of a person, usually from bad to good, or from rude to pleasant. □ *The cashier was most unpleasant until she learned that I'm a bank director. Then she changed her tune.* □ *"I shall fine you £150, and perhaps that will help change your tune," said the judge to the rude defendant.*

chapter and verse detailed sources of information. (A reference to the method of referring to biblical texts.) □ *He gave chapter and verse for his reasons for disputing that Shakespeare had written the play.* □ *The suspect gave chapter and verse of his associate's activities.*

chapter of accidents a series of misfortunes. □ *Yesterday was just a chapter of accidents—nothing went right.* □ *The play rehearsal con-*

sisted of a chapter of accidents, but the opening performance was perfect.

cheek by jowl 1. side by side; close together. □ *The walkers had to walk cheek by jowl along the narrow streets.* □ *The two families lived cheek by jowl in one house.* **2.** in co-operation; with a concerted effort. □ *The children worked cheek by jowl to make their mother's birthday gift in time.* □ *All members of the transition team worked cheek by jowl late into the night to get the job done.*

cheesed off bored; depressed; annoyed. □ *He was cheesed off with his job.* □ *She was cheesed off when she missed the bus.*

cheese-paring mean; niggardly. □ *He was too cheese-paring to eat properly.* □ *The cheese-paring old woman will not give to the poor.*

chew the cud to think deeply. (Informal. From the cow's habit of bringing food back from the first stomach into the mouth to chew it, called chewing the cud.) □ *I can't decide where to go on holiday. I'll have to chew the cud.* □ *He's chewing the cud about what to do next.*

chilled to the bone See chilled to the marrow.

chilled to the marrow AND **chilled to the bone** very cold. □ *I was chilled to the marrow in that snowstorm.* □ *The children were chilled to the bone in that unheated room.*

chink in one's armour a weakness or vulnerable point that provides an opportunity for attacking or impressing someone who is otherwise invulnerable. □ *His love for his child is the chink in his armour.* □ *Jane's insecurity is the chink in her armour.*

chip off the old block a person (usually a male) who behaves in the same way as his father or resembles his father. (Usually informal.) □ *John looks like his father—a real chip off the old block.* □ *Bill Jones is a chip off the old block. He's a banker just like his father.*

chop and change to keep changing or altering something. □ *The shop is always chopping and changing staff.* □ *The firm is constantly chopping and changing its plans.*

clap eyes on someone or something to see someone or something, perhaps for the first time; to set eyes on someone or something. (Informal.) □ *I wish she had never clapped eyes on her fiancé.* □ *I haven't clapped eyes on a red squirrel for years.*

clear the air to get rid of doubts or hostile feelings. (Sometimes this is said about an argument or other unpleasantness. The literal meaning is also used.) □ *All right, let's discuss this frankly. It'll be better if we clear the air.* □ *Mr. and Mrs. Brown always seem to have to clear the air with a big argument before they can be sociable.*

climb down to admit that one is wrong; to admit defeat. □ *They were sure they were in the right, but they climbed down when we proved them wrong.* □ *The teacher was forced to climb down and admit she had made a mistake.*

clip someone's wings to restrain someone; to reduce or put an end to someone's privileges or freedom. □ *You had better learn to get home on time, or your father will clip your wings.* □ *My mother threatened to clip my wings if I kept staying out late.*

cloak-and-dagger involving secrecy and plotting. □ *A great deal of cloak-and-dagger stuff goes on in political circles.* □ *A lot of cloak-and-dagger activity was involved in the appointment of the director.*

close one's eyes to something to ignore something; to pretend that something is not really happening. □ *You can't close your eyes to the hunger in the world.* □ *His mother closed her eyes to the fact that he was being beaten by his father.*

cloud-cuckoo-land an imaginary perfect world. □ *He thinks that he will be able to buy a house easily, but he is living in cloud-cuckoo-land.* □ *She hopes to get a job travelling abroad—she must believe in cloud-cuckoo-land.*

clutch at straws to seek something which is useless or unattainable; to make a futile attempt at something. □ *I really didn't think that I would get the job. I was clutching at straws.* □ *She won't accept that he was lost at sea. She's still clutching at straws.*

cock-and-bull story a silly, made-up story; a story which is untrue. □ *Don't give me that cock-and-bull story.* □ *I asked for an explanation, and all I got was your ridiculous cock-and-bull story!*

cock a snook at someone to show or express defiance or scorn at someone. □ *He cocked a snook at the traffic warden and tore up the ticket.* □ *The boy cocked a snook at the park attendant and walked on the grass.*

cock of the walk someone who acts in a more important manner than others in a group. □ *The deputy manager was cock of the walk until the new manager arrived.* □ *He loved acting cock of the walk and ordering everyone about.*

cold comfort no comfort or consolation at all. □ *She knows there are others worse off than her, but that's cold comfort.* □ *It was cold comfort to the student that others had failed also.*

come a cropper to have a misfortune; to fail. (Literally, to fall off one's horse.) □ *Bob invested all his money in the shares market just before it fell. Did he come a cropper!* □ *Jane was out all night before she took her exams. She really came a cropper.*

come away empty-handed to return without anything. □ *All right, go gambling if you must. Don't come away empty-handed, though.* □ *Go to the bank and ask for the loan again. This time try not to come away empty-handed.*

come down in the world to lose one's social position or financial standing. □ *Mr. Jones has really come down in the world since he lost his job.* □ *If I were unemployed, I'm certain I'd come down in the world, too.*

come down to earth to become realistic or practical, especially after a period of day-dreaming; to become alert to what is going on around one. (Informal.) □ *You have very good ideas, John, but you must come down to earth. We can't possibly afford any of your suggestions.* □ *Pay attention to what is going on. Come down to earth and join the discussion.*

come down with something to become ill with some disease. □ *I'm afraid I'm coming down with a cold.* □ *I'll probably come down with pneumonia.*

come from far and wide to come from many different places. □ *Everyone was there. They came from far and wide.* □ *We have foods that come from far and wide.*

come full circle to return to the original position or state of affairs. □ *The family sold the house generations ago, but the wheel has come full circle and one of their descendants lives there now.* □ *The employers' power was reduced by the unions at one point, but the wheel has come full circle again.*

come home to roost to return to cause trouble (for someone). □ *As I feared, all my problems came home to roost.* □ *His lies finally came home to roost. His wife discovered his adultery.*

come in for something to receive something; to acquire something. □ *Mary came in for a tremendous amount of money when her aunt died.* □ *Her new play has come in for a lot of criticism.*

come into something to inherit something. □ *Jane came into a small fortune when her aunt died.* □ *Mary does not come into her inheritance until she comes of age.*

come of age to reach an age when one is old enough to own property, get married, and sign legal contracts. □ *When Jane comes of age, she will buy her own car.* □ *Sally, who came of age last month, entered into an agreement to purchase a house.*

come off second-best to be in second place or worse; to be the loser. □ *You can fight with your brother if you like, but you'll come off second-best.* □ *Why do I always come off second-best in an argument with you?*

come out in the wash to work out all right. (Informal. This means that problems or difficulties will go away as dirt goes away in the process of washing.) □ *Don't worry about their accusation. It'll all come out in the wash.* □ *This trouble will go away. It'll come out in the wash.*

come out of nowhere to appear suddenly. □ *Suddenly, a container lorry came out of nowhere.* □ *The storm came out of nowhere, and we were unprepared.*

come out of one's shell to become more friendly; to be more sociable. □ *Ann, you should come out of your shell and spend more time with your friends.* □ *Come out of your shell, Tom. Go out and make some friends.*

(come) rain or shine no matter whether it rains or the sun shines. (Informal.) □ *Don't worry. I'll be there come rain or shine.* □ *We'll hold the picnic—rain or shine.*

come round 1. finally to agree or consent (to something). □ *I thought he'd never agree, but in the end he came round.* □ *She came round only after we argued for an hour.* **2.** to return to consciousness; to wake up. □ *He came round after we threw cold water in his face.*

□ *The boxer was knocked out, but came round in a few seconds.* **3.** to come for a visit; to stop by (somewhere). □ *Why don't you come round about eight? I'll be home then.* □ *Come round some week-end when you aren't busy.*

come to a bad end to have a disaster, perhaps one which is deserved or expected; to die an unfortunate death. □ *I just know that the young man will come to a bad end.* □ *The miserly shopkeeper came to a bad end and was declared bankrupt.*

come to a head to come to a crucial point; to come to a point when a problem must be solved. □ *Remember my problem with my neighbours? Well, last night the whole thing came to a head.* □ *The battle between the two factions of the town council came to a head yesterday.*

come to an untimely end to come to an early death. □ *Poor Mr. Jones came to an untimely end in a car accident.* □ *The older brother came to an untimely end, but the twin boys lived to a ripe old age.*

come to a pretty pass to develop into a bad, unfortunate, or difficult situation. □ *Things have come to a pretty pass when people have to beg in the streets.* □ *When parents are afraid of their children, things have come to a pretty pass.*

come to grief to fail or be unsuccessful; to have trouble or grief. □ *The artist wept when her canvas came to grief.* □ *The wedding party came to grief when the bride passed out.*

come to light to become known; to be discovered. □ *Some interesting facts about your past have just come to light.* □ *If too many bad things come to light, you may lose your job.*

come to the fore to become obvious or prominent; to become important. □ *The question of salary has now come to the fore.* □ *Since his great showing in court, my solicitor has really come to the fore in his profession.*

conspicuous by one's absence having one's absence noticed (at an event). □ *We missed you last night. You were conspicuous by your absence.* □ *How could the bride's father miss the wedding party? He was certainly conspicuous by his absence.*

contradiction in terms a seeming contradiction in the wording of something. □ *A wealthy pauper is a contradiction in terms.* □ *A straight-talking politician may seem a contradiction in terms.*

cook someone's goose to damage or ruin someone. (Informal.) □ *I cooked my own goose by not showing up on time.* □ *Sally cooked Bob's goose for treating her the way he did.*

cook the books to cheat in bookkeeping; to make the accounts appear to balance when they do not. □ *Jane was sent to jail for cooking the books of her mother's shop.* □ *It's hard to tell whether she really cooked the books or just didn't know how to add.*

cool one's heels to wait impatiently (for someone). (Informal.) □ *I spent all afternoon cooling my heels in the waiting room while the doctor talked on the telephone.* □ *All right. If you can't behave properly, just sit down here and cool your heels until I call you.*

cost a pretty penny to cost a lot of money. □ *I'll bet that diamond cost a pretty penny.* □ *You can be sure that house cost a pretty penny.*

cost the earth to cost an enormous sum of money. (Compare with pay the earth.) □ *That huge car must have cost the earth!* □ *Do I look as though I can afford a house that costs the earth?*

count heads to count people. □ *I'll tell you how many people are here after I count heads.* □ *Everyone is here. Let's count heads so we can order the drinks.*

crack a bottle to open a bottle. (Informal.) □ *Let's crack a bottle of champagne to celebrate.* □ *We always crack a bottle of port at Christmas.*

cramp someone's style to limit someone in some way. □ *Having her young sister with her rather cramped her style on the dance floor.* □ *To ask him to keep regular hours would really be cramping his style.*

cross a bridge before one comes to it to worry excessively about something before it happens. □ *There is no sense in crossing that bridge before you come to it.* □ *She's always crossing bridges before coming to them. She needs to learn to relax.*

cross one's heart (and hope to die) to pledge or vow that the truth is being told. □ *It's true, cross my heart and hope to die.* □ *It's really true—cross my heart.*

cross swords (with someone) to enter into an argument with someone. □ *I don't want to cross swords with Tom.* □ *The last time we crossed swords, we had a terrible time.*

cross the Rubicon to do something which inevitably commits one to a following course of action. (The crossing of the River Rubicon by Julius Caesar inevitably involved him in a war with the Senate in 49 B.C.) □ *Jane crossed the Rubicon by signing the contract.* □ *Find another job before you cross the Rubicon and resign from this one.*

crux of the matter the central issue of the matter. (*Crux* is Latin for "cross.") □ *All right, this is the crux of the matter.* □ *It's about time that we looked at the crux of the matter.*

cry one's eyes out to cry very hard. □ *When we heard the news, we cried our eyes out with joy.* □ *She cried her eyes out after his death.*

cry over spilled milk to be unhappy about having done something which cannot be undone. (*Spilled* can also be spelled *spilt*.) □ *I'm sorry that you broke your bicycle, Tom. But there is nothing that can be done now. Don't cry over spilled milk.* □ *Ann is always crying over spilt milk.*

cry wolf to cry out for help or to complain about something when nothing is really wrong. □ *Pay no attention. She's just crying wolf again.* □ *Don't cry wolf too often. No one will come.*

culture vulture someone whom one considers to be excessively interested in the (classical) arts. □ *She won't go to a funny film. She's a real culture vulture.* □ *They watch only highbrow television. They're culture vultures.*

cupboard love affection shown to someone just because of the things, such as food or clothes, they supply. □ *She doesn't love her husband. It's just cupboard love.* □ *Her affection for her foster-parents is a pretence—simply cupboard love.*

curl up (and die) to retreat and die; to shrink away because one is very embarrassed. □ *When I heard you say that, I could have curled up and died.* □ *Her mother's praises made her want to curl up.*

curry favour (with someone) to try to win favour from someone. □ *The solicitor tried to curry favour with the judge.* □ *It's silly to curry favour. Just act yourself.*

cut a fine figure to look good; to look elegant. □ *Tom really cuts a fine figure on the dance-floor.* □ *Bill cuts a fine figure since he bought some new clothes.*

cut a long story short to bring a story to an end. (A formula which introduces a summary of a story or a joke.) □ *And—to cut a long story short—I never got back the money that I lent him.* □ *If I can cut a long story short, let me say that everything worked out fine.*

cut and dried fixed; determined beforehand; usual and uninteresting. □ *I find your writing quite boring. It's too cut and dried.* □ *The lecture was, as usual, cut and dried. It was the same thing we've heard for years.* □ *Our plans are all cut and dried; you can't contribute anything now.*

cut and thrust intense competition. (From sword-fighting.) □ *Peter tired of the cut and thrust of business.* □ *The cut and thrust of the stock-market is not for John.*

cut both ways to affect both sides of an issue equally. □ *Remember your suggestion that costs should be shared cuts both ways. You will have to pay as well.* □ *If our side cannot take along supporters to the game, then yours cannot either. The rule has to cut both ways.*

cut corners to reduce efforts or expenditures; to do things poorly or incompletely. (From the phrase *cut the corner*, meaning to avoid going to an intersection to turn.) □ *You cannot cut corners when you are dealing with public safety.* □ *Don't cut corners, Sally. Let's do the thing properly.*

cut it (too) fine to allow scarcely enough time, money, etc., in order to accomplish something. □ *You're cutting it too fine if you want to catch the bus. It leaves in five minutes.* □ *Joan had to search her pockets for money for the bus fare. She really cut it fine.*

cut no ice to have no effect; to make no sense; to have no influence. □ *That idea cuts no ice. It won't help at all.* □ *It cuts no ice that your mother is the director.*

cut one's coat according to one's cloth AND **cut one's coat to suit one's cloth** to plan one's aims and activities in line with one's resources and circumstances. □ *We would like a bigger house, but we must cut our coat according to our cloth.* □ *They can't afford a holiday abroad—they have to cut their coat to suit their cloth.*

cut one's coat to suit one's cloth See cut one's coat according to one's cloth.

cut one's eye-teeth on something to have done something since one was very young; to have much experience at something. □ *Do I know about cars? I cut my eye-teeth on cars.* □ *I cut my eye-teeth on Bach. I can whistle everything he wrote.*

cut one's teeth on something to gain one's early experiences on something. □ *You can cut your teeth on this project before getting involved in a more major one.* □ *The young police officers cut their teeth on minor crimes.*

cut someone dead to ignore someone totally. □ *Joan was just about to speak to James when he cut her dead.* □ *Jean cut her former husband dead.*

cut someone down to size to make a person more humble. □ *John's remarks really cut me down to size.* □ *Jane is too conceited. I think her new managing director will cut her down to size.*

cut someone to the quick to hurt someone's feelings very badly. (Can be used literally when *quick* refers to the tender flesh at the base of finger- and toe-nails.) □ *Your criticism cut me to the quick.* □ *Tom's sharp words to Mary cut her to the quick.*

cut teeth [for a baby or young person] to grow teeth. □ *Billy is cross because he's cutting teeth.* □ *Ann cut her first tooth this week.*

daily dozen physical exercises done every day. (Informal.) □ *My brother always feels better after his daily dozen.* □ *She would rather do a daily dozen than go on a diet.*

daily grind the everyday work routine. (Informal.) □ *I'm getting very tired of the daily grind.* □ *When my holiday was over, I had to go back to the daily grind.*

damn someone or something with faint praise to criticize someone or something indirectly by not praising enthusiastically. □ *The critic did not say that he disliked the play, but he damned it with faint praise.* □ *Mrs. Brown is very proud of her son's achievements, but damns her daughter's with faint praise.*

damp squib something which fails to be as successful or exciting as it promised to be. (Informal.) □ *The charity ball was a bit of a damp squib.* □ *The much-publicized protest turned out to be a damp squib.*

dance attendance on someone to be always ready to tend to someone's wishes or needs. □ *That young woman has three men dancing attendance on her.* □ *Her father expects her to dance attendance on him day and night.*

Darby and Joan an old married couple living happily together. (From a couple so-called in eighteenth-century ballads.) □ *Her parents are divorced, but her grandparents are like Darby and Joan.* □ *It's good to see so many Darby and Joans at the party, but it needs some young couples to liven it up.*

dark horse someone whose abilities, plans, or feelings are little known to others. (From horse-racing.) □ *It's difficult to predict who will win the prize—there are two or three dark horses in the tournament.* □ *You're a dark horse! We didn't know you ran marathons!*

Davy Jones's locker the bottom of the sea, especially when it is the final resting place for someone or something. (From seamen's name for the evil spirit of the sea.) □ *They were going to sail around the world, but ended up in Davy Jones's locker.* □ *Most of the gold from that trading ship is in Davy Jones's locker.*

daylight robbery [an instance of] the practice of blatantly or grossly overcharging. (Informal.) □ *It's daylight robbery to charge that amount of money for a hotel room!* □ *The cost of renting a car at that place is daylight robbery.*

dead and buried gone forever. (Refers literally to persons and figuratively to ideas and other things.) □ *Now that Uncle Bill is dead and buried, we can read his will.* □ *That way of thinking is dead and buried.*

dead centre at the exact centre of something. □ *The arrow hit the target dead centre.* □ *When you put the flowers on the table, put them dead centre.*

dead on one's or its feet exhausted; worn out; no longer effective or successful. (Informal.) □ *Ann is so tired. She's really dead on her feet.* □ *He can't teach well any more. He's dead on his feet.* □ *This inefficient company is dead on its feet.*

dead set against someone or something totally opposed to someone or something. □ *I'm dead set against the new rates proposal.* □ *Everyone is dead set against the MP.*

dead to the world sleeping very soundly. (Informal.) □ *He spent the whole plane journey dead to the world.* □ *Look at her sleeping. She's dead to the world.*

death to something having a harmful effect on something; liable to ruin something. □ *This road is terribly bumpy. It's death to tyres.* □ *Stiletto heels are death to those tiles.*

die a natural death [for something] to fade away or die down. □ *I expect that all this excitement about computers will die a natural death.* □ *Most fads die a natural death.*

die laughing to laugh very long and hard. (Informal.) □ *The joke was so funny that I almost died laughing.* □ *The play was meant to be funny, but the audience didn't exactly die laughing.*

die of a broken heart to die of emotional distress, especially grief over a lost love. □ *I was not surprised to hear of her death. They say she died of a broken heart.* □ *In the film, the heroine appeared to die of a broken heart, but the audience knew she was poisoned.*

die of boredom to suffer from boredom; to be very bored. □ *I shall die of boredom if I stay here alone all day.* □ *We sat there and listened politely, even though we were dying of boredom.*

dig one's own grave to be responsible for one's own downfall or ruin. □ *The manager tried to get rid of his assistant, but he dug his own grave. He got the sack himself.* □ *The government has dug its own grave with the new taxation bill. It won't be re-elected.*

dine out on something to be asked to social gatherings because of the information one has. □ *She's been dining out on the story of her promotion for months.* □ *The journalist dines out on all the gossip he acquires.*

dirt cheap extremely cheap. (Informal.) □ *Buy some more of those plums. They're dirt cheap.* □ *In Italy, the peaches are dirt cheap.*

dirty look a look or glance expressing disapproval or dislike. (Especially with *get, give, receive*.) □ *I stopped whistling when I saw the dirty look on her face.* □ *The child who sneaked received dirty looks from the other children.* □ *Ann gave me a dirty look.* □ *I gave her a dirty look back.*

do a double take to react with surprise; to have to look twice to make sure that one really saw correctly. (Informal.) □ *When the boy led a goat into the park, everyone did a double take.* □ *When the doctor saw that the man had six toes, she did a double take.*

do an about-face to make a total reversal of opinion or action. □ *Without warning, the government did an about-face on taxation.* □ *It had done an about-face on the question of rates last year.*

dog in the manger one who prevents others from enjoying a privilege that one does not make use of or enjoy oneself. (From one of Aesop's fables in which a dog—which cannot eat hay—lay in the hay-rack [manger] and prevented the other animals from eating the hay.) □ *Jane is a real dog in the manger. She cannot drive, but she will not lend anyone her car.* □ *If Martin were not such a dog in the manger, he would let his brother have that evening suit he never wears.*

do justice to something 1. to do something well; to represent or portray something accurately. □ Sally really did justice to the contract negotiations. □ This photograph doesn't do justice to the beauty of the mountains. **2.** to eat or drink a great deal. (Informal.) □ Bill always does justice to the evening meal. □ The guests didn't do justice to the roast pig. There were nearly ten pounds of it left over.

done to a turn cooked just right. □ Yummy! This meat is done to a turn. □ I like it done to a turn, not too well done and not too raw.

donkey's ages AND **donkey's years** a very long time. (Informal.) □ The woman hasn't been seen for donkey's ages. □ We haven't had a holiday in donkey's years.

donkey's years See donkey's ages.

donkey-work hard or boring work. (Informal.) □ His wife picks flowers, but he does all the donkey-work in the garden. □ I don't only baby-sit. I do all the donkey-work around the house.

do one's bit to do one's share of the work; to do whatever one can do to help. □ Everybody must do their bit to help get things under control. □ I always try to do my bit. How can I help this time?

dose of one's own medicine the same kind of, usually bad, treatment which one gives to other people. (Often with get or have.) □ Sally is never very friendly. Someone is going to give her a dose of her own medicine someday and ignore her. □ The thief didn't like getting a dose of his own medicine when his car was stolen.

do someone down to do something to someone's disadvantage. □ He really did me down when he applied for the same job. □ Don't expect Mr. Black to help you. He enjoys doing people down.

do someone good to benefit someone. □ A nice hot bath really does me good. □ It would do you good to lose some weight.

do someone proud to treat someone generously. (Informal.) □ What a good hotel. The conference has done us proud. □ He certainly did his daughter proud. The wedding reception cost a fortune.

do someone's heart good to make someone feel good emotionally. (Informal.) □ It does my heart good to hear you talk that way. □ When she sent me a get-well card, it really did my heart good.

do the trick to do exactly what needs to be done; to be satisfactory for a purpose. (Informal.) □ *Push the car just a little more to the left. There, that does the trick.* □ *If you give me two pounds, I'll have enough to do the trick.*

double Dutch language or speech that is difficult or impossible to understand. □ *This book on English grammar is written in double Dutch. I can't understand a word.* □ *Try to find a lecturer who speaks slowly, not one who speaks double Dutch.*

doubting Thomas someone who will not easily believe something without strong proof or evidence. (From the biblical account of the apostle Thomas, who would not believe that Christ had risen from the grave until he had touched Him.) □ *Mary won't believe that I have a dog until she sees him. She's such a doubting Thomas.* □ *This school is full of doubting Thomases. They want to see his new bike with their own eyes.*

down at heel shabby; run-down; [of a person] poorly dressed. □ *The tramp was really down at heel.* □ *Tom's house needs paint. It looks down at heel.* ALSO: **down-at-heel** □ *Look at that down-at-heel tramp.*

down in the mouth sad-faced; depressed and unsmiling. □ *Ever since the party was cancelled, Barbara has been looking down in the mouth.* □ *Bob has been down in the mouth since his girlfriend left.*

down on one's luck without any money; unlucky. (Euphemistic for *poor* or *penniless*.) □ *Can you lend me twenty pounds? I've been down on my luck lately.* □ *The gambler had to get a job because he had been down on his luck and didn't earn enough money to live on.*

down to earth practical; realistic; not theoretical; not fanciful. □ *Her ideas for the boutique are always very down to earth.* □ *Those philosophers are anything but down to earth.* ALSO: **down-to-earth** □ *She's far too dreamy. We want a more down-to-earth person.*

drag one's feet to act very slowly, often deliberately. □ *The government are dragging their feet on this bill because it will lose votes.* □ *If the planning department hadn't dragged their feet, the building would have been built by now.*

draw a blank to get no response; to find nothing. (Informal.) □ *I asked him about Tom's financial problems, and I just drew a blank.* □ *We looked in the files for an hour, but we drew a blank.*

draw a line between something and something else to separate two things; to distinguish or differentiate between two things. (The *a* can be replaced with *the*.) □ *It's necessary to draw a line between bumping into people and striking them.* □ *It's very hard to draw the line between slamming a door and just closing it loudly.*

draw a red herring to introduce information which diverts attention from the main issue. (See also red herring.) □ *The accountant drew several red herrings to prevent people from discovering that he had embezzled the money.* □ *The government, as always, will draw a red herring whenever there is a monetary crisis.*

draw blood to hit or bite (a person or an animal) and make a wound that bleeds. □ *The dog chased me and bit me hard, but it didn't draw blood.* □ *The boxer landed just one punch and drew blood immediately.*

dream come true a wish or a dream which has become a reality. □ *Going to Hawaii is like having a dream come true.* □ *Having you for a friend is a dream come true.*

dressed (up) to the nines dressed in one's best clothes. (Informal. Very high on a scale of one to ten.) □ *The applicants for the job were all dressed up to the nines.* □ *The wedding party were dressed to the nines.*

dressing down a scolding. □ *After that dressing down I won't be late again.* □ *The boss gave Fred a real dressing down for breaking the machine.*

drive a hard bargain to work hard to negotiate prices or agreements in one's own favour. □ *All right, sir, you drive a hard bargain. I'll sell you this car for £12,450.* □ *You drive a hard bargain, Jane, but I'll sign the contract.*

drive someone up the wall to annoy or irritate someone. (Informal.) □ *Stop whistling that tune. You're driving me up the wall.* □ *All his talk about moving to London nearly drove me up the wall.*

drop a bombshell to announce shocking or startling news. (Informal.) □ *They really dropped a bombshell when they announced that the president had cancer.* □ *Friday is a good day to drop a bombshell like that. It gives the business world the week-end to recover.*

drop back to go back or remain back; to fall behind. □ As the crowd moved forward, the weaker ones dropped back. □ She was winning the race at first, but soon dropped back.

drop in one's tracks to stop or collapse from exhaustion; to die suddenly. □ If I keep working this way, I'll drop in my tracks. □ Uncle Bob was working in the garden and dropped in his tracks. We are all sorry that he's dead.

drop someone to stop being friends with someone, especially with one's boyfriend or girlfriend. (Informal.) □ Bob finally dropped Jane. I don't know what he saw in her. □ I'm surprised that she didn't drop him first.

drown one's sorrows to try to forget one's problems by drinking a lot of alcohol. (Informal.) □ Bill is in the bar drowning his sorrows. □ Jane is at home drowning her sorrows after losing her job.

dry run an attempt; a rehearsal. □ We had better have a dry run for the official ceremony tomorrow. □ The children will need a dry run before their procession in the pageant.

E

eager beaver someone who is very enthusiastic; someone who works very hard. □ *New volunteers are always eager beavers.* □ *The young assistant gets to work very early. She's a real eager beaver.*

eagle eye careful attention; an intently watchful eye. (From the sharp eyesight of the eagle.) □ *The pupils wrote their essays under the eagle eye of the headmaster.* □ *The umpire kept his eagle eye on the ball.*

early bird someone who gets up or arrives early or starts something very promptly, especially someone who gains an advantage of some kind by so doing. □ *The Smith family are early birds. They caught the first ferry.* □ *I was an early bird and got the best selection of flowers.*

eat humble pie to act very humbly, especially when one has been shown to be wrong; to accept humiliation. □ *I think I'm right, but if I'm wrong, I'll eat humble pie.* □ *You think you're so smart. I hope you have to eat humble pie.*

eat like a bird to eat only small amounts of food; to peck at one's food. □ *Jane is very slim because she eats like a bird.* □ *Bill is trying to lose weight by eating like a bird.*

eat like a horse to eat large amounts of food. (Informal.) □ *No wonder he's so fat. He eats like a horse.* □ *John works like a horse and eats like a horse, so he never gets fat.*

eat one's hat a phrase telling the kind of thing that one would do if a very unlikely event were actually to happen. □ *I'll eat my hat if you get a rise.* □ *He said he'd eat his hat if she got elected.*

eat one's heart out 1. to be very sad (about someone or something). □ *Bill spent a lot of time eating his heart out after his divorce.* □ *Sally ate her heart out when she had to sell her house.* **2.** to be envious (of someone or something). (Informal.) □ *Do you like my new* *watch? Well, eat your heart out. It was the last one in the shop.* □ *Eat your heart out, Jane! I've got a new girlfriend now.*

eat one's words to have to take back one's statements; to confess that one's predictions were wrong. □ *You shouldn't say that to me. I'll make you eat your words.* □ *John was wrong about the election and had to eat his words.*

eat out of someone's hands to do what someone else wants; to obey someone eagerly. (Often with *have*.) □ *Just wait! I'll have everyone eating out of my hands. They'll do whatever I ask.* □ *The treasurer has everyone eating out of his hands.* □ *A lot of people are eating out of his hands.*

eat someone out of house and home to eat a lot of food (in someone's home); to bring someone to the point of financial ruin by eating all the food in the person's house. (Informal.) □ *Billy has a huge appetite. He almost eats us out of house and home.* □ *When the young people come home from college, they always eat us out of house and home.*

either feast or famine either too much (of something) or not enough (of something). (Also without *either*.) □ *This month is very dry, and last month it rained almost every day. Our weather is either feast or famine.* □ *Sometimes we are busy, and sometimes we have nothing to do. It's feast or famine.*

elbow-grease physical exertion; hard work. (The "grease" may be the sweat that exertion produces.) □ *It'll take some elbow-grease to clean this car.* □ *Expensive polishes are all very well, but this floor needs elbow-grease.*

eleventh-hour decision a decision made at the last possible minute. □ *Eleventh-hour decisions are seldom satisfactory.* □ *The treasurer's eleventh-hour decision was made in a great hurry, but it turned out to be correct.*

enough is as good as a feast a saying that means one should be satisfied if one has enough of something to meet one's needs, and one should not seek more than one needs. □ *We have enough money to live on, and enough is as good as a feast.* □ *I cannot understand why they want a larger house. Enough is as good as a feast.*

enter the lists to begin to take part in a contest or argument. □ *He had decided not to stand for Parliament, but entered the lists at* *the last minute.* □ *The family disagreement had almost been resolved when the grandfather entered the lists.*

escape someone's notice to go unnoticed; not to have been noticed. (Usually a way to point out that someone has failed to see or respond to something.) □ *I suppose my earlier request escaped your notice, so I'm writing again.* □ *I'm sorry. Your letter escaped my notice.*

everything but the kitchen sink almost everything one can think of. □ *When Sally went off to college, she took everything but the kitchen sink.* □ *When you take a baby on holiday, you have to pack everything but the kitchen sink.*

everything from A to Z almost everything one can think of. □ *She knows everything from A to Z about decorating.* □ *The biology exam covered everything from A to Z.*

every time one turns around frequently; at every turn; with annoying frequency. □ *Somebody asks me for money every time I turn around.* □ *Something goes wrong with Bill's car every time he turns around.*

(every) Tom, Dick, and Harry everyone without discrimination; ordinary people. (Not necessarily males.) □ *The golf club is very exclusive. They don't let any Tom, Dick, or Harry join.* □ *Mary's sending out very few invitations. She doesn't want every Tom, Dick, and Harry turning up.*

expecting (a child) pregnant. (A euphemism.) □ *Tommy's mother is expecting a child.* □ *Oh, I didn't know she was expecting.*

expense is no object See money is no object.

extend one's sympathy (to someone) to express sympathy to someone. (A very polite and formal way to tell someone that you are sorry about a death in the family.) □ *Please permit me to extend my sympathy to you and your children. I'm very sorry to hear of the death of your husband.* □ *Let's extend our sympathy to Bill Jones, whose father died this week.*

eyeball to eyeball person to person; face to face. (Informal.) □ *The discussions will have to be eyeball to eyeball to be effective.* □ *Telephone conversations are a waste of time. We need to talk eyeball to eyeball.*

face the music to receive punishment; to accept the unpleasant results of one's actions. (Informal.) □ *Mary broke a dining-room window and had to face the music when her father got home.* □ *After failing a maths test, Tom had to go home and face the music.*

face value outward appearance; what something first appears to be. (From the value printed on the "face" of a coin or banknote.) □ *Don't just accept her offer at face value. Think of the implications.* □ *Joan tends to take people at face value, and so she is always getting hurt.*

fair crack of the whip a fair share of something; a fair opportunity of doing something. □ *He doesn't want to do all the overtime. He only wants a fair crack of the whip.* □ *They were supposed to share the driving equally, but James refused to give Ann a fair crack of the whip.*

fair do's fair and just treatment [done to someone]. (Informal.) □ *It's hardly fair do's to treat her like that.* □ *It's not a question of fair do's. He treats everyone in the same way.* ALSO: **Fair do's!** Be fair!; Be reasonable! □ *Fair do's! You said you would lend me your bike if I took your books home.* □ *I know I said I'd baby-sit tonight, but fair do's—I hate to work late.*

fair game someone or something that it is quite permissible to attack. □ *I don't like seeing articles exposing people's private lives, but politicians are fair game.* □ *Journalists always regard film-stars as fair game.*

fall about to laugh heartily. (Informal.) □ *We fell about at the antics of the clown.* □ *The audience were falling about during the last act of the comedy.*

fall apart at the seams to break into pieces; to fall apart. □ *This old car is about ready to fall apart at the seams.* □ *The plan won't succeed. It's falling apart at the seams already.*

fall between two stools to come somewhere between two possibilities and so fail to meet the requirements of either. □ *The material is not suitable for an academic book, and it is not suitable for a popular one either. It falls between two stools.* □ *He tries to be both teacher and friend, but falls between two stools.*

fall by the wayside to give up and quit before the end (of something); not to succeed. (As if one became exhausted and couldn't finish a foot-race.) □ *John fell by the wayside and didn't finish college.* □ *Many people start out to train for a career in medicine, but some of them fall by the wayside.*

fall down on the job to fail to do something properly; to fail to do one's job adequately. (Informal.) □ *The team kept losing because the coach was falling down on the job.* □ *Tom was sacked because he fell down on the job.*

fall foul of someone or something to do something that annoys or offends someone or something; to do something that is contrary to the rules. □ *He has fallen foul of the police more than once.* □ *The political activists fell foul of the authorities.* □ *I hope I don't fall foul of your sister. She doesn't like me.* □ *John fell foul of the law.*

fall from grace to cease to be held in favour, especially because of some wrong or foolish action. □ *He was the teacher's prize pupil until he fell from grace by failing the history exam.* □ *Mary was the favourite grandchild until she fell from grace by running away from home.*

fall into line to conform. □ *If you are going to work here, you will have to fall into line.* □ *He likes to do as he pleases. He hates having to fall into line.*

fancy someone's chances to have confidence in someone's [including one's own] ability to be successful. (Informal.) □ *We all think she will refuse to go out with him, but he certainly fancies his chances.* □ *The other contestants are so talented that I don't fancy his chances at all.*

far cry from something a thing which is very different from something else. □ *What you did was a far cry from what you said you were* *going to do.* □ *The song they played was a far cry from what I call music.*

feast one's eyes (on someone or something) to look at someone or something with pleasure, envy, or admiration. □ *Just feast your eyes on that beautiful juicy steak!* □ *Yes, feast your eyes. You won't see one like that again for a long time.*

feather in one's cap an honour; something of which one can be proud. □ *Getting a new client was really a feather in my cap.* □ *It was certainly a feather in the journalist's cap to get an interview with the president.*

feather one's (own) nest to use power and prestige selfishly to provide for oneself, often immorally or illegally. □ *The mayor seemed to be helping people, but was really feathering her own nest.* □ *The building contractor used a lot of public money to feather his nest.*

feel fit to feel well and healthy. □ *If you want to feel fit, you must eat the proper food and get enough rest.* □ *I hope I still feel fit when I get old.*

feel it beneath one (to do something) to feel that one would be humbling oneself or reducing one's status to do something. □ *Tom feels it beneath him to scrub the floor.* □ *Ann feels it beneath her to carry her own luggage.* □ *I would do it, but I feel it beneath me.*

feel like a million dollars to feel well and healthy, both physically and mentally. □ *A quick swim in the morning makes me feel like a million dollars.* □ *What a beautiful day! It makes you feel like a million dollars.*

feel like a new person to feel refreshed and renewed, especially after getting well or getting dressed up. □ *I bought a new suit, and now I feel like a new person.* □ *Bob felt like a new person when he got out of the hospital.*

feel something in one's bones to sense something; to have an intuition about something. (Informal.) □ *The train will be late. I feel it in my bones.* □ *I failed the test. I feel it in my bones.*

fiddle while Rome burns to do nothing or something trivial while something disastrous happens. (From a legend that the emperor Nero played the lyre while Rome was burning.) □ *The Opposition doesn't seem to be doing anything to stop this terrible parliamentary* *bill. It's fiddling while Rome burns.* □ *The doctor should have sent for an ambulance right away instead of examining her. He was just fiddling while Rome burned.*

fighting chance a good possibility of success, especially if every effort is made. □ *They have at least a fighting chance of winning the race.* □ *The patient could die, but he has a fighting chance since the operation.*

fight shy of something to avoid something; to keep from doing something. □ *She fought shy of borrowing money from her father, but had to in the end.* □ *He's always fought shy of marrying.*

fill dead men's shoes See step into dead men's shoes.

fill someone's shoes to take the place of some other person and perform satisfactorily in that role. (As if you were wearing the other person's shoes.) □ *I don't know how we'll be able to do without you. No one can fill your shoes.* □ *It'll be difficult to fill Jane's shoes. She did her job very well.*

fill the bill to be exactly the thing that is needed. □ *Ah, this steak is great. It really fills the bill.* □ *This new pair of shoes fills the bill nicely.*

find it in one's heart to do something to have the courage or compassion to do something; to persuade oneself to do something. □ *She couldn't find it in her heart to refuse to come home to him.* □ *Could you really find it in your heart to send her away?*

find one's feet to become used to a new situation or experience. □ *She was lonely at first when she left home, but she is finding her feet now.* □ *It takes time to learn the office routine, but you will gradually find your feet.*

find one's own level to find the position or rank to which one is best suited. (As water "seeks its own level.") □ *You cannot force junior staff to be ambitious. They will all find their own level.* □ *The new pupil is happier in the lower class. It was just a question of letting her find her own level.*

find one's tongue to be able to talk. (Informal.) □ *Tom was speechless for a moment. Then he found his tongue.* □ *Ann was unable to find her tongue. She sat there in silence.*

find time to catch one's breath See get time to catch one's breath.

fine kettle of fish AND **pretty kettle of fish** a real mess; an unsatisfactory situation. □ *The dog has eaten the steak we were going to have for dinner. This is a fine kettle of fish!* □ *This is a pretty kettle of fish. It's below freezing outside, and the boiler won't work.*

fine state of affairs an unpleasant state of affairs. □ *This is a fine state of affairs, and it's all your fault.* □ *What a fine state of affairs you've got us into.*

fish for compliments to try to get someone to pay you a compliment. (Informal.) □ *When she showed me her new dress, I could tell that she was fishing for a compliment.* □ *Tom was certainly fishing for compliments when he modelled his new haircut for his friends.*

fish in troubled waters to involve oneself in a difficult, confused, or dangerous situation, especially with a view to gaining an advantage. □ *Frank is fishing in troubled waters by buying more shares in that firm. They are supposed to be in financial difficulties.* □ *The firm could make more money by selling armaments abroad, but they would be fishing in troubled waters.*

fit for a king splendid; of a very high standard. □ *What a delicious meal. It was fit for a king.* □ *Our room at the hotel was fit for a king.*

fit someone in(to something) to succeed with difficulty in putting someone into a schedule. □ *The doctor is busy, but I can try to fit you into the appointment book.* □ *Yes, here's a free appointment. I can fit you in.*

fix someone up (with something) to arrange to provide someone with something. (Informal.) □ *We fixed John up with a room for the night.* □ *The usher fixed us up with seats at the front of the theatre.* □ *We thanked the usher for fixing us up.*

flash in the pan something that draws a lot of attention for a very brief time. (Informal.) □ *I'm afraid that my success as a painter was just a flash in the pan.* □ *Tom had hoped to be a singer, but his career was only a flash in the pan.*

flea in one's ear a severe scolding. (Informal.) □ *I got a flea in my ear when I tried to give Pat some advice.* □ *Margaret was only trying to help the old lady, but she came away with a flea in her ear.*

flesh and blood 1. a living human body, especially with reference to its natural limitations; a human being. □ *This cold weather is more* *than flesh and blood can stand.* □ *Carrying £300 is beyond mere flesh and blood.* **2.** one's own relations; one's own kin. □ *That's no way to treat one's own flesh and blood.* □ *I want to leave my money to my own flesh and blood.*

flight of fancy an idea or suggestion that is out of touch with reality or possibility. □ *What is the point in indulging in flights of fancy about foreign holidays when you cannot even afford the rent?* □ *We are tired of her flights of fancy about marrying a millionaire.*

flog a dead horse to try to continue discussing or arousing interest in something that already has been fully discussed or that is no longer of interest. □ *Stop arguing! You have won your point. You are just flogging a dead horse.* □ *There's no point in putting job-sharing on the agenda. We've already voted against it four times. Why flog a dead horse?*

fly a kite to spread rumours or suggestions about something, such as a new project, in order to find out people's attitudes to it. □ *The government is flying a kite with these stories of a new airport.* □ *No official proposal has been made about redundancies. The management is flying a kite by dropping hints.*

fly-by-night irresponsible; untrustworthy. (Refers to a person who sneaks away secretly in the night.) □ *The carpenter we employed was a fly-by-night worker who did a very bad job of work.* □ *You shouldn't deal with a fly-by-night merchant.*

flying visit a very short, often unexpected visit. □ *She paid us a flying visit before leaving town.* □ *Very few people saw her in the office. It was just a flying visit.*

fly in the face of someone or something to disregard, defy, or show disrespect for someone or something. □ *John loves to fly in the face of tradition.* □ *Ann made it a practice to fly in the face of standard procedures.*

fly in the ointment a small, unpleasant matter which spoils something; a drawback. □ *We enjoyed the play, but the fly in the ointment was not being able to find our car afterwards.* □ *It sounds like a good idea, but there must be a fly in the ointment somewhere.*

foam at the mouth to be very angry. (Informal. Related to a "mad dog"—a dog with rabies—which foams at the mouth.) □ *Bob was* *furious—foaming at the mouth. I've never seen anyone so angry.* □ *Bill foamed at the mouth in sheer rage.*

follow one's heart to act according to one's feelings; to obey one's sympathetic or compassionate inclinations. □ *I couldn't decide what to do, so I just followed my heart.* □ *I trust that you will follow your heart in this matter.*

follow one's nose 1. to go straight ahead, the direction in which one's nose is pointing. (Informal.) □ *The town that you want is straight ahead on this motorway. Just follow your nose.* □ *The chief's office is right around the corner. Turn left and follow your nose.* **2.** to follow a smell to its source. (Informal.) □ *The kitchen is at the back of the building. Just follow your nose.* □ *There was a bad smell in the basement—probably a dead mouse. I followed my nose until I found it.*

follow suit to follow in the same pattern; to follow someone else's example. (From card-games.) □ *Mary went to work for a bank, and Jane followed suit. Now they are both head cashiers.* □ *The Smiths went out to dinner, but the Browns didn't follow suit. They ate at home.*

food for thought something to think about. □ *I don't like your idea very much, but it's food for thought.* □ *Your lecture was very good. It contained much food for thought.*

fool's paradise a condition of apparent happiness that is based on false assumptions and will not last. (Treated as a place grammatically.) □ *They think they can live on love alone, but they are living in a fool's paradise.* □ *The inhabitants of the island feel politically secure, but they are living in a fool's paradise. They could be invaded at any time.*

fools rush in (where angels fear to tread) people with little experience or knowledge often get involved in difficult or delicate situations which wiser people would avoid. □ *I wouldn't ask Jean about her divorce, but Kate did. Fools rush in, as they say.* □ *Only the newest member of the committee questioned the chairman's decision. Fools rush in where angels fear to tread.*

foot the bill to pay the bill; to pay (for something). □ *Let's go out and eat. I'll foot the bill.* □ *If the insurance firm goes bankrupt, don't worry. The government will foot the bill.*

forbidden fruit someone or something that one finds attractive or desirable partly because the person or thing is unobtainable. (From the fruit in the garden of Eden that was forbidden to Adam by God.) □ *Jim is in love with his sister-in-law only because she's forbidden fruit.* □ *The boy watches that programme only when his parents are out. It's forbidden fruit.*

force someone's hand to force one to do something that one is unwilling to do or sooner than one wants to do it. (Refers to a handful of cards in card-playing.) □ *We didn't know what she was doing until Tom forced her hand.* □ *The committee didn't want to reveal their plans so soon, but we forced their hand.*

for days on end for many days without a break. □ *We kept on travelling for days on end.* □ *Doctor, I've had this pain for days on end.*

forget oneself to forget one's manners or training. (Said in formal situations in reference to bad table manners or bad taste.) □ *Sorry, Mother, I forgot myself. I didn't mean to use a swear-word.* □ *John, we are going out to dinner tonight. Please don't forget yourself and gulp down your food.*

forgive and forget to forgive someone (for something) and forget that it ever happened. □ *I'm sorry we quarrelled, John. Let's forgive and forget. What do you say?* □ *It was nothing. We'll just have to forgive and forget.*

for sale See on sale.

for the record so that (one's own version of) the facts will be known; so there will be a record of a particular fact. □ *I'd like to say—for the record—that at no time have I ever accepted a bribe from anyone.* □ *For the record, I've never been able to get anything done around city hall without bribing someone.*

foul one's own nest to harm one's own interests; to bring disadvantage upon oneself. □ *He tried to discredit a fellow MP with the prime minister, but just succeeded in fouling his own nest.* □ *The boss really dislikes Mary. She certainly fouled her own nest when she spread those rumours about him.*

foul play illegal activity; a criminal act. □ *The police investigating the death suspect foul play.* □ *Foul play cannot be ruled out.*

free and easy casual. □ *John is so free and easy. How can anyone be so relaxed?* □ *Now, take it easy. Just act free and easy. No one will know you're nervous.*

(fresh fields and) pastures new new places; new activities. (From a line in Milton's poem *Lycidas*.) □ *I used to like living here, but it's fresh fields and pastures new for me now.* □ *Peter has decided to leave teaching. He's looking for fresh fields and pastures new.* □ *It's all very well to seek pastures new, but think of the unemployment situation.*

from pillar to post from one place to another or to a series of other places. □ *My father was in the army, and we moved from pillar to post, year after year.* □ *I went from pillar to post trying to find a telephone.*

from rags to riches from poverty to wealth. □ *The princess used to be quite poor. She certainly moved from rags to riches when she married.* □ *When I inherited the money, I went from rags to riches.*

from stem to stern from one end to another. (Refers to the front and back ends of a ship. Also used literally in reference to ships.) □ *Now, I have to clean the house from stem to stern.* □ *I polished my car carefully from stem to stern.*

from the word go from the beginning. (Informal.) □ *I knew about the problem from the word go.* □ *She was doing badly in the class from the word go.*

from the year dot AND **since the year dot** for a very long time; since very far back in time. (Informal.) □ *Mr. Jones worked there from the year dot.* □ *I've known Mike since the year dot.*

full of oneself conceited; self-important. □ *Mary's very unpopular because she's so full of herself.* □ *She doesn't care about other people's feelings. She's too full of herself.*

full of the devil always making mischief. (Informal.) □ *Tom is a lot of fun, but he's certainly full of the devil.* □ *I've never seen a child get into so much mischief. He's really full of the devil.*

full steam ahead forward at the greatest speed possible; with as much energy and enthusiasm as possible. (From an instruction given on a steamship.) □ *It will have to be full steam ahead for everybody if the factory gets this order.* □ *It's going to be full steam ahead for me this year. I take my final exams.*

fun and games 1. playing around; someone's lively behaviour. (Informal.) □ *All right, Bill, the fun and games are over. It's time to get down to work.* □ *I'm tired of your fun and games. Go away and read a book.* **2.** difficulties; trouble. □ *There will be fun and games when her father sees the broken window.* □ *There will be fun and games if the children are home late.*

G

game at which two can play a manner of competing which two competitors can use; a strategy that competing sides can both use. □ *The mayor shouted at the town council, "Politics is a game at which two can play."* □ *"Flattery is a game at which two can play," said John as he returned Mary's compliment.* ALSO: **two can play at that game** two people can compete, using the same strategy. □ *I'm sorry you're being so hard to deal with. Two can play at that game.*

generous to a fault too generous. □ *My favourite uncle is generous to a fault.* □ *Sally—always generous to a fault—gave away her sandwiches.*

get a black eye to get a bruise near the eye from being struck. (Note: *Get* can be replaced with *have*. See the variations in the examples. *Get* usually means to become, to acquire, or to cause. *Have* usually means to possess, to be, or to have resulted in.) □ *I got a black eye from walking into a door.* □ *I have a black eye where John hit me.* ALSO: **give someone a black eye** to hit someone near the eye so that a dark bruise appears. □ *John became angry and gave me a black eye.*

get above oneself to think or behave as though one is better or more important than one is. □ *John has been getting a bit above himself since he was promoted. He never goes for a drink with his old colleagues.* □ *There was no need for her to get above herself just because she married a wealthy man.*

get a clean bill of health [for someone] to be pronounced healthy by a doctor. (Also with *have*. See the note at get a black eye. From the fact that ships were given a clean bill of health before sailing only after the absence of infectious disease was certified.) □ *Sally got a clean bill of health from the doctor.* □ *Now that Sally has a clean bill of health, she can go back to work.* ALSO: **give someone a clean**

bill of health [for a doctor] to pronounce someone well and healthy. □ *The doctor gave Sally a clean bill of health.*

get a good run for one's money to receive what one deserves, expects, or wants; to be well compensated for effort, money, etc., spent. (Informal. Also with *have*.) □ *If Bill gets a good run for his money, he will be satisfied.* □ *Even if she does get the sack now, she's had a good run for her money. She's been there for years.*

get a lucky break to have good fortune; to receive a bit of luck. (Informal. Also with *have*. See the note at *get a black eye*.) □ *Mary really got a lucky break when she got that job.* □ *After losing three times, John finally had a lucky break.*

get a lump in one's throat to have the feeling of something in one's throat—as if one were going to cry; to become emotional or sentimental. (Also with *have*. See the note at *get a black eye*.) □ *Whenever they play the national anthem, I get a lump in my throat.* □ *I have a lump in my throat because my friends are going away.*

get a slap on the wrist to get a light punishment (for doing something wrong). (Informal.) □ *He created quite a disturbance, but he only got a slap on the wrist.* □ *I thought I'd just get a slap on the wrist for speeding, but I got fined £200.*

get a start to receive training or a big opportunity in beginning one's career. □ *She got a start in show business in Manchester.* □ *She got a start in modelling when she was only four.* ALSO: **give someone a start** to give one training or a big opportunity in beginning one's career. □ *My career began when my father gave me a start in his act.*

get a tongue-lashing to receive a severe scolding. □ *I really got a tongue-lashing when I got home.* □ *She got a terrible tongue-lashing from her mother.* ALSO: **give someone a tongue-lashing** to give someone a severe scolding. □ *I gave Bill a real tongue-lashing when he got home late.*

get away (from it all) to get away from one's work or daily routine; to go on a holiday. □ *I just love the summer when I can take time off and get away from it all.* □ *Yes, that's the best time to get away.*

get a word in (edgeways) to succeed in saying something when other people are talking and one is being ignored. (Often in the negative.) □ *It was such an exciting conversation that I could hardly get* *a word in edgeways.* □ *Mary talks so fast that nobody can get a word in edgeways.*

get back on one's feet to become independent again; to become able to move around again. (Note the variations with *own* and *two* in the examples.) □ *He was sick for a while, but now he's getting back on his feet.* □ *My parents helped a lot when I lost my job. I'm glad I'm back on my own feet now.* □ *It feels great to be back on my own two feet again.*

get butterflies in one's stomach to get a nervous feeling in one's stomach. (Informal. Also with *have*. See the note at **get a black eye**.) □ *Whenever I have to go on stage, I get butterflies in my stomach.* □ *She always has butterflies in her stomach before a test.* ALSO: **give one butterflies in one's stomach** to cause someone to have a nervous stomach. □ *Exams give me butterflies in my stomach.*

get by (on a shoe-string) to manage to live (on very little money). □ *For the last two years, we have had to get by on a shoe-string.* □ *With so little money, it's hard to get by.*

get carried away to be overcome by emotion or enthusiasm (in one's thinking or actions). □ *Calm down, Jane. Don't get carried away.* □ *Here, Bill. Take this money and go to the sweet-shop, but don't get carried away.*

get cold feet to become timid or frightened. (Also with *have*. See the note at **get a black eye**.) □ *I usually get cold feet when I have to speak in public.* □ *John got cold feet and wouldn't run in the race.* □ *I can't give my speech now. I have cold feet.*

get credit (for something) to receive praise or recognition for one's role in something. (Especially with *a lot of, much*, etc., as in the examples.) □ *Mary should get a lot of credit for the team's success.* □ *Each of the team captains should get credit.* ALSO: **give someone credit (for something)** to praise or recognize someone for doing something. □ *The coach gave Mary a lot of credit.* □ *The director gave John much credit for his fine performance.*

get down to brass tacks to begin to talk about important things. (Informal.) □ *Let's get down to brass tacks. We've wasted too much time chatting.* □ *Don't you think that it's about time to get down to brass tacks?*

get down to business to begin to get serious; to begin to negotiate or conduct business. □ *All right, everyone. Let's get down to business. There has been enough playing around.* □ *When the president and vice-president arrive, we can get down to business.*

get in someone's hair to bother or irritate someone. (Informal.) □ *Billy is always getting in his mother's hair.* □ *I wish you'd stop getting in my hair.*

get into full swing to move into the peak of activity; to start moving fast or efficiently. (Informal.) □ *In the summer months, things really get into full swing around here.* □ *We go skiing in the mountains each winter. Things get into full swing there in November.*

get into the swing of things to join in the routine or the activities. (Informal.) □ *Come on, Bill. Try to get into the swing of things.* □ *John just couldn't seem to get into the swing of things.*

get nowhere fast not to make progress; to get nowhere. (Informal.) □ *I can't seem to make any progress. No matter what I do, I'm just getting nowhere fast.* □ *Come on. Go faster! We're getting nowhere fast.*

get off lightly to receive very little punishment (for doing something wrong). □ *It was a serious crime, but Mary got off lightly.* □ *Billy's punishment was very light. Considering what he did, he got off lightly.*

get off to a flying start to have a very successful beginning to something. □ *The new business got off to a flying start with those export orders.* □ *We shall need a large donation from the local council if the charity is to get off to a flying start.*

get one's come-uppance to get a reprimand; to get the punishment one deserves. □ *Tom is always insulting people, but he finally got his come-uppance. Bill hit him.* □ *I hope I don't get my come-uppance like that.*

get one's fill of someone or something to receive enough of someone or something. (Also with have. See the note at **get a black eye**.) □ *You'll soon get your fill of Tom. He can be quite a pest.* □ *I can never get my fill of shrimps. I love them.* □ *Three weeks of visiting grandchildren is enough. I've had my fill of them.*

get one's fingers burned to have a bad experience. (Also used literally.) □ *I tried that once before and got my fingers burned. I won't try it again.* □ *If you buy shares and get your fingers burned, you then tend to leave your money in the bank.*

get one's foot in the door to achieve a favourable position (for further action); to take the first step in a process. (People selling things from door to door used to block the door with a foot, so it could not be closed on them. Also with *have*. See the note at **get a black eye**.) □ *I think I could get the position if I could only get my foot in the door.* □ *It pays to get your foot in the door. Try to get an appointment with the managing director.* □ *I have a better chance now that I have my foot in the door.*

get one's just deserts to get what one deserves. □ *I feel better now that Jane got her just deserts. She really insulted me.* □ *Bill got back exactly the treatment which he gave out. He got his just deserts.*

get one's money's worth to get everything that has been paid for; to get the best quality for the money paid. □ *Weigh that pack of meat before you buy it. Be sure you're getting your money's worth.* □ *The show was so bad we felt we hadn't got our money's worth.*

get one's nose out of someone's business to stop interfering in someone else's business; to mind one's own business. (Informal.) □ *Go away! Get your nose out of my business!* □ *Bob just can't seem to get his nose out of other people's business.* ALSO: **keep one's nose out of someone's business** to refrain from interfering in someone else's business. □ *Let John have his privacy, and keep your nose out of my business, too!*

get one's second wind (Also with *have*. See the note at **get a black eye**.) **1.** for one's breathing to become stabilized after exerting oneself for a short time. □ *John was having a hard time running until he got his second wind.* □ *"At last," thought Ann, "I have my second wind. Now I can really swim fast." ***2.** to become more active or productive (after becoming tired for a time.) □ *I usually get my second wind early in the afternoon.* □ *Mary is a better worker now that she has her second wind.*

get one's teeth into something to start on something seriously, especially a difficult task. (Informal.) □ *Come on, Bill. You have to get your teeth into your biology.* □ *I can't wait to get my teeth into this problem.*

get on the good side of someone to get into someone's favour. □ *You had better behave properly if you want to get on the good side of Mary.* □ *If you want to get on the good side of your teacher, you must do your homework.* ALSO: **keep on the good side of someone** to stay in someone's favour. □ *You have to work hard to keep on the good side of the manager.*

get out of the wrong side of the bed to get up in the morning in a bad mood. □ *What's wrong with you? Did you get out of the wrong side of the bed today?* □ *Excuse me for being cross. I got out of the wrong side of the bed.*

get someone off the hook to free someone from an obligation. (Informal.) □ *Thanks for getting me off the hook. I didn't want to attend that meeting.* □ *I couldn't get Tom off the hook by myself.* ALSO: **get off the hook** to get free from an obligation. □ *She did everything she could to get off the hook.* □ *I couldn't get off the hook by myself.*

get someone's number to find out about a person; to learn the key to understanding a person. (Informal. Also with *have*. See the note at get a black eye.) □ *I'm going to get your number if I can. You're a real puzzle.* □ *I've got Tom's number. He's ambitious.*

get something off one's chest to tell something that has been bothering you. (Also with *have*. See the note at get a black eye.) □ *I have to get this off my chest. I broke your window with a stone.* □ *I knew I'd feel better when I had that off my chest.*

get something out of one's system to be rid of the desire to do something; to do something that you have been wanting to do so that you are not bothered by wanting to do it any more. □ *I bought a new car. I've been wanting to for a long time. I'm glad I finally got that out of my system.* □ *I can't get it out of my system! I want to go back to university and get a degree.*

get something under one's belt (Informal. Also with *have*. See the note at get a black eye.) **1.** to eat or drink something. □ *I'd feel a lot better if I had a cool drink under my belt.* □ *Come in out of the cold and get a nice warm meal under your belt.* **2.** to learn something well; to assimilate some information; to get work done. □ *I have to study tonight. I have to get a lot of algebra under my belt.* □ *I have to get all these reports under my belt before I go home.*

get the ball rolling See start the ball rolling.

get the brush-off to be ignored or sent away; to be rejected. (Informal.) □ Don't talk to Tom. You'll just get the brush-off. □ I went up to her and asked for a date, but I got the brush-off.

get the hang of something to learn how to do something; to learn how something works. (Informal. Also with *have*. See the note at get a black eye.) □ As soon as I get the hang of this computer, I'll be able to work faster. □ Now that I have the hang of starting the car in cold weather, I won't have to get up so early.

get the last laugh to laugh at or ridicule someone who has laughed at or ridiculed you; to put someone in the same bad position that you were once in. (Also with *have*. See the note at get a black eye.) □ John laughed when I got a D on the final exam. I got the last laugh, though. He failed the course. □ Mr. Smith said I was foolish when I bought an old building. I had the last laugh when I sold it a month later for twice what I paid for it.

get the runaround to receive a series of excuses, delays, and referrals. (Informal.) □ You'll get the runaround if you ask to see the manager. □ I hate it when I get the runaround. ALSO: **give someone the runaround** to give someone a series of excuses, delays, and referrals. □ If you ask to see the manager, they'll give you the runaround.

get the shock of one's life to receive a serious (emotional) shock. (Also with *have*. See the note at get a black eye.) □ I opened the telegram and got the shock of my life. □ I had the shock of my life when I won £5,000.

get the show on the road to get (something) started. (Informal.) □ Hurry up! Let's get the show on the road. □ If you don't get the show on the road now, we'll never finish today.

get time to catch one's breath AND **find time to catch one's breath** to find enough time to relax or behave normally. (See also catch one's breath.) □ When things slow down around here, I'll get time to catch my breath. □ Sally was so busy she couldn't find time to catch her breath.

getting on (in years) growing older. □ Grandfather is getting on in years. □ Yes, he's really getting on.

get to one's feet to stand up, sometimes in order to address the audience. □ *On a signal from the director, the singers got to their feet.* □ *I was so weak, I could hardly get to my feet.*

get to the bottom of something to get an understanding of the causes of something. □ *We must get to the bottom of this problem immediately.* □ *There is clearly something wrong here, and I want to get to the bottom of it.*

get under someone's skin to bother or irritate someone. (Informal.) □ *John is so annoying. He really gets under my skin.* □ *I know he's a nuisance, but don't let him get under your skin.*

get what is coming to one to get what one deserves, usually something bad. □ *If you cheat, you'll get into trouble. You'll get what's coming to you.* □ *Bill got what was coming to him when Ann left him.* ALSO: **give one what is coming to one** to give one what one deserves. □ *Jim gave Bill what was coming to him.*

get wind of something to hear about something; to receive information about something. (Informal.) □ *I just got wind of the job vacancy and have applied.* □ *Wait until the treasurer gets wind of this. Somebody is going to get in trouble.*

gild the lily to add ornament or decoration to something which is pleasing in its original state; to attempt to improve something which is already fine the way it is. (Often refers to flattery or exaggeration.) □ *Your house has lovely brickwork. Don't paint it. That would be gilding the lily.* □ *Oh, Sally. You're beautiful the way you are. You don't need make-up. You would be gilding the lily.*

give a good account of oneself to do (something) well or thoroughly. □ *John gave a good account of himself when he gave his speech last night.* □ *Mary was not hungry, and she didn't give a good account of herself at dinner.*

give as good as one gets to give as much as one receives. □ *John can hold his own in a fight. He can give as good as he gets.* □ *Sally usually wins a formal debate. She gives as good as she gets.*

give credit where credit is due to give credit to someone who deserves it; to acknowledge or thank someone who deserves it. □ *We must give credit where credit is due. Thank you very much, Sally.* □ *Let's give credit where credit is due. Mary is the one who wrote the report, not Jane.*

give ground to retreat (literally or figuratively). □ *When I argue with Mary, she never gives ground.* □ *I approached the barking dog, but it wouldn't give ground.*

give it to someone straight to tell something to someone clearly and directly. (Informal.) □ *Come on, give it to me straight. I want to know exactly what happened.* □ *Quit wasting time, and tell me. Give it to me straight!*

give of oneself to be generous with one's time and concern. □ *Tom is very good with children because he gives himself.* □ *If you want to have more friends, you have to learn to give of yourself.*

give one one's marching orders to sack someone; to dismiss someone from employment. (Informal.) □ *Tom has proved unsatisfactory. I decided to give him his marching orders.* □ *We might even give Sally her marching orders, too.*

give oneself airs to act in a conceited or superior way. □ *Sally is always giving herself airs. You'd think she had royal blood.* □ *Come on, John. Don't behave so haughtily. Stop giving yourself airs.*

give one's right arm (for someone or something) to be willing to give something of great value for someone or something. □ *I'd give my right arm for a nice cool drink.* □ *I'd give my right arm to be there.* □ *Tom really admires John. Tom would give his right arm for John.*

give someone a piece of one's mind to reprimand or scold someone; to tell someone off. □ *I've had enough from John. I'm going to give him a piece of my mind.* □ *Sally, stop it, or I'll give you a piece of my mind.*

give someone or something a wide berth to keep a reasonable distance from someone or something. (Originally referred to sailing ships.) □ *The dog we are approaching is very bad-tempered. Better give it a wide berth.* □ *Give Mary a wide berth. She's in a very bad mood.*

give someone pause for thought to cause someone to stop and think. □ *When I see a golden sunrise, it gives me pause for thought.* □ *Witnessing an accident is likely to give all of us pause for thought.*

give someone the shirt off one's back to be very generous or solicitous towards someone. □ *Tom really likes Bill. He'd give Bill* *the shirt off his back.* □ *John is so friendly that he'd give anyone the shirt off his back.*

give someone tit for tat to give someone something equal to what one has received; to exchange a series of things, one by one, with someone. (Informal.) □ *They took my car after I took theirs. It was tit for tat.* □ *He punched me, so I punched him. Every time he hit me, I hit him. I just gave him tit for tat.*

give something a lick and a promise to do something poorly—quickly and carelessly. (Informal.) □ *John! You didn't clean your room! You just gave it a lick and a promise.* □ *This time, Tom, comb your hair. It looks as if you just gave it a lick and a promise.*

give something a miss not to go to something; not to bother with something; to leave something alone. (Informal.) □ *Betty decided to give the fair a miss this year.* □ *I regretted having to give Monday's lecture a miss, but I was just too busy to attend.*

give something one's best shot to give a task one's best effort. (Informal. Often with *it*.) □ *I gave the project my best shot.* □ *Sure, try it. Give it your best shot!*

give the devil her due See give the devil his due.

give the devil his due AND **give the devil her due** to give your foe proper credit (for something). (This usually refers to a person who has acted in an evil way—like the devil.) □ *She's generally impossible, but I have to give the devil her due. She's always honest.* □ *John may squander money, but give the devil his due. He makes sure his family are well taken care of.*

give the game away to reveal a plan or strategy. (Informal.) □ *Now, all of you have to keep quiet. Please don't give the game away.* □ *If you keep giving out hints, you'll give the game away.*

give up the ghost 1. to die; to release one's spirit. (Considered formal or humorous.) □ *The old man sighed, rolled over, and gave up the ghost.* □ *I'm too young to give up the ghost.* **2.** to quit; to cease trying. □ *Don't give up the ghost. Keep trying!* □ *The runner gave up the ghost and failed to complete the race.*

give voice to something to express a feeling or an opinion in words; to speak out about something. □ *The bird gave voice to its* *joy in the golden sunshine.* □ *All the people gave voice to their anger with the government.*

glut on the market something on the market in great abundance. □ *Right now, small computers are a glut on the market.* □ *Some years ago, small transistor radios were a glut on the market.*

glutton for punishment someone who seems to like doing or seeking out difficult, unpleasant, or badly paid tasks. □ *If you work for this charity, you'll have to be a glutton for punishment and work long hours for nothing.* □ *Jane must be a real glutton for punishment. She's typing Bill's manuscript free of charge and he doesn't even thank her.*

go against the grain to go against the natural direction or inclination. □ *You can't expect me to help you cheat. That goes against the grain.* □ *Would it go against the grain for you to lend her money?*

go back on one's word to break a promise which one has made. □ *I hate to go back on my word, but I won't pay you £100 after all.* □ *Going back on your word makes you a liar.*

go begging to be unwanted or unused. (As if a thing were begging for an owner or a user.) □ *There is still food left. A whole lobster is going begging. Please eat some more.* □ *There are many excellent books in the library just going begging because people don't know they are there.*

go broke to run out of money and other assets. □ *This company is going to go broke if you don't stop spending money foolishly.* □ *I made some bad investments last year, and it looks as though I may go broke this year.*

go by the board to get ruined or lost. (This is a nautical expression meaning to fall or be washed overboard.) □ *I hate to see good food go by the board. Please eat up so we won't have to throw it out.* □ *Your plan has gone by the board. The entire project has been cancelled.*

go down fighting to continue the struggle until one is completely defeated. □ *I won't give up easily. I'll go down fighting.* □ *Sally, who is very determined, went down fighting.*

go downhill [for something] to decline and grow worse and worse. (Also used literally.) □ *This industry is going downhill. We lose money every year.* □ *As one gets older, one tends to go downhill.*

go down in history to be remembered as historically important. □ *Wellington went down in history as a famous general.* □ *This is the greatest affair of the century. I bet it'll go down in history.*

go down like a lead balloon to fail, especially to fail to be funny. □ *Your joke went down like a lead balloon.* □ *If that play was supposed to be a comedy, it went down like a lead balloon.*

go Dutch to share the cost of a meal or some other event with someone. □ *I'll go out and eat with you if we can go Dutch.* □ *It's getting expensive to have Sally for a friend. She never wants to go Dutch.*

goes without saying [something] is so obvious that it need not be said. □ *It goes without saying that you must keep the place clean.* □ *Of course. That goes without saying.*

go for someone or something to attack someone or something; to move or lunge towards someone or something. □ *The dog went for the visitor and almost bit him.* □ *He went for the door and tried to break it down.*

go from bad to worse to progress from a bad state to a worse state. □ *This is a terrible day. Things are going from bad to worse.* □ *My cold is awful. It went from bad to worse in just an hour.*

go haywire to go wrong; to malfunction; to break down. (Informal.) □ *We were all organized, but our plans suddenly went haywire.* □ *There we were, driving along, when the engine went haywire. It was two hours before the breakdown lorry came.*

go in for something to take part in something; to enjoy (doing) something. □ *John doesn't go in for sports.* □ *None of them seems to go in for swimming.*

going great guns going energetically or fast. (Informal.) □ *I'm over my cold and going great guns.* □ *Business is great. We are going great guns selling icecream.*

go in one ear and out the other [for something] to be heard and then forgotten. (Informal.) □ *Everything I say to you seems to go in one ear and out the other. Why don't you pay attention?* □ *I can't concentrate. Things people say to me just go in one ear and out the other.*

go it alone to do something by oneself. (Informal.) □ *Do you need help, or will you go it alone?* □ *I think I need a little more experience before I go it alone.*

go like clockwork to progress with regularity and dependability. □ *The building project is progressing nicely. Everything is going like clockwork.* □ *The elaborate pageant was a great success. It went like clockwork from start to finish.*

good enough for someone or something adequate or fine for someone or something. □ *This seat is good enough for me. I don't want to move.* □ *That table isn't good enough for my office.*

good-for-nothing a worthless person. □ *Tell that good-for-nothing to go home at once.* □ *Bob can't get a job. He's such a good-for-nothing.*

good riddance (to bad rubbish) [it is] good to be rid (of worthless persons or things). □ *She slammed the door behind me and said, "Good riddance to bad rubbish!"* □ *"Good riddance to you, madam," thought I.*

go off at a tangent to go off suddenly in another direction; suddenly to change one's line of thought, course of action, etc. (A reference to geometry. Plural: **go off at tangents**.) □ *Please stick to one subject and don't go off at a tangent.* □ *If Mary would settle down and deal with one subject she would be all right, but she keeps going off at tangents.*

go off at half cock to proceed without proper preparation; to speak (about something) without adequate knowledge. (Informal.) □ *Their plans are always going off at half cock.* □ *Get your facts straight before you make your presentation. There is nothing worse than going off at half cock.*

go off the deep end to become angry or hysterical; to lose one's temper. (Informal. Refers to going into a swimming-pool at the deep end—rather than the shallow end.) □ *Her father went off the deep end when she came in late.* □ *The teacher went off the deep end when she saw his work.*

go over someone's head [for the intellectual content of something] to be too difficult for someone to understand. □ *All that talk about computers went over my head.* □ *I hope my lecture didn't go over the pupils' heads.*

go over something with a fine-tooth comb AND **go through something with a fine-tooth comb; search something with a fine-tooth comb** to search through something very carefully. (As if one were searching for something very tiny which is lost in some kind of fibre.) □ *I can't find my calculus book. I went over the whole place with a fine-tooth comb.* □ *I searched this place with a fine-tooth comb and didn't find my ring.*

go round in circles to keep going over the same ideas or repeating the same actions, often resulting in confusion, without reaching a satisfactory decision or conclusion. □ *We're just going round in circles discussing the problems of the fête. We need to consult someone else to get a new point of view.* □ *Fred's trying to find out what's happened, but he's going round in circles. No one will tell him anything useful.*

go sky-high to go very high. (Informal.) □ *Prices go sky-high whenever there is inflation.* □ *Oh, it's so hot. The temperature went sky-high about midday.*

go so far as to say something to put something into words; to risk saying something. □ *I think that Bob is dishonest, but I wouldn't go so far as to say he's a thief.* □ *Red meat may be harmful in some cases, but I can't go so far as to say it causes cancer.*

go the distance AND **stay the distance** to do the whole amount; to play the entire game; to run the whole race. (Informal. Originally sports use.) □ *That horse runs fast. I hope it can go the distance.* □ *This is going to be a long, hard project. I hope I can go the distance.* □ *Jim changes jobs a lot. He never stays the distance.*

go the whole hog to do everything possible; to be extravagant. (Informal.) □ *Let's go the whole hog. Order steak and lobster.* □ *Show some restraint. Don't go the whole hog and leave yourself penniless.*

go through something with a fine-tooth comb See go over something with a fine-tooth comb.

go through the motions to make a feeble effort to do something; to pretend to do something. □ *Jane isn't doing her best. She's just going through the motions.* □ *Bill was supposed to be raking the garden, but he was just going through the motions.*

go through the proper channels to proceed by consulting the proper persons or offices. □ *If you want an answer to your question,* *you'll have to go through the proper channels.* □ *Your application will have to go through the proper channels.*

go to Davy Jones's locker to go to the bottom of the sea; to drown. (Thought of as a nautical expression.) □ *My uncle was a sailor. He went to Davy Jones's locker during a terrible storm.* □ *My camera fell overboard and went to Davy Jones's locker.*

go to hell AND **go to the devil** to go away and stop bothering (someone). (Informal. Use caution with both phrases, and especially with *hell*.) □ *He told her to go to hell, that he didn't want her.* □ *Leave me alone! Go to the devil!*

go to rack and ruin to become ruined or destroyed, especially due to neglect. □ *That lovely old house on the corner is going to go to rack and ruin.* □ *My lawn is going to rack and ruin.*

go to seed See run to seed.

go to someone's head to make someone conceited; to make someone overly proud. □ *You did a fine job, but don't let it go to your head.* □ *He let his success go to his head, and soon he became a complete failure.*

go to the devil See go to hell.

go to the limit to do as much as is possible to do. □ *Okay, we can't afford it, but we'll go to the limit.* □ *How far shall I go? Shall I go to the limit?*

go to the loo See go to the toilet.

go to the toilet AND **go to the loo** to eliminate bodily wastes through defecation or urination. (*Loo* is an informal word meaning "toilet.") □ *The child needed to go to the toilet.* □ *After drinking so much, he had to go to the loo.*

go to the wall to be defeated; to fail in business. (Informal.) □ *During the recession, many small companies went to the wall.* □ *The company went to the wall because of that contract. Now it's broke and the employees are redundant.*

go to town to make a great effort; to work with energy or enthusiasm. (Informal.) □ *They really went to town on cleaning the house. It's spotless.* □ *You've really gone to town with the food for the party.*

go to waste to be wasted; to be unused (and therefore thrown away). □ *Eat your potatoes! Don't let them go to waste.* □ *He never practises on the piano. It's sad to see talent going to waste.*

grasp the nettle to tackle a difficult or unpleasant task with firmness and determination. □ *We must grasp the nettle and do something about our overspending.* □ *The education committee is reluctant to grasp the nettle of lack of textbooks.*

Greek to me See all Greek to me.

green about the gills See pale around the gills.

green around the gills See pale around the gills.

green with envy envious; jealous. □ *When Sally saw me with Tom, she turned green with envy. She likes him a lot.* □ *I feel green with envy whenever I see you in your new car.*

grin and bear it to endure something unpleasant with good humour. □ *There is nothing you can do but grin and bear it.* □ *I hate having to work for rude people. I suppose I have to grin and bear it.*

grind to a halt to slow to a stop. □ *By the end of the day, the factory had ground to a halt.* □ *The train ground to a halt, and we got out to stretch our legs.*

grist to the mill something which can be put to good use or which can bring advantage or profit. (Grist was corn brought to a mill to be ground and so kept the mill operating.) □ *Some of the jobs that we are offered are more interesting than others, but all is grist to the mill.* □ *The firm is having to sell rather ugly souvenirs, but they are grist to the mill and keep the firm in business.*

grit one's teeth to grind one's teeth together in anger or determination; to show determination. □ *I was so angry that all I could do was stand there and grit my teeth.* □ *All through the race, Sally was gritting her teeth. She was really determined.*

grow on someone [for something] to become commonplace to a person. (The *someone* is usually *one*, *someone*, *a person*, etc., not a specific person.) □ *That music is strange, but it grows on you.* □ *I didn't think I could ever get used to this town, but after a while it grows on one.*

H

hail-fellow-well-met friendly to everyone; falsely friendly to everyone. (Usually said of males.) □ *Yes, he's friendly, sort of hail-fellow-well-met.* □ *He's not a very sincere person. Hail-fellow-well-met—you know the type.* □ *He's one of those hail-fellow-well-met people that you don't quite trust.*

hail from somewhere [for someone] to come originally from somewhere. (Informal.) □ *I'm from Edinburgh. Where do you hail from?* □ *I hail from the Southwest.*

hair of the dog (that bit one) an alcoholic drink taken when one has a hangover. (Informal.) □ *Oh, I have a terrible hangover. I need a hair of the dog.* □ *That's some hangover you've got there, Bob. Here, drink this. It's a hair of the dog that bit you.*

hale and hearty well and healthy. □ *Doesn't Ann look hale and hearty after the baby's birth?* □ *I don't feel hale and hearty. I'm really tired.*

hand in glove (with someone) very close to someone. □ *John is really hand in glove with Sally, although they pretend to be on different sides.* □ *The teacher and the headmaster work hand in glove.*

hand it to someone give credit to someone, often with some reluctance. (Informal. Often with *have to* or *must*.) □ *I must hand it to you. You did a fine job.* □ *We must hand it to Sally. She helped us a lot.*

handle someone with kid gloves to be very careful with a sensitive or touchy person. □ *Bill has become so sensitive. You really have to handle him with kid gloves.* □ *You don't have to handle me with kid gloves. I can take what you have to tell me.*

hand-me-down something, such as an article of used clothing, which has been "handed down," or given, to someone because another person no longer needs it. (Informal.) □ *Why do I always*

have to wear my brother's hand-me-downs? I want some new clothes.
□ *This is a nice shirt. It doesn't look like a hand-me-down at all.*

hand over fist [for money and merchandise to be exchanged] very rapidly. □ *What a busy day. We took in money hand over fist.* □ *They were buying things hand over fist.*

hand over hand [moving] one hand after the other (again and again). □ *Sally pulled in the rope hand over hand.* □ *The man climbed the rope hand over hand.*

hang by a hair AND **hang by a thread** to be in an uncertain position; to depend on something very insubstantial. (Informal.) □ *Your whole argument is hanging by a thread.* □ *John hasn't yet failed geometry, but his fate is hanging by a hair.*

hang by a thread See hang by a hair.

hang fire to delay or wait; to be delayed. □ *I think we should hang fire and wait for other information.* □ *Our plans have to hang fire until we get planning permission.*

hang in the balance to be in an undecided state; to be between two equal possibilities. □ *The prisoner stood before the judge, his life hanging in the balance.* □ *The fate of the entire project is hanging in the balance.*

hang on by an eyebrow AND **hang on by one's eyebrows** to be just hanging on or just surviving. □ *He hasn't yet failed, but he is just hanging on by an eyebrow.* □ *The manager is just about to get sacked. She is hanging on by her eyebrows.*

hang on by one's eyebrows See hang on by an eyebrow.

hang one's hat up somewhere to take up residence somewhere. (Informal.) □ *George loves London. He's decided to buy a flat and hang his hat up there.* □ *Bill moves from place to place and never hangs his hat up anywhere.*

hang on someone's every word to listen carefully and obsequiously to everything someone says. □ *He gave a great lecture. We hung on his every word.* □ *Look at the way John hangs on Mary's every word. He must be in love with her.*

hang on to someone's coat-tails to gain good fortune or success through another person's success, rather than through one's own efforts. □ *Bill isn't very creative, so he hangs on to John's coat-tails.* □ *Some people just have to hang on to somebody else's coat-tails.*

Hang on to your hat! AND **Hold on to your hat!** Prepare for a sudden surprise or shock. (Informal.) □ *Are you ready to hear the final score? Hang on to your hat! We won ten–nil!* □ *Guess who got married. Hold on to your hat!*

hard-and-fast rule a strict rule. □ *It's a hard-and-fast rule that you must be home by midnight.* □ *You should have your project completed by the end of the month, but it's not a hard-and-fast rule.*

hard cash cash, not cheques or credit. (Informal.) □ *I want to be paid in hard cash, and I want to be paid now!* □ *No plastic money for me. I want hard cash.*

hardly have time to breathe to be very busy. □ *This was such a busy day. I hardly had time to breathe.* □ *They made him work so hard that he hardly had time to breathe.*

hard on someone's heels following someone very closely. (Informal.) □ *I ran as fast as I could, but the dog was still hard on my heels.* □ *Here comes Sally, and John is hard on her heels.*

hard on the heels of something soon after something. (Informal.) □ *There was a rainstorm hard on the heels of the high winds.* □ *They had a child hard on the heels of getting married.*

hark(en) back to something (*Harken* is an old form of *hark*, which is an old word meaning "listen.") **1.** to have originated as something; to have started out as something. □ *The word icebox harks back to the old-fashioned refrigerators which were cooled by ice.* □ *Our modern breakfast cereals hark back to the porridge and gruel of our ancestors.* **2.** to remind one of something. □ *Seeing a horse and buggy in the park harks back to the time when horses drew milk wagons.* □ *Sally says it harkens back to the time when everything was delivered by horse-drawn wagon.*

hate someone's guts to hate someone very much. (Informal.) □ *Oh, Bob is terrible. I hate his guts!* □ *You may hate my guts for saying so, but I think you're getting grey hairs.*

haul someone over the coals to give someone a severe scolding. □ *My mother hauled me over the coals for coming in late last night.* □ *The manager hauled me over the coals for being late again.*

have a bee in one's bonnet to have an idea or a thought remain in one's mind; to have an obsession. □ *She has a bee in her bonnet about table manners.* □ *I had a bee in my bonnet about swimming. I couldn't stop wanting to go swimming.*

have a big mouth to be a gossiper; to be a person who tells secrets. (Informal.) □ *Mary has a big mouth. She told Bob what I was getting him for his birthday.* □ *You shouldn't say things like that about people all the time. Everyone will say you have a big mouth.*

have a bone to pick (with someone) to have a matter to discuss with someone; to have something to argue about with someone. □ *Look, Bill. I've got a bone to pick with you. Where is the money you owe me?* □ *I had a bone to pick with her, but she was so sweet that I forgot about it.* □ *Ted and Alice have a bone to pick.*

have a brush with something to have a brief contact with something; to have a brief experience of something, especially with the law. (Sometimes a *close* brush.) □ *Ann had a close brush with the law. She was nearly arrested for speeding.* □ *When I was younger, I had a brush with death in a car accident, but I recovered.*

have a case (against someone) to have much evidence which can be used against someone in court. (*Have* can be replaced with *build, gather, assemble,* etc.) □ *Do the police have a case against John?* □ *No, they don't have a case.* □ *They are trying to build a case against him.* □ *My solicitor is busy assembling a case against the other driver.*

have a chip on one's shoulder to feel resentful; to bear resentment. □ *What are you angry about? You always seem to have a chip on your shoulder.* □ *John has had a chip on his shoulder about the police ever since he got his speeding ticket.*

have a down on someone to treat someone in an unfair or hostile way; to have hostile feelings towards someone; to resent and oppose someone. □ *That teacher's had a down on me ever since I was expelled from another school.* □ *The supervisor has a down on anyone who refuses to work overtime.*

have a familiar ring [for a story or an explanation] to sound familiar. □ *Your excuse has a familiar ring. Have you done this before?* □ *This exam paper has a familiar ring. I think it has been copied.*

have a foot in both camps to have an interest in or to support each of two opposing groups of people. □ *The shop steward had been* *promised promotion and so had a foot in both camps during the strike—workers and management.* □ *Mr. Smith has a foot in both camps in the parents/teachers dispute. He teaches maths, but he has a son at the school.*

have a go (at something) to give something a try. (Informal.) □ *I've never fished before, but I'd like to have a go at it.* □ *Great, have a go now. Take my fishing rod and give it a try.*

have a good command of something to know something well. □ *Bill has a good command of French.* □ *Jane has a good command of economic theory.*

have a good head on one's shoulders to have common sense; to be sensible and intelligent. □ *Mary doesn't do well in school, but she's got a good head on her shoulders.* □ *John has a good head on his shoulders and can be depended on to give good advice.*

have a heart to be compassionate; to be generous and forgiving. □ *Oh, have a heart! Give me some help!* □ *If Ann had a heart, she'd have made us feel more welcome.*

have a heart of gold to be generous, sincere, and friendly. □ *Mary is such a lovely person. She has a heart of gold.* □ *You think Tom stole your watch? Impossible! He has a heart of gold.*

have a heart of stone to be cold and unfriendly. □ *Sally has a heart of stone. She never even smiles.* □ *The villain in the play had a heart of stone. He was an ideal villain.*

have a heart-to-heart (talk) to have a sincere and intimate talk. □ *I had a heart-to-heart talk with my father before I went off to college.* □ *I have a problem, John. Let's sit down and have a heart-to-heart.*

have a lot going for one to have many things working to one's benefit. (Informal.) □ *Jane is so lucky. She has a lot going for her.* □ *He's made a mess of his life, even though he had a lot going for him.*

have a low boiling-point to get angry easily. (Informal.) □ *Be nice to John. He's upset and has a low boiling-point.* □ *Mr. Jones certainly has a low boiling-point. I hardly said anything, and he got angry.*

have an axe to grind to have something to complain about or discuss with someone. (Informal.) □ *Tom, I need to talk to you. I have an axe to grind.* □ *Bill and Bob went into the other room to discuss the matter. They each had an axe to grind.*

have a near miss nearly to crash or collide. □ *The planes—flying much too close—had a near miss.* □ *I had a near miss while driving over here.*

have an itching palm See have an itchy palm.

have an itchy palm AND **have an itching palm** to be in need of a tip; to tend to ask for tips. (Informal. As if placing money in the palm would stop its itching. Note the variations in the examples.) □ *All the waiters at that restaurant have itchy palms.* □ *The taxi-driver was troubled by an itching palm. Since he refused to carry my bags, I gave him nothing.*

have another think coming to have to rethink something because one was wrong the first time. (Informal.) □ *She's quite wrong. She's got another think coming if she wants to walk in here like that.* □ *You've got another think coming if you think you can treat me like that!*

have an out to have an excuse; to have a (literal or figurative) means of escape or avoiding something. (Informal.) □ *He's very clever. No matter what happens, he always has an out.* □ *I agreed to go to the party, but now I don't want to go. I wish I had an out.*

have ants in one's pants to become restless; to fidget. (Informal.) □ *Sit still! Have you got ants in your pants?* □ *The children have ants in their pants. It's time to go home.*

have a penchant for doing something to have a taste, desire, or inclination for doing something. □ *John has a penchant for eating fattening foods.* □ *Ann has a penchant for buying clothes.*

have a price on one's head to be wanted by the authorities, who have offered a reward for one's capture. □ *We captured a thief who had a price on his head, and the police gave us the reward.* □ *The crook was so mean, he turned in his own brother, who had a price on his head.*

have a say (in something) AND **have a voice (in something)** to have a part in making a decision. □ *I'd like to have a say in choosing the carpet.* □ *John wanted to have a voice in deciding on the result also.* □ *He says he seldom gets to have a say.*

have a snowball's chance in hell to have no chance at all. (A snowball would melt in hell. Use *hell* with caution.) □ *He has a snow-*

ball's chance in hell of passing the test. □ *You don't have a snowball's chance in hell of her agreeing to marry you.*

have a soft spot for someone or something to be fond of someone or something. □ *John has a soft spot for Mary.* □ *I have a soft spot for the countryside.*

have a sweet tooth to have the desire to eat many sweet foods—especially candy and pastries. □ *I have a sweet tooth, and if I don't watch it, I'll really get fat.* □ *John eats sweets all the time. He must have a sweet tooth.*

have a thin time (of it) to experience a difficult or unfortunate time, especially because of a shortage of money. □ *Jack had a thin time of it when he was a student. He didn't have enough to eat.* □ *The Browns had a thin time of it when the children were small and Mr. Brown was poorly paid.*

have a voice (in something) See have a say (in something).

have a word with someone to speak to someone, usually privately. □ *The manager asked to have a word with me when I was not busy.* □ *John, could I have a word with you? We need to discuss something.*

have bats in one's belfry to be slightly crazy. □ *Poor old Tom has bats in his belfry.* □ *Don't act so silly, John. People will think you have bats in your belfry.*

have been through the mill to have been badly treated; to have suffered hardship or difficulties. (Informal.) □ *This has been a rough day. I've really been through the mill.* □ *She's quite well now, but she's been really through the mill with her illness.*

have clean hands to be guiltless. □ *Don't look at me. I have clean hands.* □ *The police took him in, but let him go again because he had clean hands.*

have egg on one's face to be embarrassed because of an error which is obvious to everyone. (Informal.) □ *Bob has egg on his face because he wore jeans to the affair and everyone else wore formal clothing.* □ *John was completely wrong about the weather for the picnic. It snowed! Now he has egg on his face.*

have eyes in the back of one's head to seem to be able to sense what is going on beyond one's vision. □ *My teacher seems to have* *eyes in the back of her head.* □ *My teacher doesn't need to have eyes in the back of his head. He watches us very carefully.*

have feet of clay to have a defect of character. □ *All human beings have feet of clay. No one is perfect.* □ *Sally prided herself on her complete honesty. She was nearly fifty before she learned that she, too, had feet of clay.*

have green fingers to have the ability to grow plants well. □ *Just look at Mr. Simpson's garden. He has green fingers.* □ *My mother has green fingers when it comes to house-plants.*

have half a mind to do something to have almost decided to do something, especially something unpleasant. (Informal.) □ *I have half a mind to go off and leave you here.* □ *The cook had half a mind to serve cold chicken.*

have (high) hopes of something to be expecting something. □ *I have hopes of getting there early.* □ *We have high hopes that John and Mary will have a girl.*

have it both ways to have both of two seemingly incompatible things. (See also *want it both ways.*) □ *John wants the security of marriage and the freedom of being single. He wants to have it both ways.* □ *John thinks he can have it both ways—the wisdom of age and the vigour of youth.*

have money to burn to have lots of money; to have more money than one needs. (Informal.) □ *Look at the way Tom buys things. You'd think he had money to burn.* □ *If I had money to burn, I'd just put it in the bank.*

have no business doing something to be wrong to do something; to be extremely unwise to do something. □ *You have no business bursting in on me like that!* □ *You have no business spending money like that!*

have none of something to tolerate or endure no amount of something. □ *I'll have none of your talk about leaving school.* □ *We'll have none of your gossip.*

have no staying-power to lack endurance; not to be able to last. □ *Sally can swim fast for a short distance, but she has no staying-power.* □ *That horse can race fairly well, but it has no staying-power.*

have one's back to the wall to be in a defensive position; to be in (financial) difficulties. (Informal.) □ *He'll have to give in. He has his back to the wall.* □ *How can I bargain when I've got my back to the wall?*

have one's ear to the ground AND **keep one's ear to the ground** to listen carefully, hoping to get advance warning of something. □ *John had his ear to the ground, hoping to find out about new ideas in computers.* □ *Keep your ear to the ground for news of possible jobs.*

have one's feet on the ground AND **keep one's feet on the ground** to be or remain realistic or practical. □ *Sally will have no trouble keeping her feet on the ground even when she is famous.* □ *They are ambitious but have their feet firmly on the ground.*

have one's finger in the pie to be involved in something. □ *I like to have my finger in the pie so I can make sure things go my way.* □ *As long as John has his finger in the pie, things will happen slowly.*

have one's hand in the till to be stealing money from a company or an organization. (Informal. The *till* is a cash box or drawer.) □ *Mr. Jones had his hand in the till for years before he was caught.* □ *I think that the new shop assistant has her hand in the till. There is cash missing every morning.*

have one's head in the clouds to be unaware of what is going on. □ *"Bob, do you have your head in the clouds?" said the teacher.* □ *She walks around all day with her head in the clouds. She must be in love.*

have one's heart in one's boots to be very depressed; to have little or no hope. □ *My heart's in my boots when I think of going back to work.* □ *Jack's heart was in his boots when he thought of leaving home.*

have one's nose in a book to be reading a book; to read books all the time. (Informal.) □ *Bob has his nose in a book every time I see him.* □ *His nose is always in a book. He never gets any exercise.*

have one's nose in the air AND **keep one's nose in the air** to be conceited or aloof. □ *Mary always seems to have her nose in the air.* □ *She keeps her nose in the air and never notices him.*

have one's wits about one to concentrate; to have one's mind working. □ *You have to have your wits about you when you are dealing with John.* □ *She had to have her wits about her when living in the city.* ALSO: **keep one's wits about one** to keep one's mind operating, especially in a time of stress. □ *If Jane hadn't kept her wits about her during the fire, things would have been much worse.*

have one's work cut out (for one) to have a large and difficult task prepared for one. □ *They sure have their work cut out for them, and it's going to be hard.* □ *There is a lot for Bob to do. He has his work cut out.* ALSO: **one's work is cut out (for one)** one's task is prepared for one; one has a lot of work to do. □ *This is a big job. My work is certainly cut out for me.*

have other fish to fry to have other things to do; to have more important things to do. (Informal. *Other* can be replaced by *bigger, better, more important,* etc.) □ *I don't have time for your problems. I have other fish to fry.* □ *I won't waste time on your question. I have bigger fish to fry.*

have seen better days to be worn or worn out. (Informal.) □ *This coat has seen better days. I need a new one.* □ *Oh, my old legs ache. I've seen better days, but everyone has to grow old.*

have someone in one's pocket to have control over someone. (Informal.) □ *Don't worry about the mayor. She'll co-operate. I've got her in my pocket.* □ *John will do just what I tell him. I've got him and his brother in my pocket.*

have someone on a string to have someone waiting for one's decision or actions. (Informal.) □ *Sally has John on a string. He has asked her to marry him, but she hasn't replied yet.* □ *Yes, it sounds as if she has him on a string.* ALSO: **keep someone on a string** to keep someone waiting for a decision. □ *Sally kept John on a string for weeks while she made up her mind.* □ *Please don't keep me on a string waiting for a final decision.*

have someone or something on 1. [with *someone*] to kid or deceive someone. (Informal.) □ *You can't be serious. You're having me on!* □ *Bob is such a joker. He's always having someone on.* **2.** [with *something*] to have plans for a particular time. (Note the variation with *anything* in the examples.) □ *I can't get to your party. I have something on.* □ *I have something on almost every Saturday.* □ *Mary rarely has anything on during the week.*

have someone's hide to scold or punish someone. (Informal. Refers to skinning an animal.) □ *If you ever do that again, I'll have your hide.* □ *He said he'd have my hide if I entered his garage again.*

have someone under one's thumb to have control over someone; to dominate someone. □ *His wife has him under her thumb.* □ *The younger child has the whole family under his thumb.*

have something at one's fingertips to have all the knowledge or information one needs; to know something very well, so the knowledge is readily available and can be remembered quickly. □ *He has lots of gardening hints at his fingertips.* □ *They have all the tourist information at their fingertips.*

have something coming to one to deserve punishment for something. (Informal. See also get what is coming to one.) □ *Bill broke a window, so he has a reprimand coming to him.* □ *You've got a lot of criticism coming to you.*

have something hanging over one's head to have something bothering or worrying one; to have a deadline worrying one. (Informal. Also used literally.) □ *I keep worrying about being declared redundant. I hate to have something like that hanging over my head.* □ *I have a history essay hanging over my head. I must write it tonight because it's due tomorrow.*

have something in hand to be prepared to take action on something. □ *I have the matter in hand.* □ *The management has your complaint in hand.*

have something in mind to be thinking of something; to have an idea or image (of something) in one's mind. □ *I have something in mind for dinner.* □ *Do you have something in mind for your mother's birthday?*

have something in stock to have merchandise available and ready for sale. □ *Do you have extra-large sizes in stock?* □ *Of course, we have all sizes and colours in stock.*

have something in store (for someone) to have something planned for one's future. □ *Tom has a large inheritance in store for him when his uncle dies.* □ *I wish I had something like that in store.*

have something on file to have a written record of something in storage. □ *I'm certain I have your letter on file. I'll check again.* □ *We have your application on file somewhere.*

have something on one's hands to be burdened with something. □ *I run a record shop. I sometimes have a large number of unwanted records on my hands.* □ *I have too much time on my hands.*

have something on the brain to be obsessed with something. (Informal.) □ *They have good manners on the brain.* □ *Mary has money on the brain. She wants to earn as much as possible.*

have something out (with someone) to clear the air; to settle a disagreement or a complaint. (Informal.) □ *John has been angry with Mary for a week. He finally had it out with her today.* □ *I'm glad we are having this out today.*

have something up one's sleeve to have a secret or surprise plan or solution (to a problem). (Refers to cheating at cards by having a card hidden up one's sleeve.) □ *He hasn't lost yet. He has something up his sleeve.* □ *The manager has something up her sleeve. She'll surprise us with it later.*

have the courage of one's convictions to have enough courage and determination to carry out one's aims. □ *It's fine to have noble goals in life and to believe in great things. If you don't have the courage of your convictions, you'll never succeed.* □ *Others don't trust him, but I do. I have the courage of my convictions.*

have the Midas touch to have the ability to be successful, especially the ability to make money easily. (From the name of a legendary king whose touch turned everything to gold.) □ *Bob is a merchant banker and really has the Midas touch.* □ *The poverty-stricken boy turned out to have the Midas touch and was a millionaire by the time he was twenty-five.*

have the right of way to possess the legal right to occupy a particular space or proceed before others on a public roadway. □ *I had a traffic accident yesterday, but it wasn't my fault. I had the right of way.* □ *Don't pull out on to a motorway if you don't have the right of way.*

have the time of one's life to have a very good or entertaining time; to have the most exciting time in one's life. (Informal.) □ *What* *a great party! I had the time of my life.* □ *We went to Florida last winter and had the time of our lives.*

have the wherewithal (to do something) to have the means to do something, especially money. □ *He has good ideas, but he doesn't have the wherewithal to carry them out.* □ *I could do a lot if only I had the wherewithal.*

have to live with something to have to endure something. □ *I have a slight limp in the leg that I broke last year. The doctor says I'll have to live with it.* □ *We don't like the new carpet in the living-room, but we'll have to live with it.*

have too many irons in the fire to be doing too many things at once. □ *Tom had too many irons in the fire and missed some important deadlines.* □ *It's better if you don't have too many irons in the fire.*

have turned the corner to have passed a critical point in a process. □ *The patient has turned the corner. She should begin to show improvement now.* □ *The project has turned the corner. The rest should be easy.*

have what it takes to have the courage, stamina, or ability (to do something). □ *Bill has what it takes. He can swim for miles.* □ *Tom won't succeed. He doesn't have what it takes.*

head and shoulders above someone or something clearly superior to someone. (Often with *stand*, as in the example.) □ *This wine is head and shoulders above that one.* □ *John stands head and shoulders above the others.*

head over heels in love (with someone) very much in love with someone. □ *John is head over heels in love with Mary.* □ *They are head over heels in love with each other.* □ *They are head over heels in love.*

heads will roll some people will get into trouble. (Informal. From the use of the guillotine to execute people.) □ *When company's end-of-year results are known, heads will roll.* □ *Heads will roll when the headmaster sees the damaged classroom.*

heavy going difficult to do, understand, or make progress with. (Informal.) □ *Jim finds maths heavy going.* □ *Talking to Mary is heavy going. She has nothing to say.*

hell for leather moving or behaving recklessly. (Informal.) □ *They took off after the horse thief, riding hell for leather.* □ *They ran hell for leather for the train.*

help oneself to take whatever one wants or needs. □ *Please have some sweets. Help yourself.* □ *When you go to a cafeteria, you help yourself to the food.* □ *Bill helped himself to dessert.*

hem and haw AND **hum and haw** to be uncertain about something; to be evasive; to say "ah" and "eh" when speaking—avoiding saying something meaningful. □ *Stop hemming and hawing. I want an answer.* □ *Don't just hem and haw. Speak up. We want to hear what you think.* □ *Stop humming and hawing and say whether you are coming or not.* □ *Jean hummed and hawed for a long time before deciding to marry Henry.*

here's to someone or something an expression used as a toast, wishing the best to someone or something. □ *Here's to Jim and Mary! May they be very happy!* □ *Here's to your new job!*

hide one's face in shame to cover one's face because of shame or embarrassment. □ *Mary was so embarrassed. She could only hide her face in shame.* □ *When Tom broke Ann's crystal vase, he wanted to hide his face in shame.*

hide one's light under a bushel to conceal one's good ideas or talents. (A biblical theme.) □ *Jane has some good ideas, but she doesn't speak very often. She hides her light under a bushel.* □ *Don't hide your light under a bushel. Share your gifts with other people.*

high and mighty proud and powerful. (Informal. Especially with *be* or *act*.) □ *Why does the doctor always have to act so high and mighty?* □ *If Sally didn't act so high and mighty, she'd have more friends.* □ *Don't be so high and mighty!*

high-flyer a person who is ambitious or who is very likely to be successful. (Informal.) □ *Jack was one of the high-flyers of our university year and he is now in the Foreign Office.* □ *Tom is a high-flyer and has applied for the post of managing director.*

hit a snag to run into a problem. (Informal.) □ *We've hit a snag with the building project.* □ *I stopped working on the project when I hit a snag.*

hitch a lift See thumb a lift.

hit it off (with someone) to quickly become good friends with someone. (Informal.) □ *Look how John hit it off with Mary.* □ *Yes, they really hit it off.*

hit rock bottom to reach the lowest or worst point. (Informal.) □ *Our profits have hit rock bottom. This is our worst year ever.* □ *After my life hit rock bottom, I gradually began to feel much better. I knew that if there was going to be any change, it would be for the better.*

hit (someone) below the belt to do something unfair or unsporting to someone. (Informal. From boxing, where a blow below the belt line is not permitted. Also used literally.) □ *You really hit me below the belt when you told my sister about my health problems.* □ *In business, Bill is difficult to deal with. He hits below the belt.*

hit someone (right) between the eyes to become completely apparent; to surprise or impress someone. (Informal. Also with *right*, as in the examples. Also used literally.) □ *Suddenly, it hit me right between the eyes. John and Mary were in love.* □ *Then—as he was talking—the exact nature of the evil plan hit me between the eyes.*

hit the bull's-eye 1. to hit the centre area of a circular target. □ *The archer hit the bull's-eye three times in a row.* □ *I didn't hit the bull's-eye even once.* **2.** to achieve the goal perfectly. (Informal.) □ *Your idea really hit the bull's-eye. Thank you!* □ *Jill has a lot of insight. She hit the bull's-eye in her choice of flowers for her mother.*

Hobson's choice the choice between taking what is offered and getting nothing at all. (From the name of a stable owner in the seventeenth century who offered customers the hire of the horse nearest the door.) □ *We didn't really want that holiday cottage, but it was a case of Hobson's choice. We booked very late and there was nothing else left.* □ *If you want a yellow car, it's Hobson's choice. The garage has only one.*

hold forth to speak, usually at length. (Informal.) □ *The guide held forth about the city.* □ *I've never seen anyone who could hold forth so long.* □ *The professor held forth about economic theory for nearly an hour.*

hold no brief for someone or something not to care about someone or something; not to support someone or something; to dislike someone or something. □ *I hold no brief for people who cheat the company.* □ *My father says he holds no brief for the new plans.*

hold one's fire 1. to refrain from shooting (a gun, etc.). □ *The sergeant told the soldiers to hold their fire.* □ *Please hold your fire until I get out of the way.* **2.** to postpone one's criticism or commentary. (Informal.) □ *Now, now, hold your fire until I've had a chance to explain.* □ *Hold your fire, Bill. You're too quick to complain.*

hold one's own 1. to do as well as anyone else. □ *I can hold my own in a running race any day.* □ *She was unable to hold her own, and she had to leave.* **2.** [for someone] to remain in a stable physical condition. □ *Mary is still seriously ill, but she is holding her own.* □ *We thought Jim was holding his own after the accident, but he died suddenly.*

hold one's peace to remain silent. □ *Bill was unable to hold his peace any longer. "Don't do it!" he cried.* □ *Quiet, John. Hold your peace for a little while longer.*

hold one's tongue to refrain from speaking; to refrain from saying something unpleasant. □ *I felt like scolding her, but I held my tongue.* □ *Hold your tongue, John. You can't talk to me that way.*

Hold on to your hat! See **Hang on to your hat!**

hold out the olive branch to offer to end a dispute and be friendly; to offer reconciliation. (The olive branch is a symbol of peace and reconciliation. A biblical reference.) □ *Jill was the first to hold out the olive branch after our argument.* □ *I always try to hold out the olive branch to someone I have hurt. Life is too short for a person to bear grudges for very long.*

hold true [for something] to be true; [for something] to remain true. □ *Does this rule hold true all the time?* □ *Yes, it holds true no matter what.*

hold water to be able to be proved; to be correct or true. (Usually negative.) □ *Jack's story doesn't hold water. It sounds too unlikely.* □ *I don't think the police's theory will hold water. The suspect has an alibi.*

hole-and-corner AND **hole-in-the-corner** secretive; secret and dishonourable. □ *Jane is tired of the hole-and-corner affair with Tom. She wants him to marry her.* □ *The wedding was a hole-in-the-corner occasion because the bride's parents refused to have anything to do with it.*

hole-in-the-corner See **hole-and-corner.**

holier-than-thou excessively pious; acting as though one is more virtuous than other people. □ *Jack always adopts a holier-than-thou attitude to other people, but people say he has been in prison.* □ *Jane used to be holier-than-thou, but she is marrying Tom, who is a crook.*

home and dry having been successful in one's aims. □ *There is the cottage we are looking for. We are home and dry.* □ *We need £100 to reach our target. Then we are home and dry.*

hope against hope to have hope even when the situation appears to be hopeless. □ *We hope against hope that she'll see the right thing to do and do it.* □ *There is little point in hoping against hope, except that it makes you feel better.*

horse of a different colour See horse of another colour.

horse of another colour AND **horse of a different colour** another matter altogether. □ *I was talking about trees, not bushes. Bushes are a horse of another colour.* □ *Gambling is not the same as investing in the shares market. It's a horse of a different colour.*

horse-play physically active and frivolous play. (Informal.) □ *Stop that horse-play and get to work.* □ *I won't tolerate horse-play in my living-room.*

horse sense common sense; practical thinking. □ *Jack is no scholar but he has a lot of horse sense.* □ *Horse sense tells me I should not be involved in that project.*

hot and bothered excited; anxious. (Informal.) □ *Now don't get hot and bothered. Take it easy.* □ *John is hot and bothered about the tax rate increase.*

hot on something enthusiastic about something; very much interested in something; knowledgeable about something. (Informal.) □ *Meg's hot on animal rights.* □ *Jean is hot on modern ballet just now.*

hot under the collar very angry. (Informal.) □ *The solicitor was really hot under the collar when you told him you lost the contract.* □ *I get hot under the collar every time I think about it.*

house-proud extremely or excessively concerned about the appearance of one's house. □ *Mrs. Smith is so house-proud that she makes her guests take their shoes off at the front door.* □ *Mrs. Brown keeps plastic covers over her chairs. She's much too house-proud.*

hue and cry a loud public protest or opposition. □ *There was a hue and cry when the council wanted to build houses in the playing-field.* □ *The decision to close the local school started a real hue and cry.*

hum and haw See hem and haw.

hush-money money paid as a bribe to persuade someone to remain silent and not reveal certain information. (Informal.) □ *Bob gave his younger sister hush-money so that she wouldn't tell Jane that he had gone to the cinema with Sue.* □ *The crooks paid Fred hush-money to keep their whereabouts secret.*

I

ill at ease uneasy; anxious. □ *I feel ill at ease about the interview.* □ *You look ill at ease. Do relax.*

ill-gotten gains money or other possessions acquired in a dishonest or illegal fashion. □ *Fred cheated at cards and is now living on his ill-gotten gains.* □ *Mary is also enjoying her ill-gotten gains. She deceived an old lady into leaving money to her in her will.*

in a bad mood sad; depressed; cross; with low spirits. □ *He's in a bad mood. He may shout at you.* □ *Please try to cheer me up. I'm in a bad mood.*

in a bad way in a critical or bad state. (Can refer to health, finances, mood, etc.) □ *Mr. Smith is in a bad way. He may have to go to hospital.* □ *My bank account is in a bad way. It needs some help from a millionaire.* □ *My life is in a bad way, and I'm depressed about it.*

in a dead heat [finishing a race] at exactly the same time; tied. □ *The two horses finished the race in a dead heat.* □ *They ended the contest in a dead heat.*

in a fix in a bad situation. (Informal. *In* can be replaced with *into.* See comment at *in a jam* and the examples below.) □ *I really got myself into a fix. I owe a lot of money on my car.* □ *John is in a fix because he lost his wallet.* □ *John certainly has got into a fix.*

in a flash quickly; immediately. □ *I'll be there in a flash.* □ *It happened in a flash. Suddenly my wallet was gone.*

in a huff in an angry or offended manner or state. (Informal. *In* can be replaced with *into.* See comment at *in a jam* and the examples below.) □ *He heard what we had to say, then left in a huff.* □ *She came in a huff and ordered us to bring her something to eat.* □ *She gets into a huff very easily.*

in a jam in a tight or difficult situation. (*In* can be replaced with *into* to show movement towards or into the state described by *a jam*. Especially *get into*.) □ *I'm in a jam. I owe a lot of money.* □ *Whenever I get into a jam, I ask my supervisor for help.*

in a jiffy very fast; very soon. (Informal.) □ *Just wait a minute. I'll be there in a jiffy.* □ *I'll be finished in a jiffy.*

in all one's born days ever; in all one's life. □ *I've never been so angry in all my born days.* □ *Have you ever heard such a thing in all your born days?*

in all probability very likely; almost certainly. □ *He'll be here on time in all probability.* □ *In all probability, they'll finish the work today.*

in a mad rush in a hurry. □ *I ran around all day today in a mad rush looking for a present for Bill.* □ *Why are you always in such a mad rush?*

in a nutshell in a few words; briefly; concisely. □ *I don't have time for the whole explanation. Please give it to me in a nutshell.* □ *Well, in a nutshell, we have to work late.*

in a (pretty) pickle in a mess; in trouble. (Informal. *In* can be replaced with *into*. See comment at **in a jam** and the examples below.) □ *John has got himself into a pickle. He has two dates for the party.* □ *Now we are in a pretty pickle. We are out of petrol.*

in a quandary uncertain about what to do; confused. (*In* can be replaced with *into*. See comment at **in a jam** and the examples below.) □ *Mary was in a quandary about which college to go to.* □ *I couldn't decide what to do. I was in such a quandary.* □ *I got myself into a quandary about where to go on holiday.*

in arrears overdue; late, especially in reference to bills and money. □ *This bill is three months in arrears. It must be paid immediately.* □ *I was in arrears on my car payments, so the bank threatened to take my car away.*

in a sense in a way. □ *In a sense, cars make life better.* □ *But, in a sense, they also make life worse.*

in a split second in an instant. □ *The lightning struck, and in a split second the house burst into flames.* □ *Just wait. I'll be there in a split second.*

in a stage whisper in a loud whisper which everyone can hear. □ *John said in a stage whisper, "This play is boring."* □ *"When do we eat?" asked Billy in a stage whisper.*

in a stew (about someone or something) upset or bothered about someone or something. (Informal. *In* can be replaced with *into*. See comment at in a jam and the examples below.) □ *I'm in such a stew about my dog. She ran away last night.* □ *Now, now. Don't be in a stew. She'll be back when she gets hungry.* □ *I hate to get into a stew worrying about my children.*

in a (tight) spot caught in a problem; in a jam. (Informal. *In* can be replaced with *into*. See comment at in a jam and the examples below.) □ *Look, John, I'm in a tight spot. Can you lend me £20?* □ *I'm in a spot too. I need £300.* □ *He's always getting into a tight spot financially.*

in at the kill present at the end of some activity, usually an activity with negative results. (Literally, present when a hunted animal is put to death. Informal when used about any other activity.) □ *I went to the final hearing on the proposed ring-road. I knew it would be shouted down strongly, and I wanted to be in at the kill.* □ *The judge will sentence the criminal today, and I'm going to be in at the kill.*

in black and white official, in writing or printing. (Said of something, such as an agreement or a statement, which has been recorded in writing. *In* can be replaced with *into*. See comment at in a jam and the examples below.) □ *I have it in black and white that I'm entitled to three weeks' holiday each year.* □ *It says right here in black and white that oak trees produce acorns.* □ *Please put the agreement into black and white.*

in broad daylight publicly visible in the daytime. □ *The thief stole the car in broad daylight.* □ *There they were, selling drugs in broad daylight.*

inch along (something) to move slowly along something little by little. □ *The cat inched along the carpet towards the mouse.* □ *Traffic was inching along.*

in clover with good fortune; in a very good situation, especially financially. (Informal.) □ *If I get this contract, I'll be in clover for the rest of my life.* □ *I have very little money saved, so when I retire I won't exactly be in clover.*

in deep water in a dangerous or vulnerable situation; in a serious situation; in trouble. (As if one were swimming in or had fallen into water which is over one's head. *In* can be replaced with *into*. See comment at in a jam and the examples below.) □ *John is having trouble with his wife. He's in deep water.* □ *Bill is in deep water in the algebra class. He's almost failing.* □ *He really got himself into deep water when he ran away from school.*

in dribs and drabs in small irregular quantities. (*In* can be replaced with *by*.) □ *The cheques for the charity are coming in in dribs and drabs.* □ *The members of the orchestra arrived by dribs and drabs.*

in fear and trembling with anxiety or fear; with dread. □ *In fear and trembling, I went into the room to take the exam.* □ *The witness left the courtroom in fear and trembling.*

in fine feather in good humour; in good health. (*In* can be replaced with *into*. See comment at in a jam and the examples below.) □ *Hello, John. You appear to be in fine feather.* □ *Of course I'm in fine feather. I get lots of sleep.* □ *Good food and lots of sleep put me into fine feather.*

in force in a very large group. □ *The entire group arrived in force.* □ *The mosquitoes will attack in force this evening.*

in full swing in progress; operating or running without restraint. (Informal. *In* can be replaced with *into*. See comment at in a jam and the examples below.) □ *We can't leave now! The party is in full swing.* □ *Our programme to help the starving people is in full swing. You should see results soon.* □ *Just wait until our project gets into full swing.*

in high gear (*In* can be replaced with *into*. See comment at in a jam and the examples below.) **1.** [for a machine, such as a car] to be set in its highest gear, giving the greatest speed. □ *When my car is in high gear, it goes very fast.* □ *You can't start out in high gear. You must work up through the low ones.* □ *You don't go into high gear soon enough.* **2.** very fast and active. (Informal.) □ *When Jane is in high gear, she's a superb athlete.* □ *When Jane changed into high gear, I knew she'd win the race.*

in (just) a second in a very short period of time. □ *I'll be there in a second.* □ *I'll be with you in just a second. I'm on the telephone.*

in league (with someone) in co-operation with someone; in a conspiracy with someone. □ *The mayor is in league with the Coun-*

cil Treasurer. They are misusing public money. □ *Those two have been in league for years.*

in leaps and bounds See *by leaps and bounds*.

in less than no time very quickly. □ *I'll be there in less than no time.* □ *Don't worry. This won't take long. It'll be over in less than no time.*

in lieu of something in place of something; instead of something. (The word *lieu* occurs only in this phrase.) □ *They gave me roast beef in lieu of steak.* □ *We gave money to charity in lieu of sending flowers to the funeral.*

in luck fortunate; lucky. □ *You want a red one? You're in luck. There is one red one left.* □ *I had an accident, but I was in luck. It was not serious.*

in mint condition in perfect condition. (Refers to the perfect state of a coin which has just been minted. *In* can be replaced with *into*. See comment at *in a jam* and the examples below.) □ *This is a fine car. It runs well and is in mint condition.* □ *We found a first edition in mint condition and decided to buy it.* □ *We put our house into mint condition before we sold it.*

in name only nominally; not actual, only by terminology. □ *The president is head of the country in name only.* □ *Mr. Smith is the managing director of the Smith Company in name only. Mrs. Smith handles all the business affairs.*

in no mood to do something not to feel like doing something; to wish not to do something. □ *I'm in no mood to cook dinner tonight.* □ *Mother is in no mood to put up with our arguing.*

in one ear and out the other [for something to be] ignored; [for something to be] unheard or unheeded. (Informal. *In* can be replaced with *into*. See the explanation at *in a jam* and the examples below.) □ *Everything I say to you goes into one ear and out the other!* □ *Bill just doesn't pay attention. Everything is in one ear and out the other.*

in one's birthday suit See *in the altogether*.

in one's blood See *in the blood*.

in one's book in one's opinion. (Informal.) □ *He's okay in my book.* □ *In my book, this is the best that money can buy.*

in one's cups drunk. □ *She doesn't make much sense when she's in her cups.* □ *The speaker—who was in his cups—could hardly be understood.*

in one's mind's eye in one's mind. (Refers to visualizing something in one's mind.) □ *In my mind's eye, I can see trouble ahead.* □ *In her mind's eye, she could see a beautiful building beside the river. She decided to design such a building.*

in one's opinion according to one's belief or judgement. □ *In my opinion, that is a very ugly picture.* □ *That isn't a good idea in my opinion.*

in one's (own) backyard (figuratively) very close to one. (Informal.) □ *That kind of thing is quite rare. Imagine it happening right in your backyard.* □ *You always think of something like that happening to someone else. You never expect to find it in your own backyard.*

in one's own time not while one is at work. □ *My employer made me write the report in my own time. That's not fair.* □ *Please make your personal telephone calls in your own time.*

in one's right mind sane; rational and sensible. (Often in the negative. See also *out of one's mind.*) □ *That was a stupid thing to do. You're not in your right mind.* □ *You can't be in your right mind! That sounds crazy!*

in one's second childhood being interested in things or people which normally interest children. □ *My father bought himself a toy train, and my mother said he was in his second childhood.* □ *Whenever I go to the river and throw stones, I feel as though I'm in my second childhood.*

in one's spare time in one's leisure time; in the time not reserved for doing something else. □ *I write novels in my spare time.* □ *I'll try to paint the house in my spare time.*

in other words said in another, simpler way. □ *Cease! Desist! In other words, stop!* □ *Our cash flow is negative, and our assets are worthless. In other words, we are broke.*

in over one's head with more difficulties than one can manage. (Informal.) □ *Calculus is very hard for me. I'm in over my head.* □ *Ann is too busy. She's really in over her head.*

in part partly; to a lesser degree or extent. □ *I was not there, in part because of my disagreement about the purpose of the meeting, but I also had a previous appointment.* □ *I hope to win, in part because I want the prize money.*

in place in the proper place or location. □ *Everything was in place for the ceremony.* □ *It's good to see everything in place again.*

in plain English in simple, clear, and straightforward language. (*In* can be replaced with *into*. See comment at in a jam and the examples below.) □ *That's too confusing. Please say it again in plain English.* □ *Tell me again in plain English.* □ *Please put it into plain English.*

in progress happening now; taking place at this time. □ *You can't go into that room. There is a meeting in progress.* □ *Please tell me about the work you have in progress.*

in Queer Street in a difficult situation, especially because of lack of money. (Informal.) □ *We're in Queer Street. We've no money to pay the rent.* □ *No wonder Jack's in Queer Street. He spends more than he earns.*

in rags in worn-out and torn clothing. □ *The beggars were in rags.* □ *I think the new casual fashions make you look as though you're in rags.*

in seventh heaven in a very happy state. □ *Ann was really in seventh heaven when she got a car of her own.* □ *I'd be in seventh heaven if I had a million pounds.*

(in) single file queued up, one behind the other; in a queue that is one person or one thing wide. (*In* can be replaced with *into*. See comment at in a jam and the examples below.) □ *Have you ever seen ducks walking in single file?* □ *No, do they usually walk single file?* □ *Please march in single file.* □ *Please get into single file.*

in stock readily available, as with goods in a shop. □ *I'm sorry, I don't have that in stock. I'll have to order it for you.* □ *We have all our Christmas merchandise in stock now.*

instrumental in doing something playing an important part in doing something. □ *John was instrumental in getting the contract to* *build the new building.* □ *Our MP was instrumental in defeating the proposal.*

in the air everywhere; all about. (Also used literally.) □ *There is such a feeling of joy in the air.* □ *We felt a sense of tension in the air.*

in the altogether AND **in the buff; in the raw; in one's birthday suit** naked; nude. (Informal.) □ *We often went swimming in the altogether down at the lake.* □ *The museum has a painting of some ladies in the buff.* □ *Bill says he sleeps in the raw.* □ *It's too cold in here to sleep in your birthday suit.*

in the balance in an undecided state. □ *He is waiting for the operation. His life is in the balance.* □ *With his fortune in the balance, John rolled the dice.*

in the best of health very healthy. □ *Bill is in the best of health. He eats well and exercises.* □ *I haven't been in the best of health. I think I have the flu.*

in the blood AND **in one's blood** built into one's personality or character. □ *John's a great runner. It's in his blood.* □ *The whole family is very athletic. It's in the blood.*

in the buff See *in the altogether.*

in the dark (about someone or something) uninformed about someone or something; ignorant about someone or something. □ *I'm in the dark about who is in charge around here.* □ *I can't imagine why they are keeping me in the dark.* □ *You won't be in the dark long. I'm in charge.* □ *She's in the dark about how this machine works.*

in the doghouse in trouble; in (someone's) disfavour. (Informal.) □ *I'm really in the doghouse. I was late for an appointment.* □ *I hate being in the doghouse all the time. I don't know why I can't stay out of trouble.*

in the doldrums sluggish; inactive; in low spirits. □ *He's usually in the doldrums in the winter.* □ *I had some bad news yesterday which put me in the doldrums.*

in the family restricted to one's own family, as with private or embarrassing information. (Especially with *keep.*) □ *Don't tell anyone else about the bankruptcy. Please keep it in the family.* □ *He told only his brother because he wanted it to remain in the family.*

in the family way pregnant. (Informal.) □ *I've heard that Mrs. Smith is in the family way.* □ *Our daughter is in the family way.*

in the flesh really present; in person. □ *I've heard that the Queen will be here in the flesh.* □ *Is she really here? In the flesh?* □ *The old man wanted to see the Pope in the flesh.*

in the lap of luxury in luxurious surroundings. □ *John lives in the lap of luxury because his family is very wealthy.* □ *When I retire, I'd like to live in the lap of luxury.*

in the light of something because of certain knowledge; considering something. (As if knowledge or information shed light on something.) □ *In the light of what you have told us, I think we must abandon the project.* □ *In the light of the shop assistant's rudeness, we didn't return to that shop.*

in the limelight at the centre of attention. (*In* can be replaced with *into*. See comment at **in a jam** and the examples below. *Limelight* is an obsolete form of *spotlight*, and the word occurs only in this phrase.) □ *John will do almost anything to get himself into the limelight.* □ *All elected officials spend a lot of time in the limelight.*

in the line of duty as part of one's expected (military, police, or other) duties. □ *When soldiers fight people in a war, it's in the line of duty.* □ *Police officers have to do things they may not like in the line of duty.*

in the long run over a long period of time; ultimately. □ *We'd be better off in the long run buying a car instead of hiring one.* □ *In the long run, we'd be happier in the South.*

in the market (for something) wanting to buy something. □ *I'm in the market for a video recorder.* □ *If you have a boat for sale, we're in the market.*

in the middle of nowhere in a very remote place. (Informal. *In* can be replaced with *into*. See comment at **in a jam** and the examples below.) □ *We found a nice place to eat, but it's out in the middle of nowhere.* □ *To get to my house, you have to drive into the middle of nowhere.*

in the money wealthy. (Informal.) □ *John is really in the money. He's worth millions.* □ *If I am ever in the money, I'll be generous to others.*

in the near future in the time immediately ahead. □ *I don't plan to go to Florida in the near future.* □ *What do you intend to do in the near future?*

in the nick of time just in time; at the last possible instant; just before it is too late. □ *The doctor arrived in the nick of time. The patient's life was saved.* □ *I reached the airport in the nick of time.*

in the offing happening at some time in the future. □ *There is a big investigation in the offing, but I don't know when.* □ *It's hard to tell what's in the offing if you don't keep track of things.*

in the peak of condition See in the pink (of condition).

in the pink (of condition) AND **in the peak of condition** in very good health; in very good condition, physically and emotionally. (Informal. *In* can be replaced with *into*. See comment at in a jam and the examples below.) □ *The garden is lovely. All the flowers are in the pink of condition.* □ *Jane has to exercise hard to get into the peak of condition.* □ *She's been ill, but she's in the pink now.*

in the public eye publicly; visible to all; conspicuous. (*In* can be replaced with *into*. See comment at in a jam and the examples below.) □ *Elected officials find themselves constantly in the public eye.* □ *The mayor made it a practice to get into the public eye as much as possible.*

in the raw See in the altogether.

in the same boat in the same situation; having the same problem. □ *"I'm broke. Can you lend me twenty pounds?" "Sorry. I'm in the same boat."* □ *Jane and Mary are both in the same boat. They both have been called to the boss's office.*

in the same breath [stated or said] almost at the same time. □ *He told me I was lazy, but then in the same breath he said I was doing a good job of work.* □ *The teacher said that the pupils were working hard and, in the same breath, that they were not working hard enough.*

in the soup in a bad situation. (Informal.) □ *Now I'm really in the soup. I broke Mrs. Franklin's window.* □ *The child's always in the soup. He attracts trouble.*

in the swim (of things) fully involved in or participating in events or happenings. (The *in* can be replaced with *into*. See the explanation at in a jam and the examples below.) □ *I've been ill, but soon*

I'll be back in the swim of things. □ *He can't wait to grow up and get into the swim of things.* □ *Mary loves to be in the swim socially.*

in the wind about to happen. (Also used literally.) □ *There are some major changes in the wind. Expect these changes to happen soon.* □ *There is something in the wind. We'll find out what it is soon.*

in thing (to do) the fashionable thing to do. (Informal. In this phrase, the word *in* is always stressed.) □ *Eating low-fat food is the in thing to do.* □ *Bob is very old-fashioned. He never does the in thing.*

in this day and age presently; currently; nowadays. □ *You don't expect people to be polite in this day and age.* □ *Young people don't care for their parents in this day and age.*

into the bargain in addition to what was agreed on. □ *I bought a car, and they threw a trailer into the bargain.* □ *When I bought the house, I asked the seller to include the furniture into the bargain.*

in turn 1. one at a time in sequence. □ *Each of us can read the book in turn.* □ *We cut the hair of every child in turn.* **2.** in return (for doing something). □ *I took Sally out to lunch, and she took me out in turn.* □ *They invited us to their house in turn.*

in two shakes of a lamb's tail in a very short time. □ *Jane returned in two shakes of a lamb's tail.* □ *Fred was able to solve the problem in two shakes of a lamb's tail.*

in vain for no purpose; with no success. □ *They rushed her to the hospital, but they did it in vain.* □ *We tried in vain to get her there on time.* □ *They tried and tried, but their efforts were in vain.*

iron hand in a velvet glove a strong, ruthless type of control that gives the appearance of being gentle and liberal. □ *In that family, it is a case of the iron hand in a velvet glove. The father looks gentle and loving, but he is a tyrant.* □ *It is a case of the iron hand in a velvet glove in that country. The president pretends to be liberal, but his people have little freedom.*

jack-of-all-trades someone who can do several different jobs instead of specializing in one. □ *John can do plumbing, joinery, and roofing—a real jack-of-all-trades. He isn't very good at any of them.* □ *Take your car to a trained mechanic, not a jack-of-all-trades.*

jam tomorrow good things in the future. (It is suggested that the future never comes. From Lewis Carroll's *Through the Looking-Glass*, in which the White Queen offers Alice "jam every other day . . . jam tomorrow and jam yesterday but never jam today.") □ *The politicians promised the people jam tomorrow during the hard times.* □ *Jack was tired of working for a firm that kept promising him a large salary in the future—jam tomorrow.*

Jekyll and Hyde someone with both an evil and a good personality. (From *The Strange Case of Dr. Jekyll and Mr. Hyde* by Robert Louis Stevenson.) □ *Bill thinks Mary is so soft and gentle, but she can be very cruel—she is a real Jekyll and Hyde.* □ *Jane doesn't know that Fred is a Jekyll and Hyde. She sees him only when he is being kind and generous, but he can be very mean and miserly.*

job lot a mixed collection of varying quality. (Informal.) □ *Mike found a valuable vase in that job lot he bought at the auction.* □ *There was nothing but junk in the job lot that I bought.*

Job's comforter someone who makes matters worse when trying to comfort or console someone. (Biblical.) □ *Jane is a Job's comforter. She told me how many other people were looking for jobs when I lost mine.* □ *John's a Job's comforter, too. He told Mary that there were lots of other unattached girls in the district when her engagement was broken off.*

jockey for position to try to push or manoeuvre one's way into an advantageous position at the expense of others. □ *All the staff in that firm are jockeying for position. They all want the manager's job.*

□ *It is unpleasant working for a firm where people are always jockeying for position.*

johnny-come-lately someone who joins in (something) after it is under way. □ *Don't pay any attention to Sally. She's just a johnny-come-lately and doesn't know what she's talking about.* □ *We've been here for thirty years. Why should some johnny-come-lately tell us what to do?*

joking apart being serious for a moment; in all seriousness. □ *I know I laugh at him but, joking apart, he's a very clever scientist.* □ *I know I threatened to leave and go round the world, but, joking apart, I need a holiday.*

jolly someone along to keep someone happy and satisfied in order to obtain compliance with one's wishes. □ *If you jolly Jim along, he will help you with the garden.* □ *You'll have to jolly Bert along if you want his help. If he's in a bad mood, he'll refuse.*

jump at the chance (to do something) AND **leap at the chance (to do something); jump at the opportunity (to do something); leap at the opportunity (to do something)** to take advantage of a chance to do something. (*To do something* can be replaced with *of doing something.*) □ *John jumped at the chance to go to England.* □ *I don't know why I didn't jump at the opportunity myself.* □ *I should have leapt at the chance.*

jump at the opportunity (to do something) See jump at the chance (to do something).

jump down someone's throat AND **jump on someone** to scold someone severely. (Informal.) □ *If I disagree with them, my parents will jump down my throat.* □ *Don't jump on me! I didn't do it!*

jumping-off point a point or place from which to begin a venture. □ *The local library is a good jumping-off point for your research.* □ *The office job in that firm would be a good jumping-off point for a job in advertising.*

jump on someone See jump down someone's throat.

jump out of one's skin to react strongly to shock or surprise. (Informal. Usually with *nearly, almost,* etc.) □ *Oh! You really scared me. I nearly jumped out of my skin.* □ *Bill was so startled he almost jumped out of his skin.*

jump the gun 1. to start before the starting signal, as in a race. (Informal. Originally used in sports contests which are started by firing a gun.) □ *We all had to start the race again because Jane jumped the gun.* □ *When we took the test, Tom jumped the gun and started early.* **2.** to start before the starting time. (Figurative on sense 1.) □ *You jumped the gun with your proposal.* □ *We jumped the gun and turned in our application early.*

just the job exactly what is required. (Informal.) □ *Those pills were just the job for Jean's headache.* □ *That jacket was just the job for wet weather.*

just what the doctor ordered exactly what is required, especially for health or comfort. □ *That meal was delicious, Bob. Just what the doctor ordered.* □ *A glass of cold water would be just what the doctor ordered.*

K

keen on someone or something enthusiastic about someone or something. ☐ *I'm not too keen on going to London.* ☐ *Sally is fairly keen on getting a new job.* ☐ *Mary isn't keen on her new assignment.*

keep a civil tongue (in one's head) to speak decently and politely. ☐ *Please, John. Don't talk like that. Keep a civil tongue in your head.* ☐ *John seems unable to keep a civil tongue.*

keep an eye out (for someone or something) to watch for the arrival or appearance of someone or something. (The *an* can be replaced by *one's*.) ☐ *Please keep an eye out for the bus.* ☐ *Keep an eye out for rain.* ☐ *Okay. I'll keep my eye out.*

keep a stiff upper lip to be cool and unmoved by unsettling events. ☐ *John always keeps a stiff upper lip.* ☐ *Now, Billy, don't cry. Keep a stiff upper lip.*

keep a straight face to make one's face stay free from laughter or smiling. ☐ *It's hard to keep a straight face when someone tells a funny joke.* ☐ *I knew it was John who played the trick. He couldn't keep a straight face.*

keep a weather eye open to watch for something (to happen); to be on the alert (for something); to be on guard. ☐ *Some trouble is brewing. Keep a weather eye open.* ☐ *Try to be more alert. Learn to keep a weather eye open.*

keep body and soul together to feed, clothe, and house oneself. ☐ *I hardly have enough money to keep body and soul together.* ☐ *How the old man was able to keep body and soul together is beyond me.*

keep house to manage a household. ☐ *I hate to keep house. I'd rather live in a tent than keep house.* ☐ *My grandmother kept house for nearly sixty years.*

keep in with someone to remain friendly with a person, especially a person who might be useful. (Informal.) □ *Jack keeps in with Jane because he likes to borrow her car.* □ *The children keep in with Peter because his father has a sweet-shop.*

keep late hours to stay up or stay out until very late. □ *I'm always tired because I keep late hours.* □ *If I didn't keep late hours, I wouldn't sleep so late in the morning.*

keep one's cards close to one's chest See play one's cards close to one's chest.

keep one's chin up to keep one's spirits high; to act brave and confident. (Informal.) □ *Keep your chin up, John. Things will get better.* □ *Just keep your chin up and tell the judge exactly what happened.*

keep one's distance (from someone or something) to maintain a respectful or cautious distance from someone or something. (The distance can be figurative or literal.) □ *Keep your distance from John. He's in a bad mood.* □ *Keep your distance from the fire.* □ *Okay. I'll tell Sally to keep her distance, too.*

keep one's ear to the ground See have one's ear to the ground.

keep oneself to oneself to remain private; not to mix with other people very much. □ *We never see our neighbours. They keep themselves to themselves.* □ *Jean used to go out a lot, but she has kept herself to herself since her husband died.*

keep one's eye on the ball to remain alert to the events occurring around one. (Informal.) □ *If you want to get along in this office, you're going to have to keep your eye on the ball.* □ *Bill would do better in his classes if he would just keep his eye on the ball.*

keep one's feet on the ground See have one's feet on the ground.

keep one's hand in (something) to retain one's control of something. □ *I want to keep my hand in the business.* □ *Mrs. Johnson has retired from the library, but she still wants to keep her hand in. She works part-time.*

keep one's head above water to stay ahead of one's problems; to keep up with one's work or responsibilities. (Also used literally. Also with *have.*) □ *I can't seem to keep my head above water. Work just keeps piling up.* □ *Now that I have more space to work in, I can easily keep my head above water.*

keep one's mouth shut (about someone or something) to keep quiet about someone or something; to keep a secret about someone or something. (Informal.) □ *They told me to keep my mouth shut about the problem or I'd be in big trouble.* □ *I think I'll keep my mouth shut.*

keep one's nose in the air See have one's nose in the air.

keep one's nose to the grindstone to keep busy doing one's work. (Also with *have* and *get*, as in the examples.) □ *The manager told me to keep my nose to the grindstone or be sacked.* □ *I've had my nose to the grindstone ever since I started working here.* □ *If the other people in this office would get their noses to the grindstone, more work would get done.*

keep one's own counsel to keep one's thoughts and plans to oneself; not to tell other people about one's thoughts and plans. □ *Jane is very quiet. She tends to keep her own counsel.* □ *I advise you to keep your own counsel.*

keep one's side of the bargain to do one's part as agreed; to attend to one's responsibilities as agreed. □ *Tom has to learn to cooperate. He must keep his side of the bargain.* □ *If you don't keep your side of the bargain, the whole project will fail.*

keep one's wits about one See under have one's wits about one.

keep one's word to uphold one's promise. □ *I told her I'd be there to collect her, and I intend to keep my word.* □ *Keeping one's word is necessary in the legal profession.*

keep someone in line to make certain that someone behaves properly. (Informal.) □ *It's very hard to keep Bill in line. He's sort of rowdy.* □ *The teacher had to struggle to keep the class in line.*

keep someone in stitches to cause someone to laugh loud and hard, over and over. (Informal. Also with *have*. See the examples.) □ *The comedian kept us in stitches for nearly an hour.* □ *The teacher kept the class in stitches, but the pupils didn't learn anything.* □ *The clown had the crowd in stitches.*

keep someone on a string See under have someone on a string.

keep someone on tenterhooks to keep someone anxious or in suspense. (Also with *have*. See the examples.) □ *Please tell me now.*

Don't keep me on tenterhooks any longer! □ Now that we have her on tenterhooks, shall we let her worry, or shall we tell her?

keep someone posted to keep someone informed (of what is happening); to keep someone up to date. □ *If the price of corn goes up, I need to know. Please keep me posted. □ Keep her posted about the patient's condition.*

keep something under one's hat to keep something a secret; to keep something in one's mind (only). (Informal. If the secret stays under your hat, it stays in your mind.) □ *Keep this under your hat, but I'm getting married. □ I'm getting married, but keep it under your hat.*

keep something under wraps to keep something concealed (until some future time). □ *We kept the plan under wraps until after the election. □ The car company kept the new model under wraps until most of the old models had been sold.*

keep the ball rolling See under start the ball rolling.

keep the home fires burning to keep things going at one's home or other central location. □ *My uncle kept the home fires burning when my sister and I went to school. □ The manager stays at the office and keeps the home fires burning while I'm out selling our products.*

keep the lid on something to restrain something; to keep something quiet or under control. (Informal.) □ *The politician worked hard to keep the lid on the scandal. □ Try to keep the lid on the situation. Don't let it get out of hand.*

keep the wolf from the door to maintain oneself at a minimal level; to keep from starving, freezing, etc. □ *I don't make a lot of money, just enough to keep the wolf from the door. □ We have a small amount of money saved, hardly enough to keep the wolf from the door.*

kick oneself (for doing something) to regret doing something. (Informal.) □ *I could just kick myself for going off and not locking the car door. Now the car's been stolen. □ James felt like kicking himself when he missed the train.*

kick one's heels to be kept waiting for someone or something; to have nothing to do. (Informal.) □ *They left me kicking my heels while they had lunch. □ Mary is just kicking her heels until the university reopens.*

kick up a fuss AND **kick up a row** to become a nuisance; to misbehave and disturb (someone). (Informal. *Row* rhymes with *cow*.) □ *The customer kicked up such a fuss about the food that the manager came to apologize.* □ *I kicked up such a row that they kicked me out.*

kick up a row See kick up a fuss.

kick up one's heels to act in a frisky way; to be lively and have fun. (Informal.) □ *I like to go to an old-fashioned dance and really kick up my heels.* □ *For an old man, your uncle is really kicking up his heels by going on a cruise.*

kids' stuff a very easy task. (Informal.) □ *Climbing that hill is kids' stuff.* □ *Driving an automatic car is kids' stuff.*

kill the fatted calf to prepare an elaborate banquet (in someone's honour). (From the biblical story recounting the return of the prodigal son.) □ *When Bob got back from college, his parents killed the fatted calf and threw a great party.* □ *Sorry this meal isn't much, John. We didn't have time to kill the fatted calf.*

kill time to waste time. (Informal.) □ *Stop killing time. Get to work!* □ *We went over to the record shop just to kill time.*

kiss of death an act that puts an end to someone or something. (Informal.) □ *The mayor's veto was the kiss of death for the new law.* □ *Fainting on stage was the kiss of death for my acting career.*

knit one's brow to wrinkle one's brow, especially by frowning. □ *The woman knitted her brow and asked us what we wanted from her.* □ *While he read his book, John knitted his brow occasionally. He must not have agreed with what he was reading.*

knock about (somewhere) AND **knock around (somewhere)** to travel around; to act as a vagabond. (Informal.) □ *I'd like to take off a year and knock about Europe.* □ *If you're going to knock around, you should do it when you're young.*

knock around (somewhere) See knock about (somewhere).

knock people's heads together to scold some people; to get some people to do what they are supposed to be doing. (Informal.) □ *If you children don't quieten down and go to sleep, I'm going to come up there and knock your heads together.* □ *The government is in a mess. We need to go down to London and knock the ministers' heads together.*

knock someone cold 1. to knock someone out. (Informal.) □ *The blow knocked the boxer cold.* □ *The attacker knocked the old man cold.* **2.** to stun someone; to shock someone. □ *The news of his death knocked me cold.* □ *Pat was knocked cold by the imprisonment of her son.*

knock someone dead to put on a stunning performance or display for someone. (Informal. *Someone* is often replaced by *'em* from them.) □ *This band is going to do great tonight. We're going to knock them dead.* □ *"See how your sister is all dressed up!" said Bill. "She's going to knock 'em dead."*

knock someone down with a feather to push over a person who is stunned, surprised, or awed by something extraordinary. □ *I was so surprised, you could have knocked me down with a feather.* □ *When she heard the news, you could have knocked her down with a feather.*

know all the tricks of the trade to possess the skills and knowledge necessary to do something. (Also without *all*.) □ *Tom can repair car engines. He knows the tricks of the trade.* □ *If I knew all the tricks of the trade, I could be a better plumber.*

know a thing or two (about someone or something) to be well informed about someone or something; to know something, often something unpleasant, about someone or something. (Informal.) □ *I know a thing or two about cars.* □ *I know a thing or two about Mary that would really shock you.*

know one's ABC to know the alphabet; to know the most basic things (about something). (Informal.) □ *Bill can't do it. He doesn't even know his ABC.* □ *You can't expect to write novels when you don't know your ABC.*

know one's place to know and accept the behaviour appropriate to one's position or status in life. □ *I know my place. I won't speak unless spoken to.* □ *People around here are expected to know their place. You have to follow all the rules.*

know the ropes to know how to do something. (Informal.) □ *I can't do the job because I don't know the ropes.* □ *Ask Sally to do it. She knows the ropes.* ALSO: **show someone the ropes** to tell or show someone how something is to be done. □ *Since this was my first day on the job, the manager spent a lot of time showing me the ropes.*

labour of love a task which is either unpaid or poorly paid and which one does simply for one's own satisfaction or pleasure or to please someone whom one likes or loves. □ *Jane made no money out of the biography she wrote. She was writing about the life of a friend, and the book was a labour of love.* □ *Mary hates knitting, but she made a sweater for her boyfriend. What a labour of love!*

lady-killer a man who likes to flirt and make love to women, and who is popular with them. □ *Fred used to be a real lady-killer, but now women laugh at him.* □ *Jack's wife doesn't know that he's a lady-killer who goes out with other women.*

lag behind (someone or something) to fall behind someone or something; to linger behind someone or something. □ *John always lags behind the person marching in front of him.* □ *"Don't lag behind!" shouted the leader.*

lame duck someone or something that is helpless, useless, or inefficient. □ *Jack is always having to help his brother, who is a lame duck.* □ *The best firms will survive, but the lame ducks will not.*

land a blow (somewhere) to strike someone or something with the hand or fist. □ *Bill landed a blow on Tom's chin.* □ *When Bill wasn't looking, Tom landed a blow.*

land of Nod sleep. (Humorous. From the fact that people sometimes nod when they are falling asleep. This is a pun, because the *land of Nod* is also the name of a place referred to in the Bible.) □ *The baby is in the land of Nod.* □ *Look at the clock! It's time we were all in the land of Nod.*

land on both feet See land on one's feet.

land on one's feet AND **land on both feet** to recover satisfactorily from a trying situation or a setback. (Informal.) □ *Her first year* *was terrible, but she landed on both feet.* □ *It's going to be a hard day. I only hope I land on my feet.*

last but not least last in sequence, but not last in importance. (Often said in introductions.) □ *The speaker said, "And now, last but not least, I'd like to present Bill Smith, who will give us some final words."* □ *And last but not least, here is the owner of the firm.*

last-ditch effort a final effort; the last possible attempt. □ *I made one last-ditch effort to get her to stay.* □ *It was a last-ditch effort. I didn't expect it to work.*

late in life when one is old. □ *She injured her hip running. She's taken to exercising rather late in life.* □ *Isn't it rather late in life to buy a house?*

late in the day far on in a project or activity; too late in a project or activity for action, decisions, etc., to be taken. □ *It was a bit late in the day for him to apologize.* □ *It's late in the day to change the plans.*

laugh something out of court to dismiss something as ridiculous. □ *The committee laughed the suggestion out of court.* □ *Jack's request for a large salary increase was laughed out of court.*

laugh up one's sleeve to laugh secretly; to laugh quietly to oneself. (Informal.) □ *Jane looked very serious, but I knew she was laughing up her sleeve.* □ *They pretended to admire her singing voice, but they were laughing up their sleeves at her. She screeches.*

law unto oneself one who makes one's own laws or rules; one who sets one's own standards of behaviour. □ *You can't get Bill to follow the rules. He's a law unto himself.* □ *Jane is a law unto herself. She's totally unwilling to co-operate.*

lay about one to strike at people and things in all directions around one; to hit everyone and everything near one. □ *When the police tried to capture the robber, he laid about him wildly.* □ *In trying to escape, the prisoner laid about him and injured several people.*

lay down the law 1. to state firmly what the rules are (for something). □ *Before the meeting, the managing director laid down the law. We all knew exactly what to do.* □ *The way she laid down the law means that I'll remember her rules.* **2.** to express one's opinions with force. □ *When the teacher caught us, he really laid down the law.* □ *Poor Bob. He really got it when his mother laid down the law.*

lay something on the line to speak very firmly and directly about something. □ *She was very angry. She laid it on the line, and we had no doubt about what she meant.* □ *All right, you lot! I'm going to lay it on the line. Don't ever do that again if you know what's good for you.*

lay the table See set the table.

lead a dog's life to lead a miserable life. □ *Poor Jane really leads a dog's life.* □ *I've been working so hard. I'm tired of leading a dog's life.*

lead someone by the nose to force someone to go somewhere (with you); to lead someone by coercion. (Informal.) □ *John had to lead Tom by the nose to get him to the opera.* □ *I'll go, but you'll have to lead me by the nose.*

lead someone (on) a merry chase AND **lead someone (on) a merry dance** to lead someone in a purposeless pursuit. □ *What a waste of time. You really led me on a merry chase.* □ *Jane led Bill a merry dance trying to find an antique lamp.*

lead someone (on) a merry dance See lead someone (on) a merry chase.

lead someone to believe something to imply something to someone; to cause someone to believe something untrue, without lying. □ *But you led me to believe that this watch was guaranteed!* □ *Did you lead her to believe that she was employed as a cook?*

lead someone to do something to cause someone to do something. □ *This agent led me to purchase a worthless piece of land.* □ *My illness led me to resign.*

lead someone up the garden path to deceive someone. □ *Now, be honest with me. Don't lead me up the garden path.* □ *That swindler really led her up the garden path.*

leap at the chance (to do something) See jump at the chance (to do something).

leap at the opportunity (to do something) See jump at the chance (to do something).

learn something by heart to learn something so well that it can be written or recited without thinking; to memorize something. □ *The director told me to learn my speech by heart.* □ *I had to go over* *it many times before I learned it by heart.* ALSO: **know something by heart** to know something perfectly; to have memorized something perfectly. □ *I know my speech by heart.* □ *I went over and over it until I knew it by heart.*

learn something by rote to learn something without giving any thought to what is being learned. □ *I learned history by rote, and then I couldn't pass the examination, which required me to think.* □ *If you learn things by rote, you'll never understand them.*

learn the ropes to learn how to do something; to learn how to work something. (Informal.) □ *I'll be able to do my job very well as soon as I learn the ropes.* □ *John is very slow to learn the ropes.*

leave a bad taste in someone's mouth [for something] to leave a bad feeling or memory with someone. (Informal.) □ *The whole business about the missing money left a bad taste in his mouth.* □ *It was a very nice affair, but something about it left a bad taste in my mouth.*

leave no stone unturned to search in all possible places. (As if one might find something under a rock.) □ *Don't worry. We'll find your stolen car. We'll leave no stone unturned.* □ *In searching for a nice place to live, we left no stone unturned.*

leave oneself wide open for something AND **leave oneself wide open to something** to invite criticism or joking about oneself; to fail to protect oneself from criticism or ridicule. □ *Yes, that was a harsh remark, Jane, but you left yourself wide open to it.* □ *I can't complain about your joke. I left myself wide open for it.*

leave oneself wide open to something See leave oneself wide open for something.

leave someone holding the baby to leave someone with the responsibility for something, especially something difficult or unpleasant, often when it was originally someone else's responsibility. (Informal. Note passive use in the examples.) □ *We all promised to look after the house when the owner was away, but I was left holding the baby on my own.* □ *It was her brother who promised to finish the work, and it was he who then left her holding the baby.*

leave someone in the lurch to leave someone waiting on or anticipating your actions. □ *Where were you, John? You really left me in* *the lurch.* □ *I didn't mean to leave you in the lurch. I thought we had cancelled our meeting.*

leave well alone See let well alone.

leave word (with someone) to leave a message with someone (who will pass the message on to someone else.) □ *If you decide to go to the convention, please leave word with my secretary.* □ *Leave word before you go.* □ *I left word with your brother. Didn't he give you the message?*

left, right, and centre everywhere; to an excessive extent. (Informal.) □ *John lent money left, right, and centre.* □ *Mary spent her money on clothes, left, right, and centre.*

lend (someone) a hand to give someone some help, not necessarily with the hands. □ *Could you lend me a hand with this piano? I need to move it across the room.* □ *Could you lend a hand with this maths problem?* □ *I'd be happy to lend a hand.*

less than pleased displeased. □ *We were less than pleased to learn of your comments.* □ *Bill was less than pleased at the outcome of the election.*

let down one's hair See let one's hair down.

let off steam AND **blow off steam** to release excess energy or anger. (Informal.) □ *Whenever John gets a little angry, he blows off steam by jogging.* □ *Don't worry about John. He's just letting off steam. He won't sack you.*

let one's hair down AND **let down one's hair** to become less formal and more intimate, and to begin to speak frankly. (Informal.) □ *Come on, Jane, let your hair down and tell me all about it.* □ *I have a problem. Do you mind if I let down my hair?*

let someone have it to strike someone or attack someone verbally. (Informal.) □ *I really let Tom have it. I told him he had better not do that again if he knows what's good for him.* □ *Bob let John have it— right on the chin.*

let someone off (the hook) to release someone from a responsibility. (Informal.) □ *Please let me off the hook for Saturday. I have other plans.* □ *Okay, I'll let you off.*

let something ride to allow something to continue or remain as it is. (Informal.) □ *It isn't the best plan, but we'll let it ride.* □ *I disagree with you, but I'll let it ride.*

let something slide to neglect something. (Informal.) □ *John let his lessons slide.* □ *Jane doesn't let her work slide.*

let something slip (out) to tell a secret by accident. □ *I didn't let it slip out on purpose. It was an accident.* □ *John let the plans slip when he was talking to Bill.*

let the cat out of the bag AND **spill the beans** to reveal a secret or a surprise by accident. (Informal.) □ *When Bill glanced at the door, he let the cat out of the bag. We knew then that he was expecting someone to arrive.* □ *We are planning a surprise party for Jane. Don't let the cat out of the bag.* □ *It's a secret. Try not to spill the beans.*

let the chance slip by to lose the opportunity (to do something). □ *When I was younger, I wanted to become a doctor, but I let the chance slip by.* □ *Don't let the chance slip by. Do it now!*

let the grass grow under one's feet to do nothing; to stand still. □ *Mary doesn't let the grass grow under her feet. She's always busy.* □ *Bob is too lazy. He's letting the grass grow under his feet.*

let well alone AND **leave well alone** to leave things as they are (and not try to improve them). □ *There isn't much more you can accomplish here. Why don't you just let well alone?* □ *This is as good as I can do. I'll stop and leave well alone.*

lick one's lips to show eagerness or pleasure about a future event. (Informal. From the habit of people licking their lips when they are about to enjoy eating something.) □ *The children licked their lips at the sight of the cake.* □ *The author's readers were licking their lips in anticipation of her new novel.* □ *The journalist was licking his lips when he went off to interview the disgraced politician.*

lick something into shape AND **whip something into shape** to put something into good condition, usually with difficulty. (Informal.) □ *I have to lick this report into shape this morning.* □ *Let's all lend a hand and whip this house into shape. It's a mess.*

lie down on the job to do one's job poorly or not at all. (Informal.) □ *Tom was sacked because he was lying down on the job.* □ *The* *telephonist was not answering the phone. She was lying down on the job.*

lie through one's teeth to lie boldly. (Informal.) □ *I knew she was lying through her teeth, but I didn't want to say so just then.* □ *I'm not lying through my teeth! I never do!*

life (and soul) of the party the type of person who is lively and helps make a party fun and exciting. □ *Bill is always the life and soul of the party. Be sure to invite him.* □ *Bob isn't exactly the life of the party, but he's polite.*

like a bolt out of the blue suddenly and without warning. (Refers to a bolt of lightning coming out of a clear blue sky.) □ *The news came to us like a bolt out of the blue.* □ *Like a bolt out of the blue, the managing director came and sacked us all.*

like a fish out of water awkward; in a foreign or unaccustomed environment. □ *At a formal dance, John is like a fish out of water.* □ *Mary was like a fish out of water at the bowling tournament.*

like a sitting duck AND **like sitting ducks** unguarded; unsuspecting and unaware. □ *He was waiting there like a sitting duck—a perfect target for a mugger.* □ *The soldiers were standing at the top of the hill like sitting ducks. It's a wonder they weren't all killed.*

like looking for a needle in a haystack engaged in a hopeless search. □ *Trying to find a white dog in the snow is like looking for a needle in a haystack.* □ *I tried to find my lost contact lens on the beach, but it was like looking for a needle in a haystack.*

like one of the family as if someone (or a pet) were a member of one's family. (Informal.) □ *We treat our dog like one of the family.* □ *We are very happy to have you stay with us, Bill. I hope you don't mind if we treat you like one of the family.*

like sitting ducks See *like a sitting duck*.

likes of someone the type of person that someone is; anyone like someone. (Informal. Almost always in a negative sense.) □ *I don't like Bob. I wouldn't do anything for the likes of him.* □ *Nobody wants the likes of him around.*

like water off a duck's back without any apparent effect. □ *Insults rolled off John like water off a duck's back.* □ *There's no point in scolding the children. It's like water off a duck's back.*

lion's share (of something) the larger share of something. □ *The elder boy always takes the lion's share of the food.* □ *Jim was supposed to divide the cake in two equal pieces, but he took the lion's share.*

listen to reason to yield to a reasonable argument; to take the reasonable course. □ *Please listen to reason, and don't do something you'll regret.* □ *She got into trouble because she wouldn't listen to reason and was always late.*

live and let live not to interfere with other people's business or preferences. □ *I don't care what they do! Live and let live, I always say.* □ *Your parents are strict. Mine prefer to live and let live.*

live by one's wits to survive by being clever. □ *When you're in the kind of business I'm in, you have to live by your wits.* □ *John was orphaned at the age of ten and grew up living by his wits.*

live from hand to mouth to live in poor circumstances; to be able to get only what one needs for the present and not save for the future. (Informal.) □ *When both my parents were out of work, we lived from hand to mouth.* □ *We lived from hand to mouth during the war. Things were very difficult.*

live in an ivory tower to be aloof or separated from the realities of living. (*Live* can be replaced by certain other expressions meaning to dwell or spend time, as in the examples.) □ *If you didn't spend so much time in your ivory tower, you'd know what people really think!* □ *Many professors are said to live in ivory towers. They don't know what the real world is like.*

live off the fat of the land to live in a very affluent or luxurious way. (Biblical.) □ *If I had a million pounds, I'd invest it and live off the fat of the land.* □ *Jean married a wealthy man and lived off the fat of the land.*

live on borrowed time to live longer than circumstances warrant; to live longer than expected; to remain in a situation longer than circumstances warrant. □ *John has a terminal disease. He's living on borrowed time.* □ *The student's living on borrowed time. If he doesn't pass this exam, he will be asked to go.*

load off one's mind relief from something which has been worrying one. (Informal.) □ *It will be a load off Jane's mind when her mother leaves hospital.* □ *You aren't going to like what I'm going to say, but it will be a load off my mind.*

lock horns (with someone) to get into an argument with someone. (Informal.) □ *Let's settle this peacefully. I don't want to lock horns with your lawyer.* □ *The judge doesn't want to lock horns either.*

lock, stock, and barrel everything. □ *We had to move everything out of the house—lock, stock, and barrel.* □ *We lost everything—lock, stock, and barrel—in the fire.*

look as if butter wouldn't melt in one's mouth to appear to be very innocent, respectable, honest, etc. □ *Sally looks as if butter wouldn't melt in her mouth, but she is going out with a married man.* □ *The child looks as though butter wouldn't melt in his mouth, but he bullies the other children.*

look daggers at someone to give someone an unpleasant or nasty look. □ *Tom must have been angry with Ann from the way he was looking daggers at her.* □ *Don't you dare look daggers at me! I haven't done anything.*

look forward to something to anticipate something with pleasure. □ *I'm really looking forward to your visit next week.* □ *We all look forward to your new book on gardening.*

look like a million dollars to look very good. □ *Oh, Sally, you look like a million dollars.* □ *Your new hair-do looks like a million dollars.*

look like the cat that swallowed the canary AND **look like the cat that swallowed the cream** to appear self-satisfied, as if one had just had a great success. □ *After the meeting John looked like the cat that swallowed the canary. I knew he must have been a success.* □ *What happened? You look like the cat that swallowed the canary.* □ *Jean must have won. She looks like the cat that swallowed the cream.*

look like the cat that swallowed the cream See look like the cat that swallowed the canary.

look the other way to ignore (something) on purpose. □ *John could have prevented the problem, but he looked the other way.* □ *By looking the other way, he actually made the problem worse.*

look to one's laurels to take care not to lower or diminish one's reputation or position, especially in relation to that of someone else potentially better. □ *With the arrival of the new member of the football team, James will have to look to his laurels to remain the highest* *scorer.* □ *The older members of the team will have to look to their laurels when young people join.*

look up to someone to view someone with respect and admiration. □ *Bill really looks up to his father.* □ *Everyone in the class looked up to the teacher.*

loom large to be of great importance, especially when referring to a possible problem, danger, or threat. □ *The exams were looming large.* □ *Eviction was looming large when the students could not pay their rent.*

lord it over someone to dominate someone; to direct and control someone. □ *Mr. Smith seems to lord it over his wife.* □ *The old man lords it over everyone in the office.*

lose face to lose status; to become less respectable. □ *John is more afraid of losing face than losing money.* □ *Things will go better if you can explain to him where he was wrong without making him lose face.*

lose heart to lose one's courage or confidence. □ *Now, don't lose heart. Keep trying.* □ *What a disappointment! It's enough to make one lose heart.*

lose one's grip to lose control (over something). □ *I can't seem to run things like I used to. I'm losing my grip.* □ *They replaced the board of directors because it was losing its grip.*

lose one's reason to lose one's power of reasoning, possibly in anger. □ *I was so confused that I almost lost my reason.* □ *Bob seems to have lost his reason when he struck John.*

lose one's temper to become angry. □ *Please don't lose your temper. It's not good for you.* □ *I'm sorry that I lost my temper.*

lose one's train of thought to forget what one was talking or thinking about. □ *Excuse me, I lost my train of thought. What was I talking about?* □ *You made the speaker lose her train of thought.*

lost in thought busy thinking. □ *I'm sorry, I didn't hear what you said. I was lost in thought.* □ *Bill—lost in thought as always—went into the wrong room.*

lost on someone having no effect on someone; wasted on someone. (Informal.) □ *The joke was lost on Jean. She didn't understand* *it.* □ *The humour of the situation was lost on Mary. She was too upset to see it.*

love at first sight love established when two people first see one another. □ *Bill was standing at the door when Ann opened it. It was love at first sight.* □ *It was love at first sight when they met, but it didn't last long.*

lovely weather for ducks rainy weather. □ *It's raining and it's lovely weather for ducks.* □ *I don't like this weather, but it's lovely weather for ducks.*

lower one's sights to set one's goals or aims lower. □ *Even though you get frustrated, don't lower your sights.* □ *I shouldn't lower my sights. If I work hard, I can do what I want.*

lower one's voice to speak more softly. □ *Please lower your voice, or you'll disturb the people who are working.* □ *He wouldn't lower his voice, so everyone heard what he said.*

lucky dip a situation in which one is given no choice in what one is given, what happens, etc. (From the name of a fairground sideshow in which children choose a parcel at random from a tub of bran.) □ *The allocation of jobs is a lucky dip. You can't choose.* □ *Which coach you go back to school on is a lucky dip.*

maiden speech a first public speech, especially a British Member of Parliament's first speech to the House of Commons. □ *The new MP makes his maiden speech tonight.* □ *Our professor made her maiden speech to the conference yesterday.*

maiden voyage the first voyage of a ship or boat. □ *The liner sank on its maiden voyage.* □ *Jim is taking his yacht on its maiden voyage.*

make a beeline for someone or something to head straight towards someone or something. (Informal.) □ *Billy came into the kitchen and made a beeline for the biscuits.* □ *After the game, we all made a beeline for John, who was serving cold drinks.*

make a clean breast of something to confess something. □ *You'll feel better if you make a clean breast of it. Now tell us what happened.* □ *I was forced to make a clean breast of the whole affair.*

make a clean sweep to do something completely or thoroughly, with no exceptions. (Informal.) □ *The managing director decided to sack everybody, so he made a clean sweep.* □ *The council decided to make a clean sweep and repair all the roads in the district.*

make a comeback to return to one's former (successful) career. (Informal.) □ *After ten years in retirement, the singer made a comeback.* □ *You're never too old to make a comeback.*

make a face See pull a face.

make a go of it to make something work out all right. (Informal.) □ *It's a tough situation, but Ann is trying to make a go of it.* □ *We don't like living here, but we have to make a go of it.*

make a great show of something to make something obvious; to do something in a showy fashion. □ *Ann made a great show of wiping up the drink that John spilled.* □ *Jane displayed her irritation* *at our late arrival by making a great show of serving the overcooked dinner.*

make a mountain out of a molehill to make a major issue out of a minor one; to exaggerate the importance of something. □ *Come on, don't make a mountain out of a molehill. It's not that important.* □ *Mary is always making mountains out of molehills.*

make a name for oneself to make oneself famous; to become famous. □ *Sally wants to work hard and make a name for herself.* □ *It's hard to make a name for oneself without a lot of talent and hard work.*

make an example of someone to punish someone as a public warning to others. □ *The judge decided to make an example of John, so he fined him the full amount.* □ *The teacher made an example of Mary, who disturbed the class constantly with her whispering. She sent Mary out of the room.*

make a pitch for someone or something to say something in support of someone or something; to attempt to promote or advance someone or something. (Informal.) □ *Bill is making a pitch for his friend's new product again.* □ *The theatrical agent came in and made a pitch for her client.*

make a point of (doing) something to make an effort to do something. □ *Please make a point of posting this letter. It's very important.* □ *The hostess made a point of thanking me for bringing flowers.*

make (both) ends meet to manage to live on a small amount of money. □ *It's hard these days to make ends meet.* □ *I have to work overtime to make both ends meet.*

make cracks (about someone or something) to ridicule or make jokes about someone or something. (Informal.) □ *Please stop making cracks about my haircut. It's the new style.* □ *Some people can't help making cracks. They are just rude.*

make do (with someone or something) to do as well as possible with someone or something. □ *You'll have to make do with less money next year. The economy is very weak.* □ *We'll have to make do with John even though he's a slow worker.* □ *Yes, we'll have to make do.*

make eyes at someone to flirt with someone. □ *Tom spent all afternoon making eyes at Ann.* □ *How could they sit there in class making eyes at each other?*

make fun of someone or something to ridicule someone or something. □ *Please stop making fun of me. It hurts my feelings.* □ *Billy teases and makes fun of people a lot, but he means no harm.*

make good as something to succeed in a particular role. □ *I hope I make good as a teacher.* □ *John made good as a soccer player.*

make good money to earn a large amount of money. (Informal.) □ *Ann makes good money at her job.* □ *I don't know what she does, but she makes good money.*

make good time to proceed at a fast or reasonable rate. (Informal.) □ *On our trip to Brighton, we made good time.* □ *I'm making good time, but I have a long way to go.*

make it worth someone's while to make something profitable enough for someone to do. □ *If you deliver this parcel for me, I'll make it worth your while.* □ *The boss said he'd make it worth our while if we worked late.*

make light of something to treat something as if it were unimportant or humorous. □ *I wish you wouldn't make light of his problems. They're quite serious.* □ *I make light of my problems, and that makes me feel better.*

make merry to have fun; to have an enjoyable time. □ *The guests certainly made merry at the wedding.* □ *The children were making merry in the garden.*

make mischief to cause trouble. □ *Bob loves to make mischief and get other people into trouble.* □ *Don't believe what Mary says. She's just trying to make mischief.*

make no bones about something to have no hesitation in saying or doing something; to be open about something. (*Something* is often *it.*) □ *Fred made no bones about his dislike of games.* □ *Make no bones about it, Mary is a great singer.*

make nothing of it not to understand something; not to get the significance of something. □ *I could make nothing of his statement.* □ *I saw him leave, but I made nothing of it.*

make oneself at home to make oneself comfortable as if one were in one's own home. □ *Please come in and make yourself at home.* □ *I'm glad you're here. During your visit, just make yourself at home.*

make or break someone to improve or ruin someone. (Informal.) □ *The army will either make or break him.* □ *It's a tough assignment, and it will either make or break her.*

make someone look good to cause someone to appear successful or competent (especially when this is not the case). □ *John arranges all his affairs to make himself look good.* □ *The manager didn't like the quarterly report because it didn't make her look good.*

make someone's blood boil to make someone very angry. (Informal.) □ *It just makes my blood boil to think of the amount of food that gets wasted in this house.* □ *Whenever I think of that dishonest man, it makes my blood boil.*

make someone's blood run cold to shock or horrify someone. □ *The terrible story in the newspaper made my blood run cold.* □ *I could tell you things about prisons which would make your blood run cold.*

make someone's hair stand on end to cause someone to be very frightened. (Informal.) □ *The horrible scream made my hair stand on end.* □ *The ghost story made our hair stand on end.*

make someone's head spin See make someone's head swim.

make someone's head swim AND **make someone's head spin** **1.** to make someone dizzy or disoriented. □ *Riding in your car so fast makes my head spin.* □ *Breathing the gas made my head swim.* **2.** to confuse or overwhelm someone. □ *All these numbers make my head swim.* □ *The physics lecture made my head spin.*

make someone's mouth water to make someone hungry (for something); to make someone desirous of something. (Informal.) □ *That beautiful salad makes my mouth water.* □ *Talking about food makes my mouth water.* □ *Seeing those holiday brochures makes my mouth water.*

make something from scratch to make something by starting with the basic ingredients. (Informal.) □ *We made the cake from scratch, not using a cake mix.* □ *I didn't have a ladder, so I made one from scratch.*

make something to order to put something together only when someone requests it. (Usually said about clothing.) □ *This shop only makes suits to order.* □ *Our shirts fit perfectly because each one is made to order.*

make the feathers fly See make the fur fly.

make the fur fly AND **make the feathers fly** to cause a fight or an argument. (Informal.) □ *When your mother gets home and sees what you've done, she'll really make the fur fly.* □ *When those two get together, they'll make the feathers fly. They hate each other.*

make the grade to be satisfactory; to be what is expected. (Informal.) □ *I'm sorry, but your work doesn't exactly make the grade.* □ *Jack will never make the grade as a teacher.*

make up for lost time to do much of something; to make up for not doing much before; to do something fast. □ *At the age of sixty, Bill learned to play golf. Now he plays it all the time. He's making up for lost time.* □ *Because we spent too much time eating lunch, we have to drive faster to make up for lost time. Otherwise we won't arrive when we should.*

mark my word(s) remember what I'm telling you. □ *Mark my word, you'll regret this.* □ *This whole project will fail—mark my words.*

matter-of-fact businesslike; unfeeling. □ *Don't expect a lot of sympathy from Ann. She's very matter-of-fact.* □ *Don't be so matter-of-fact. It hurts my feelings.*

matter of life and death a matter of great urgency; an issue that will decide between living and dying. (Usually an exaggeration; sometimes humorous.) □ *We must find a doctor. It's a matter of life and death.* □ *I must have some water. It's a matter of life and death.*

matter of opinion the question of how good or bad someone or something is. □ *It's a matter of opinion how good the company is. John thinks it's great and Fred thinks it's poor.* □ *How efficient the committee is is a matter of opinion.*

mealy-mouthed not frank or direct. (Informal.) □ *Jane's too mealy-mouthed to tell Frank she dislikes him. She just avoids him.* □ *Don't be so mealy-mouthed. It's better to speak plainly.*

meet one's end to die. □ *The dog met his end under the wheels of a car.* □ *I hope I don't meet my end until I'm one hundred years old.*

meet one's match to meet one's equal. □ *John played tennis with Bill yesterday, and it looks as if John has finally met his match.* □ *Listen to Jane and Mary argue. I always thought that Jane was aggressive, but she has finally met her match.*

meet one's Waterloo to meet one's final and insurmountable challenge. (Refers to Napoleon at Waterloo.) □ *This teacher is being very hard on Bill, unlike the previous one. It seems that Bill has met his Waterloo.* □ *John was more than Sally could handle. She had finally met her Waterloo.*

meet someone half-way to offer to compromise with someone. □ *No, I won't give in, but I'll meet you half-way.* □ *They settled the argument by agreeing to meet each other half-way.*

melt in one's mouth to taste very good. (Informal.) □ *This cake is so good it'll melt in your mouth.* □ *John said that the food didn't exactly melt in his mouth.*

mend (one's) fences to restore good relations (with someone). (Also used literally.) □ *I think I had better get home and mend my fences. I had an argument with my daughter this morning.* □ *Sally called up her uncle to apologize and try to mend fences.*

mend one's ways to improve one's behaviour. □ *John used to be very wild, but he's mended his ways.* □ *You'll have to mend your ways if you go out with Mary. She hates people to be late.*

method in one's madness [for there to be] purpose in what one is doing. (From Shakespeare's *Hamlet*.) □ *What I'm doing may look strange, but there is method in my madness.* □ *Wait until she finishes; then you'll see that there is method in her madness.*

middle-of-the-road half-way between two extremes, especially political extremes. □ *Jane is very left-wing, but her husband is politically middle-of-the-road.* □ *I don't want to vote for either the left-wing or the right-wing candidate. I prefer someone with more middle-of-the-road views.*

milk of human kindness natural kindness and sympathy shown to others. (From Shakespeare's play *Macbeth*.) □ *Mary is completely hard and selfish—she has no milk of human kindness in her.* □ *Roger is too full of the milk of human kindness, and people take advantage of him.*

millstone around one's neck a continual burden or handicap. □ *This huge and expensive house is a millstone around my neck.* □ *Bill's huge family is a millstone around his neck.*

mind one's own business to attend only to the things that personally concern one. □ *Leave me alone, Bill. Mind your own business.* □ *I'd be fine if John would mind his own business.*

mind one's P's and Q's to mind one's manners. □ *When we go to the mayor's reception, please mind your P's and Q's.* □ *I always mind my P's and Q's when I eat at formal restaurants.*

mind you you must also take into consideration the fact that .... □ *He's very well dressed, but mind you he's got plenty of money to buy clothes.* □ *Jean is unfriendly to me, but mind you she's never very nice to anyone.*

mine of information someone or something that is full of information. □ *Grandfather is a mine of information about World War I.* □ *The new encyclopaedia is a positive mine of useful information.*

miss the point to fail to understand the point. □ *I'm afraid you missed the point. Let me explain it again.* □ *You keep explaining, and I keep missing the point.*

mixed bag a varied collection of people or things. (Refers to a bag of game brought home after a day's hunting.) □ *The new pupils are a mixed bag—some bright, some positively stupid.* □ *The furniture I bought is a mixed bag. Some of it is valuable and the rest is worthless.*

moment of truth the point at which someone has to face the reality or facts of a situation. □ *The moment of truth is here. Turn over your exam papers and begin.* □ *Now for the moment of truth, when we find out whether we have got planning permission or not.*

money for jam AND **money for old rope** payment for very little; money very easily obtained. (Informal.) □ *Baby-sitting is money for jam if the child does not wake up.* □ *Jack finds getting paid to caretake the house money for old rope.*

money for old rope See money for jam.

money is no object AND **expense is no object** it does not matter how much something costs. □ *Please show me your finest car. Money is no object.* □ *I want the finest earrings you have. Don't worry about how much they cost because expense is no object.*

money talks money gives one power and influence to help get things done or get one's own way. (Informal.) □ *Don't worry, I have a way of getting things done. Money talks.* □ *I can't compete against rich old Mrs. Jones. She'll get her way because money talks.*

monkey business peculiar or out of the ordinary activities, especially mischievous or illegal ones. □ *There's been some monkey business in connection with the firm's accounts.* □ *Bob left the firm quite suddenly. I think there was some monkey business between him and the boss's wife.*

More fool you! You are extremely foolish! □ *More fool you for agreeing to lend John money.* □ *You've offered to work for nothing. More fool you!*

more's the pity it is a great pity or shame; it is sad. □ *Jack can't come, more's the pity.* □ *Jane had to leave early, more's the pity.*

move heaven and earth to do something to make a major effort to do something. □ *"I'll move heaven and earth to be with you, Mary," said Bill.* □ *I had to move heaven and earth to get there on time.*

much ado about nothing a lot of excitement about nothing. (This is the title of a play by Shakespeare.) □ *All the commotion about the new law turned out to be much ado about nothing.* □ *Your complaints always turn out to be much ado about nothing.*

much of a muchness very alike or similar; not much different. □ *I don't mind whether we go to the restaurant in the high street or the one by the cinema. They're much of a muchness.* □ *We can go via Edinburgh or Glasgow. The two journeys are much of a muchness.*

much sought after wanted or desired very much. □ *This kind of crystal is much sought after. It's very rare.* □ *Sally is a great singer. She's much sought after.*

mum's the word don't spread the secret. (Informal.) □ *Don't tell anyone what I told you. Remember, mum's the word.* □ *Okay, mum's the word. Your secret is safe with me.*

N

nail in someone's or something's coffin something which will harm or destroy someone or something. □ *Every word of criticism that Bob said about the firm was a nail in his coffin. I knew the boss would sack him.* □ *Losing the export order was the final nail in the company's coffin.*

nail one's colours to the mast to commit oneself to a particular course of action or to a particular point of view. (A ship's flag—its colours—could not be lowered to indicate surrender when it was nailed to the mast.) □ *Fred nailed his colours to the mast by publicly declaring for strike action.* □ *Mary really believes in socialism, but she refuses to nail her colours to the mast and join the Labour Party.*

naked eye the human eye, unassisted by optics such as a telescope, microscope, or spectacles. □ *I can't see the bird's markings with the naked eye.* □ *The scientist could see nothing in the liquid with the naked eye, but with the aid of a microscope, she identified the bacteria.*

name of the game the goal or purpose; the important or central thing. (Informal.) □ *The name of the game is sell. You must sell, sell, sell if you want to make a living.* □ *Around here, the name of the game is look out for yourself.*

near the bone AND **near the knuckle** (Informal.) **1.** coming too close to mentioning something which should not be mentioned, for example because it might hurt or offend someone. □ *Jack's remark about prisons was a bit near the bone. Jane's father is on trial just now.* □ *Mike's speech about traffic safety was near the knuckle. Joan—who just had a serious car crash—was in the first row of the audience.* **2.** rather indecent. □ *The comedian's jokes were a bit near the bone.* □ *Uncle Fred's stories are always near the knuckle.*

near the knuckle See near the bone.

neck and neck exactly even, especially in a race or a contest. (Informal.) □ John and Tom finished the race neck and neck. □ Mary and Ann were neck and neck in the spelling contest.

needs must if it is absolutely necessary for something to be done, then it must be done. □ I don't want to sell the car, but needs must. I can't afford to run it. □ Needs must. Mary'll have to go out to work now that her husband's died.

neither fish nor fowl not any recognizable thing. □ The car that they drove up in was neither fish nor fowl. It must have been made out of spare parts. □ This proposal is neither fish nor fowl. I can't tell what you're proposing.

neither hide nor hair no sign or indication (of someone or something). □ We could find neither hide nor hair of him. I don't know where he is. □ I could see neither hide nor hair of the children.

never darken my door again See not to darken someone's door.

never fear do not worry; have confidence. □ I'll be there on time—never fear. □ I'll help you, never fear.

never had it so good [have] never had so much good fortune. (Informal.) □ No, I'm not complaining. I've never had it so good. □ Mary is pleased with her new job. She's never had it so good.

never in one's life not in one's experience. □ Never in my life have I been so insulted! □ He said that he had never in his life seen such an ugly painting.

never mind forget it; pay no more attention (to something). □ I wanted to talk to you, but never mind. It wasn't important. □ Never mind. I'm sorry to bother you.

new lease of life a renewed and revitalized outlook on life. □ Getting the offer of employment gave James a new lease of life. □ When I got out of the hospital, I felt I had a new lease of life.

new one on someone something one has not heard before and that one is not ready to believe. (Informal. The *someone* is often *me*.) □ Jack's poverty is a new one on me. He always seems to have plenty of money. □ The firm's difficulties are a new one on me. I thought that they were doing very well.

night on the town a night of celebrating (at one or more places in a town). (Informal.) □ *Did you enjoy your night on the town?* □ *After we got the contract signed, we celebrated with a night on the town.*

night-owl someone who usually stays up very late. (Informal.) □ *Ann's a real night-owl. She never goes to bed before 2 a.m. and sleeps until midday.* □ *Jack's a night-owl and is at his best after midnight.*

nine days' wonder something that is of interest to people only for a short time. □ *Don't worry about the story about you in the newspaper. It'll be a nine days' wonder and then people will forget.* □ *The elopement of Jack and Ann was a nine days' wonder. Now people never mention it.*

nine-to-five job a job with regular and normal hours. □ *I wouldn't want a nine-to-five job. I like the freedom I have as my own employer.* □ *I used to work night-shifts, but now I have a nine-to-five job.*

nip something in the bud to put an end to something at an early stage. □ *John is getting into bad habits, and it's best to nip them in the bud.* □ *There was trouble in the classroom, but the teacher nipped it in the bud.*

nobody's fool a sensible and wise person who is not easily deceived. □ *Mary's nobody's fool. She knows Jack would try to cheat her.* □ *Ann looks as though she's not very bright, but she's nobody's fool.*

no hard feelings no anger or resentment. (Informal. *No* can be replaced with *any*.) □ *I hope you don't have any hard feelings.* □ *No, I have no hard feelings.*

no holds barred with no restraints. (Informal. From wrestling.) □ *I intend to argue it out with Mary, no holds barred.* □ *When Ann negotiates a contract, she goes in with no holds barred and comes out with a good contract.*

no ifs or buts about it absolutely no discussion, dissension, or doubt about something. □ *I want you there exactly at eight, no ifs or buts about it.* □ *This is the best television set available for the money, no ifs or buts about it.*

no love lost between someone and someone else AND **no love lost between people** no friendship wasted between someone and someone else (because they are enemies). □ *Ever since their big argument, there has been no love lost between Tom and Bill.* □ *You can* *tell by the way that Jane is acting towards Ann that there is no love lost between them.*

none the wiser not knowing any more. □ *I was none the wiser about the project after the lecture. It was a complete waste of time.* □ *Ann tried to explain the situation tactfully to Jack, but in the end, he was none the wiser.*

none the worse for wear no worse because of use or effort. □ *I lent my car to John. When I got it back, it was none the worse for wear.* □ *I had a hard day today, but I'm none the worse for wear.*

none too something not very; not at all. □ *The towels in the bathroom were none too clean.* □ *It was none too warm in their house.*

no skin off someone's nose no difficulty for someone; no concern of someone. □ *It's no skin off my nose if she wants to act that way.* □ *She said it was no skin off her nose if we wanted to sell the house.*

no sooner said than done done quickly and obediently. (Informal.) □ *When Sally asked for someone to open the window, it was no sooner said than done.* □ *As Jane opened the window, she said, "No sooner said than done."*

no spring chicken not young (any more). (Informal.) □ *I don't get around very well any more. I'm no spring chicken, you know.* □ *Even though John is no spring chicken, he still plays tennis twice a week.*

Not a bit (of it). Not at all. □ *Am I unhappy? Not a bit.* □ *She said she was not disappointed. Not a bit, in fact.* □ *You needn't apologize— not a bit of it.*

not able See the entries beginning with *can't* as well as those listed below.

not able to call one's time one's own too busy; so busy as not to be in charge of one's own schedule. (Informal. *Not able to* is often expressed as *can't.*) □ *It's been so busy around here that I haven't been able to call my time my own.* □ *She can't call her time her own these days.*

not able to see the wood for the trees allowing many details of a problem to obscure the problem as a whole. (*Not able to* is often expressed as *can't.*) □ *The solution is obvious. You missed it because you can't see the wood for the trees.* □ *She suddenly realized that she hadn't been able to see the wood for the trees.*

not able to wait 1. too anxious to wait; excited (about something in the future). (*Not able to* is often expressed as *can't*.) □ *I'm so excited. I can't wait.* □ *Billy couldn't wait for his birthday.* **2.** to have to go to the toilet urgently. (Informal.) □ *Mum, I can't wait.* □ *Driver, stop the bus! My little boy can't wait.*

not born yesterday experienced; knowledgeable in the ways of the world. (Informal.) □ *I know what's going on. I wasn't born yesterday.* □ *Sally knows the score. She wasn't born yesterday.*

not breathe a word (about someone or something) to keep a secret about someone or something. □ *Don't worry. I won't breathe a word about it.* □ *Please don't breathe a word about Bob and his problems.*

not breathe a word (of something) not to tell something (to anyone). □ *Don't worry. I won't breathe a word of it.* □ *Tom won't breathe a word.*

not by a long shot not by a great amount; not at all. □ *Did I win the race? Not by a long shot.* □ *Not by a long shot did she complete the task.*

not for anything in the world See not for the world.

not for love nor money See not for the world.

not for the world AND **not for anything in the world; not for love nor money** not for anything (no matter what its value). □ *I won't do it for love nor money.* □ *He said he wouldn't do it—not for the world.* □ *She said no, not for anything in the world.*

not give someone the time of day to ignore someone (usually out of dislike). (Informal.) □ *Mary won't speak to Sally. She won't give her the time of day.* □ *I couldn't get an appointment with Mr. Smith. He wouldn't even give me the time of day.*

not half bad okay; pretty good. (Informal.) □ *Say, this roast beef isn't half bad.* □ *Well, Sally! You're not half bad!*

not have a care in the world free and casual; unworried and carefree. □ *I really feel good today—as if I didn't have a care in the world.* □ *Ann always acts as though she doesn't have a care in the world.*

nothing but skin and bones AND **all skin and bones** very thin or emaciated. (Informal.) □ *Bill has lost so much weight. He's noth-*

ing but skin and bones. □ *That old horse is all skin and bones. I won't ride it.*

nothing of the kind no; absolutely not. □ *I didn't insult him—nothing of the kind!* □ *Were we rude? Nothing of the kind!*

nothing short of something more or less the same as something bad; as bad as something. □ *His behaviour was nothing short of criminal.* □ *Climbing those mountains alone is nothing short of suicide.*

nothing to it it is easy; no difficulty involved. □ *Driving a car is easy. There's nothing to it.* □ *Geometry is fun to learn. There's nothing to it.*

nothing to write home about nothing exciting or interesting. (Informal.) □ *I've been busy, but nothing to write home about.* □ *I had a dull week—nothing to write home about.*

not hold water to make no sense; to be illogical. (Said of ideas or arguments. Like a vessel or container that leaks, the idea has flaws or "holes" in it.) □ *Your argument doesn't hold water.* □ *This scheme won't work because it won't hold water.*

not in the same league as someone or something not nearly as good as someone or something. □ *John isn't in the same league as Bob and his friends. He is not nearly as talented.* □ *This house isn't in the same league as our old one.*

not know someone from Adam not to know someone at all. □ *I wouldn't recognize John if I saw him. I don't know him from Adam.* □ *What does she look like? I don't know her from Adam.*

not lift a finger (to help someone) to do nothing to help someone. □ *They wouldn't lift a finger to help us.* □ *Can you imagine that they wouldn't lift a finger?*

not long for this world about to die. □ *Our dog is nearly twelve years old and not long for this world.* □ *I'm so tired. I think I'm not long for this world.*

not move a muscle to remain perfectly motionless. □ *Be quiet. Sit there and don't move a muscle.* □ *I was so tired I couldn't move a muscle.*

not open one's mouth AND **not utter a word** not to say anything at all; not to tell something (to anyone). □ *Don't worry, I'll* *keep your secret. I won't even open my mouth.* □ *Have no fear. I won't utter a word.* □ *I don't know how they found out. I didn't even open my mouth.*

no trespassing do not enter. (Usually seen on a sign. Not usually spoken.) □ *The sign on the tree said "No Trespassing." So we didn't go in.* □ *The angry farmer chased us out of the field, shouting, "Get out! Don't you see the No Trespassing sign?"*

not see further than the end of one's nose not to care about what is not actually present or obvious; not to care about the future or about what is happening elsewhere or to other people. □ *Mary can't see further than the end of her nose. She doesn't care about what will happen to the environment in the future, as long as she's comfortable now.* □ *Jack's been accused of not seeing further than the end of his nose. He refuses to expand the firm and look for new markets.*

not set foot somewhere not to go somewhere. □ *I wouldn't set foot in John's room. I'm very angry with him.* □ *He never set foot here.*

not show one's face not to appear (somewhere). □ *After what she said, she had better not show her face around here again.* □ *If I don't say I'm sorry, I'll never be able to show my face again.*

not sleep a wink not to sleep at all. (Informal.) □ *I couldn't sleep a wink last night.* □ *Ann hasn't been able to sleep a wink for a week.*

not someone's cup of tea not something one likes or prefers. (Informal.) □ *Playing cards isn't her cup of tea.* □ *Sorry, that's not my cup of tea.*

not take no for an answer not to accept someone's refusal. (A polite way of being insistent.) □ *Now, you must drop over and see us tomorrow. We won't take no for an answer.* □ *I had to go. They just wouldn't take no for an answer.*

not to darken someone's door AND **never darken my door again** to go away and not come back. □ *The heroine of the drama told the villain not to darken her door again.* □ *She touched the back of her hand to her forehead and said, "Get out and never darken my door again!"*

not up to scratch not adequate. (Informal.) □ *Sorry, your essay isn't up to scratch. Please do it over again.* □ *The performance was not up to scratch.*

not utter a word See *not open one's mouth*.

not worth a candle See *not worth a penny*.

not worth a penny AND **not worth a candle** worthless. (Informal.) □ *This land is all swampy. It's not worth a penny.* □ *This vase is not worth a candle.*

no two ways about it no choice about it; no other interpretation of it. (Informal.) □ *You have to go to the doctor whether you like it or not. There's no two ways about it.* □ *This letter means you're in trouble with the Inland Revenue. There's no two ways about it.*

null and void cancelled; worthless. □ *I tore the contract up, and the entire agreement became null and void.* □ *The judge declared the whole business null and void.*

nuts and bolts (of something) the basic facts about something; the practical details of something. □ *Tom knows all about the nuts and bolts of the chemical process.* □ *Ann is familiar with the nuts and bolts of public relations.*

odd man out an unusual or atypical person or thing. □ *I'm odd man out because I'm not wearing a tie.* □ *You had better learn to work a computer unless you want to be odd man out.*

odour of sanctity AND **air of sanctity** an atmosphere of excessive holiness or piety. (Derogatory.) □ *I hate their house. There's such an odour of sanctity, with Bibles and holy pictures everywhere.* □ *People are nervous of Jane's air of sanctity. She's always praying for people or doing good works and never has any fun.*

off-centre not exactly in the centre or middle. □ *The arrow hit the target a little off-centre.* □ *The picture hanging over the chair is a little off-centre.*

off colour not very well; slightly ill. □ *Mary is a bit off colour after the long journey.* □ *Fred went to the doctor when he was feeling off colour.*

off the beaten track in an unfamiliar place; on a route which is not often travelled. □ *Their home is in a quiet neighbourhood, off the beaten track.* □ *We like to stop there and admire the scenery. It's off the beaten track, but it's worth the trip.*

of the first water of the finest quality. □ *This is a very fine pearl— a pearl of the first water.* □ *Tom is a musician of the first water.*

of the old school holding attitudes and ideas that were popular and important in the past, but are no longer considered relevant or in line with modern trends. □ *Grammar was not taught much in my son's school, but fortunately he had a teacher of the old school.* □ *Aunt Jane is of the old school. She never goes out without wearing a hat and gloves.*

old enough to be someone's father See old enough to be someone's mother.

old enough to be someone's mother AND **old enough to be someone's father** as old as someone's parents. (Usually a way of saying that one person is much older than the other, especially when the difference in age is considered inappropriate.) □ *You can't go out with Bill. He's old enough to be your father!* □ *He married a woman who is old enough to be his mother.*

old hand at doing something someone who is experienced at doing something. (Informal.) □ *I'm an old hand at fixing clocks.* □ *With four children, he's an old hand at changing nappies.*

on active duty in battle or ready to go into battle. (Military.) □ *The soldier was on active duty for ten months.* □ *That was a long time to be on active duty.*

on a first-name basis (with someone) AND **on first-name terms (with someone)** knowing someone very well; good friends with someone. (Refers to using a person's given name rather than a surname or title.) □ *I'm on a first-name basis with John.* □ *John and I are on first-name terms.*

on a fool's errand involved in a useless journey or task. □ *Bill went for an interview, but he was on a fool's errand. The job had already been filled.* □ *I was sent on a fool's errand to buy some flowers. I knew the shop would be shut by then.*

on all fours on one's hands and knees. □ *I dropped a contact lens and spent an hour on all fours looking for it.* □ *The baby can walk, but is on all fours most of the time.*

on a par with someone or something equal to someone or something. □ *Your effort is simply not on a par with what's expected from you.* □ *John's work is not on a par with Bob's.*

on average generally; usually. □ *On average, you can expect about a 10 percent failure.* □ *On average, we see about ten people a day.*

on behalf of someone AND **on someone's behalf** [doing something] as someone's agent; [doing something] in place of someone; for the benefit of someone. □ *I'm writing on behalf of Mr. Smith, who has applied for a position with your company.* □ *I'm calling on behalf of my client, who wishes to complain about your actions.* □ *I'm acting on your behalf.*

once and for all finally and irreversibly. □ *I want to get this problem settled once and for all.* □ *I told him once and for all that he has to start studying.*

once in a blue moon very rarely. □ *I seldom go to the cinema—maybe once in a blue moon.* □ *I don't go into the city except once in a blue moon.*

once-in-a-lifetime chance a chance that will never occur again in one's lifetime. □ *This is a once-in-a-lifetime chance. Don't miss it.* □ *She offered me a once-in-a-lifetime chance, but I turned it down.*

once in a while occasionally. □ *I go to see a film once in a while.* □ *Once in a while we have lamb, but not very often.*

once upon a time once in the past. (A formula used to begin a fairy-tale.) □ *Once upon a time, there were three bears.* □ *Once upon a time, I had a puppy of my own.*

on cloud nine very happy. (Informal.) □ *When I got my promotion, I was on cloud nine.* □ *When the cheque came, I was on cloud nine for days.*

one for the record (books) a record-breaking act. □ *What a dive! That's one for the record books.* □ *I've never heard such a funny joke. That's really one for the record.*

one in a hundred See one in a thousand.

one in a million See one in a thousand.

one in a thousand AND **one in a hundred; one in a million** unique; one of a very few. □ *He's a great friend. He's one in a million.* □ *Mary's one in a hundred—such a hard worker.*

one's days are numbered [for someone] to face death, dismissal, or ruin. (Informal.) □ *If I don't get this contract, my days are numbered at this firm.* □ *His days as a member of the club are numbered.* □ *Uncle Tom has a terminal disease. His days are numbered.*

one's eyes are bigger than one's stomach [for one] to take more food than one can eat. (Informal.) □ *I can't eat all this. I'm afraid that my eyes were bigger than my stomach when I ordered.* □ *Try to take less food. Your eyes are bigger than your stomach at every meal.* ALSO: **have eyes bigger than one's stomach** to have a desire for more food than one could possibly eat. □ *I know I have eyes bigger than my stomach, so I won't take a lot of food.*

one's old stamping-ground the place where one was raised or where one has spent a lot of time. (Informal.) □ *Ann should know about that place. It's near her old stamping-ground.* □ *I can't wait to get back to my old stamping-ground and see old friends.*

one's way of life one's life-style; one's pattern of living. □ *That kind of thing just doesn't fit into my way of life.* □ *Children change one's way of life.*

one's words stick in one's throat one finds it difficult to speak because of emotion. □ *My words stick in my throat whenever I try to say something kind or tender.* □ *I wanted to apologize, but the words stuck in my throat.*

one-up (on someone) ahead of someone; with an advantage over someone. (Informal.) □ *Tom is one-up on Sally because he got a job and she didn't.* □ *Yes, it sounds like Tom is one-up.*

on first-name terms (with someone) See on a first-name basis (with someone).

on holiday away, having a holiday; on holiday. □ *Where are you going on holiday this year?* □ *I'll be away on holiday for three weeks.*

only have eyes for someone to be loyal to only one person, in the context of romance; to be interested in only one person. □ *Oh, Jane! I only have eyes for you!* □ *Don't waste any time on Tom. He only has eyes for Ann.*

on one's feet 1. standing up. □ *Get on your feet. They are playing the national anthem.* □ *I've been on my feet all day, and they hurt.* **2.** in improving health, especially after an illness. □ *I hope to be back on my feet next week.* □ *I can help out as soon as I'm back on my feet.*

on one's guard cautious; watchful. □ *Be on your guard. There are pickpockets around here.* □ *You had better be on your guard.*

on one's honour on one's solemn oath; promised sincerely. □ *On my honour, I'll be there on time.* □ *He promised on his honour that he'd pay me back next week.*

on one's mind occupying one's thoughts; currently being thought about. □ *You've been on my mind all day.* □ *Do you have something on your mind? You look so serious.*

on one's (own) head be it one must take the responsibility for one's actions. □ *On your head be it if you set fire to the house.* □ *James insisted on going to the party uninvited. On his head be it if the host is annoyed.*

on one's toes alert. (Informal.) □ *You have to be on your toes if you want to be in this business.* □ *My job keeps me on my toes.*

on order ordered with delivery expected. □ *Your car is on order. It'll be here in a few weeks.* □ *I don't have the part in stock, but it's on order.*

on record recorded for future reference. □ *We had the coldest winter on record last year.* □ *This is the fastest race on record.*

on sale AND **for sale** offered for sale; able to be bought. □ *There are antiques on sale at the market.* □ *There is a wide range of fruit for sale.*

on second thoughts having given something more thought; having reconsidered something. □ *On second thoughts, maybe you should sell your house and move into a flat.* □ *On second thoughts, let's not go to a film.*

on someone's behalf See on behalf of someone.

on the air broadcasting (a radio or television programme). □ *The radio station came back on the air shortly after the storm.* □ *We were on the air for two hours.*

on the alert (for someone or something) watchful and attentive for someone or something. □ *Be on the alert for pickpockets.* □ *You should be on the alert when you cross the street in heavy traffic.*

on the cards in the future. (Informal.) □ *Well, what do you think is on the cards for tomorrow?* □ *I asked the managing director if there was a rise on the cards for me.*

on the dot exactly right; in exactly the right place; at exactly the right time. (Informal.) □ *That's it! You're right on the dot.* □ *He got here at one o'clock on the dot.*

on the eve of something just before something, possibly the evening before something. □ *John decided to leave college on the eve of his graduation.* □ *The team held a party on the eve of the tournament.*

on the face of it superficially; from the way it looks. □ *This looks like a serious problem on the face of it. It probably is minor, however.* □ *On the face of it, it seems worthless.*

on the horns of a dilemma having to decide between two things, people, etc. □ *Mary found herself on the horns of a dilemma. She didn't know which dress to choose.* □ *I make up my mind easily. I'm not on the horns of a dilemma very often.*

on the loose running around free. (Informal.) □ *Look out! There is a bear on the loose from the zoo.* □ *Most young people enjoy being on the loose when they go to college.*

on the mend getting well; healing. (Informal.) □ *My cold was terrible, but I'm on the mend now.* □ *What you need is some hot chicken soup. Then you'll really be on the mend.*

on the off-chance because of a slight possibility that something may happen, might be the case, etc.; just in case. □ *I went to the theatre on the off-chance that there were tickets for the show left.* □ *We didn't think we would get into the football ground, but we went on the off-chance.*

on the sly slyly or sneakily. (Informal.) □ *He was seeing Mrs. Smith on the sly.* □ *She was supposed to be losing weight, but she was eating chocolate on the sly.*

on the spot (Informal.) **1.** at exactly the right place; in the place where one is needed. □ *Fortunately the ambulance men were on the spot when the accident happened at the football match.* □ *I expect the police to be on the spot when and where trouble arises.* **2.** at once; then and there. □ *She liked the house so much that she bought it on the spot.* □ *He was fined on the spot for parking illegally.*

on the spur of the moment suddenly; spontaneously. □ *We decided to go on the spur of the moment.* □ *I went on holiday on the spur of the moment.*

on the strength of something because of the support of something, such as a promise or evidence; owing to something. □ *On*

the strength of your comment, I decided to give John another chance.
□ *On the strength of my neighbour's testimony, my case was dismissed.*

on the tip of one's tongue about to be said; almost remembered.
□ *I have his name right on the tip of my tongue. I'll think of it in a
second.* □ *John had the answer on the tip of his tongue, but Ann said
it first.*

on thin ice See skating on thin ice.

on tiptoe standing or walking on the front part of the feet (the balls
of the feet) with no weight put on the heels. (This is done to gain
height or to walk quietly.) □ *I had to stand on tiptoe to see over the
fence.* □ *I came in late and walked on tiptoe so I wouldn't wake any-
body up.*

on top of the world See sitting on top of the world.

open a can of worms to uncover a set of problems or complications; to create unnecessary complications. (Informal.) □ *If you start
asking questions about the firm's accounts, you'll open a can of worms.*
□ *How about clearing up this mess before you open up a new can of
worms?*

open-and-shut case something, usually a law-case or problem,
that is simple and straightforward without complications. □ *The
murder trial was an open-and-shut case. The defendant was caught
with the murder weapon.* □ *Jack's death was an open-and-shut case
of suicide. He left a suicide note.*

open book someone or something that is easy to understand. □
Jane's an open book. I always know what she is going to do next. □
The council's intentions are an open book. They want to save money.

open fire (on someone) to start (doing something, such as asking questions or criticizing). (Informal. Also used literally.) □ *The
reporters opened fire on the mayor.* □ *When the reporters opened fire,
the film-star was smiling, but not for long.* □ *The soldiers opened fire
on the villagers.*

open one's heart (to someone) to reveal one's most private
thoughts to someone. □ *I always open my heart to my wife when I
have a problem.* □ *It's a good idea to open your heart every now and
then.*

open Pandora's box to uncover a lot of unsuspected problems. □ *When I asked Jane about her problems, I didn't know I had opened Pandora's box.* □ *You should be cautious with people who are upset. You don't want to open Pandora's box.*

open season for something unrestricted hunting of a particular game animal. □ *It's always open season for rabbits around here.* □ *Is it ever open season for deer?*

open secret something which is supposed to be secret, but which is known to a great many people. □ *Their engagement is an open secret. Only their friends are supposed to know, but in fact, the whole town knows.* □ *It's an open secret that Fred's looking for a new job.*

open the door to something to permit or allow something to become a possibility. (Also used literally.) □ *Your policy opens the door to cheating.* □ *Your statement opens the door to John's candidacy.*

order of the day something necessary or usual at a certain time. □ *Warm clothes are the order of the day when camping in the winter.* □ *Going to bed early was the order of the day when we were young.*

other way round the reverse; the opposite. □ *No, it won't fit that way. Try it the other way round.* □ *It doesn't make any sense like that. It belongs the other way round.*

out of kilter out of working order; malfunctioning. (Informal.) □ *My furnace is out of kilter. I have to call someone to fix it.* □ *This computer is out of kilter. It doesn't work.*

out of line 1. improper; inappropriate. □ *I'm afraid that your behaviour was quite out of line. I do not wish to speak further about this matter.* □ *Bill, that remark was out of line. Please be more respectful.* **2.** See the following entry.

out of line (with something) 1. not properly lined up in a line of things. □ *One of those books on the shelf is out of line with the others. Please fix it.* □ *The files are out of line also.* **2.** unreasonable when compared with something else; not fitting with what is usual. □ *The cost of this meal is out of line with what other restaurants charge.* □ *Your request is out of line with company policy.*

out of luck without good luck; having bad fortune. (Informal.) □ *If you wanted some icecream, you're out of luck.* □ *I was out of luck. I got there too late to get a seat.*

out of necessity because of necessity; because it was necessary. □ *I bought this hat out of necessity. I needed one, and this was all there was.* □ *We sold our car out of necessity.*

out of one's mind silly and senseless; crazy; irrational. □ *Why did you do that? You must be out of your mind!* □ *Good grief, Tom! You're out of your mind!*

out of order 1. not in the correct order. □ *This book is out of order. Please put it in the right place on the shelf.* □ *You're out of order, John. Please get in the queue after Jane.* **2.** not following correct procedure. □ *My question was declared out of order by the president.* □ *Ann inquired, "Isn't a motion to table the question out of order at this time?"*

out of place 1. not in the usual or proper place. □ *The salt was out of place in the cupboard, so I couldn't find it.* □ *Billy, you're out of place. Please sit next to Tom.* **2.** improper and impertinent. □ *That kind of behaviour is out of place in church.* □ *Your rude remark is quite out of place.*

out-of-pocket expenses the actual amount of money spent. (Refers to the money one person pays while doing something on someone else's behalf. One is usually paid back this money.) □ *My out-of-pocket expenses for the party were nearly £175.* □ *My employer usually pays all out-of-pocket expenses for a business trip.*

out of practice performing poorly because of a lack of practice. □ *I used to be able to play the piano extremely well, but now I'm out of practice.* □ *The players lost the game because they were out of practice.*

out of print no longer available for sale. (Said of a book or periodical.) □ *The book you want is out of print, but perhaps I can find a used copy for you.* □ *It was published nearly ten years ago, so it's probably out of print.*

out of season 1. not now available for sale. □ *Sorry, oysters are out of season. We don't have any.* □ *Watermelon is out of season in the winter.* **2.** not now legally able to be hunted or caught. □ *Are salmon out of season?* □ *I caught a trout out of season and had to pay a fine.*

out of service not now operating. □ *Both lifts are out of service, so I had to use the stairs.* □ *The toilet is temporarily out of service.*

out of sorts not feeling well; cross and irritable. □ *I've been out of sorts for a day or two. I think I'm coming down with flu.* □ *The baby is out of sorts. Maybe she's cutting a tooth.*

out of stock not immediately available in a shop; [for goods] to be temporarily unavailable. □ *Those items are out of stock, but a new supply will be delivered on Thursday.* □ *I'm sorry, but the red ones are out of stock. Would a blue one do?*

out of the blue suddenly; without warning. □ *Then, out of the blue, he told me he was leaving.* □ *Mary appeared on my doorstep out of the blue.*

out of the corner of one's eye [seeing something] at a glance; glimpsing (something). □ *I saw someone do it out of the corner of my eye. It might have been Jane who did it.* □ *I only saw the accident out of the corner of my eye. I don't know who is at fault.*

out of the frying-pan into the fire from a bad situation to a worse situation. □ *When I tried to argue about my fine for a traffic violation, the judge charged me with contempt of court. I really went out of the frying-pan into the fire.* □ *I got deeply in debt. Then I really got out of the frying-pan into the fire when I lost my job.*

out of the question not possible; not permitted. □ *I'm sorry, but leaving early is out of the question.* □ *You can't go to France this spring. We can't afford it. It's out of the question.*

out of the running no longer being considered; eliminated from a contest. □ *After the first part of the diving competition, three of our team were out of the running.* □ *After the scandal was made public, I was no longer in the running. I pulled out of the election.*

out of the swim of things not in the middle of activity; not involved in things. (Informal.) □ *While I had my cold, I was out of the swim of things.* □ *I've been out of the swim of things for a few weeks. Please bring me up to date.*

out of the woods past a critical phase; no longer at risk. (Informal.) □ *When the patient got out of the woods, everyone relaxed.* □ *I can give you a better prediction for your future health when you are out of the woods.*

out of thin air out of nowhere; out of nothing. (Informal.) □ *Suddenly—out of thin air—the messenger appeared.* □ *You just made that up out of thin air.*

out of this world wonderful; extraordinary. □ *This pie is just out of this world.* □ *Look at you! How lovely you look—simply out of this world.*

out of turn not at the proper time; not in the proper order. □ *We were permitted to be served out of turn, because we had to leave early.* □ *Bill tried to register out of turn and was sent away.*

out of work unemployed, temporarily or permanently. □ *How long have you been out of work?* □ *My brother has been out of work for nearly a year.*

out on a limb [in or into a situation of] doing something differently from the way others do it, and thus taking a chance or a risk. (Often with go.) □ *She really went out on a limb when she gave him permission to leave early.* □ *As the only one who supported the plan, Bill was out on a limb.*

out on parole out of jail but still under police supervision. □ *Bob got out on parole after serving only a few years of his sentence.* □ *He was out on parole because of good behaviour.*

over and done with finished. □ *I'm glad that's over and done with.* □ *Now that I have college over and done with, I can find a job.*

over my dead body not if I can stop you; you'll have to kill me first (so that I won't stop you). □ *You'll sell this house over my dead body!* □ *You want to leave college? Over my dead body!*

over the hill over age; too old to do something. (Informal.) □ *Now that Mary's forty, she thinks she's over the hill.* □ *My grandfather was over eighty before he felt he was over the hill.*

over the hump over the difficult part. (Informal.) □ *This is a difficult project, but we're over the hump now.* □ *I'm half-way through—over the hump—and it looks as though I may finish after all.*

over the odds more than one would expect to pay. (From betting in horse-racing.) □ *We had to pay over the odds for a house in the area where we wanted to live.* □ *It's a nice car, but the owner's asking well over the odds for it.*

over the top exaggerated; excessive. (Informal.) □ *Her reaction to my statement was a bit over the top. She hugged me.* □ *Everyone thought her behaviour was over the top.* ALSO: **go over the top** to do something in an exaggerated or excessive way; to overreact. □ *Jane really went over the top with the dinner she prepared for us. It took her hours to prepare.* □ *Uncle Jack went completely over the top when he bought my baby's present. It must have been incredibly expensive.*

P

packed out very crowded; containing as many people as possible. (Informal.) □ *The theatre was packed out.* □ *The cinema was packed out twenty minutes before we arrived.*

pack someone off (to somewhere) to send someone away to somewhere, often with the suggestion that one is glad to do so. □ *His parents packed him off to boarding-school as soon as possible.* □ *John finally has left for France. We packed him off last week.*

pack them in to draw a lot of people. (Informal.) □ *It was a good night at the theatre. The play really packed them in.* □ *The circus manager knew he could pack them in if he advertised the lion tamer.*

paddle one's own canoe to do (something) by oneself; to be alone. □ *I've been left to paddle my own canoe since I was a child.* □ *Sally didn't stay with the group. She wanted to paddle her own canoe.*

pain in the neck a bother; an annoyance. (Informal.) □ *This assignment is a pain in the neck.* □ *Your little brother is a pain in the neck.*

pale around the gills AND **green around the gills; green about the gills** looking sick. (Informal.) □ *John is looking a little pale around the gills. What's wrong?* □ *Oh, I feel a little green about the gills.*

paper over the cracks (in something) to try to hide faults or difficulties, often in a hasty or not very successful way. □ *The politician tried to paper over the cracks in his party's economic policy.* □ *Tom tried to paper over the cracks in his relationship with the boss, but it was not possible.*

par for the course typical; about what one could expect. (This refers to a golf-course.) □ *So he went off and left you? Well, that's about par for the course. He's no friend.* □ *I worked for days on this project, but it was rejected. That's par for the course around here.*

parrot-fashion without understanding the meaning of what one has learnt, is saying, etc. □ *The child learnt the poem by heart and repeated it parrot-fashion.* □ *Jean never thinks for herself. She just repeats what her father says, parrot-fashion.*

part and parcel of something an essential part of something; something that is unavoidably included as part of something else. □ *This point is part and parcel of my whole argument.* □ *Bill refused to accept pain and illness as part and parcel of growing older.*

parting of the ways a point at which people separate and go their own ways. (Often with *come to a, arrive at a, reach a,* etc.) □ *Jane and Bob finally came to a parting of the ways and divorced.* □ *Bill and his parents reached a parting of the ways and he left home.*

party line the official ideas and attitudes which are adopted by the leaders of a particular group, usually political, and which the other members are expected to accept. □ *Tom has left the club. He refused to follow the party line.* □ *Many politicians agree with the party line without thinking.*

pass as someone or something to succeed in being accepted as someone or something. □ *The spy was able to pass as a normal citizen.* □ *The thief was arrested when he tried to pass as a priest.*

pass muster to measure up to the required standards. □ *I tried my best, but my efforts didn't pass muster.* □ *If you don't wear a suit, you won't pass muster at that expensive restaurant. They won't let you in.*

pass the buck to pass the blame (to someone else); to give the responsibility (to someone else). (Informal.) □ *Don't try to pass the buck! It's your fault, and everybody knows it.* □ *Some people try to pass the buck whenever they can. They won't accept responsibility.*

pass the hat round to attempt to collect money for some (charitable) project. □ *Bob is passing the hat round to collect money to buy flowers for Ann.* □ *He's always passing the hat round for something.*

pass the time of day (with someone) to chat or talk informally with someone. (Informal.) □ *I saw Mr. Brown in town yesterday. I stopped and passed the time of day with him.* □ *No, we didn't have a serious talk; we just passed the time of day.*

past it See past someone's or something's best.

past someone's or something's best AND **past someone's or something's sell-by date; past it** less good or efficient now than someone or something was before. (Past it and past someone's or something's sell-by date are informal.) □ *Joan was a wonderful singer, but she's past her best now.* □ *This old car's past it. I'll need to get a new one.* □ *Mary feels she's past her sell-by date when she sees so many young women joining the company.* □ *This cooker's past its sell-by date. We'll have to get a new one.*

past someone's or something's sell-by date See past someone's or something's best.

pay an arm and a leg (for something) AND **pay through the nose (for something)** to pay too much money for something. (Informal.) □ *I hate to have to pay an arm and a leg for a tank of petrol.* □ *If you shop around, you won't have to pay an arm and a leg.* □ *Why should you pay through the nose?* ALSO: **cost an arm and a leg** to cost too much. □ *It cost an arm and a leg, so I didn't buy it.*

pay lip-service (to something) to express loyalty, respect, or support for something insincerely. □ *You don't really care about politics. You're just paying lip-service to the candidate.* □ *The students pay lip-service to the new rules, but they plan to ignore them in practice.*

pay one's debt to society to serve a sentence for a crime, usually in prison. □ *The judge said that Mr. Simpson had to pay his debt to society.* □ *Mr. Brown paid his debt to society in prison.*

pay one's dues to pay the fees required to belong to an organization. □ *If you haven't paid your dues, you can't come to the club picnic.* □ *How many people have paid their dues?*

pay someone a back-handed compliment to give someone an apparent compliment that is really an insult. □ *John said that he had never seen me looking better. I think he was paying me a back-handed compliment.* □ *I'd prefer that someone insulted me directly. I hate it when someone pays me a back-handed compliment—unless it's a joke.*

pay someone a compliment to compliment someone. □ *Sally thanked me for paying her a compliment.* □ *When Tom did his job well, I paid him a compliment.*

pay the earth to pay a great deal of money for something. (Informal. Compare with cost the earth.) □ *Bob paid the earth for that ugly old sideboard.* □ *You have to pay the earth for property in that area.*

pay the piper to provide the money for something and so have some control over how the money is spent. (From the expression "He who pays the piper calls the tune.") □ *The parents at a fee-paying school pay the piper and so should have a say in how the school is run.* □ *Hotel guests pay the piper and should be treated politely.*

pay through the nose (for something) See pay an arm and a leg (for something).

pick and choose to choose very carefully from a number of possibilities; to be selective. □ *You must take what you are given. You cannot pick and choose.* □ *Meg is so beautiful. She can pick and choose from a whole range of suitors.*

pick a quarrel (with someone) to start an argument with someone. □ *Are you trying to pick a quarrel with me?* □ *No, I'm not trying to pick a quarrel.*

pick holes in something to criticize something severely; to find all the flaws or fallacies in an argument. (Informal.) □ *The solicitor picked holes in the witness's story.* □ *They will pick holes in your argument.*

pick on someone to criticize someone or something constantly; to abuse someone or something. (Informal.) □ *Stop picking on me!* □ *Why are you always picking on the office junior?*

piece of cake something very easy. (Informal.) □ *No, it won't be any trouble. It's a piece of cake.* □ *Climbing this is easy! Look here—a piece of cake.*

pie in the sky a supposed future reward which one is not likely to get. (From "You'll get pie in the sky when you die," a line from a song by U.S. radical labour organizer Joe Hill.) □ *The firm have promised him a large reward, but I think it's just pie in the sky.* □ *Don't hold out for a big reward, you know—pie in the sky.*

pig(gy)-in-the-middle a person who is in a position between two opposing groups. □ *Jack and Tom share a secretary who is always pig-in-the-middle because they are always disagreeing with each other.* □

Fred's mother is piggy-in-the-middle when Fred and his father start to argue. She tries to please both of them.

pigs might fly a saying indicating that something is extremely unlikely to happen. □ *Pam might marry Tom, but there again, pigs might fly.* □ *Do you really believe that Jack will lend us his car? Yes, and pigs might fly.*

pile in(to something) to climb in or get in roughly. (Informal.) □ *Okay, children, pile in!* □ *The children piled into the car and slammed the door.*

pinch and scrape to live on very little money, sometimes to save money. □ *Bob has to pinch and scrape all the time because of his low wages.* □ *Students have to pinch and scrape to buy books.*

pin one's faith on someone or something to put one's hope, trust, or faith in someone or something. □ *I'm pinning my faith on your efforts.* □ *Don't pin your faith on Tom. He's not dependable.*

pins and needles a tingling feeling in some part of one's body. □ *I've got pins and needles in my legs.* □ *Mary gets pins and needles if she crosses her arms for long.*

pipe down to be quiet; to get quiet. (Informal.) □ *Okay, you lot, pipe down!* □ *I've heard enough from you. Pipe down!*

pipe-dream a wish or an idea which is impossible to achieve or carry out. (From the dreams or visions induced by the smoking of an opium pipe.) □ *Going to the West Indies is a pipe-dream. We'll never have enough money.* □ *Your hopes of winning a lot of money are just a silly pipe-dream.*

pipped at the post beaten in the final stages of a race or competition; defeated in some activity at the last minute. (Informal. From horse-racing.) □ *Tom led the race for most of the time, but he was pipped at the post by his rival.* □ *Jane nearly bought that house, but she was pipped at the post by the present owner.*

pitch in (and help) to get busy and help (with something). (Informal.) □ *Pick up a paintbrush and pitch in and help.* □ *Why don't some of you pitch in? We need all the help we can get.*

pit someone or something against someone or something to set someone or something in opposition to someone or something. □ *The rules of the tournament pit their team against ours.* □ *John* *pitted Mary against Sally in the tennis match.* □ *In the illegal dog fight, large dogs were pitted against small ones.*

plain sailing progress made without any difficulty; an easy situation. □ *Once you've passed that exam, it will be plain sailing.* □ *Working there was not all plain sailing. The boss had a very hot temper.*

play both ends (against the middle) [for one] to scheme in a way that pits two sides against each other (for one's own gain). (Informal.) □ *I told my brother that Mary doesn't like him. Then I told Mary that my brother doesn't like her. They broke up, so now I can have the car this week-end. I succeeded in playing both ends against the middle.* □ *If you try to play both ends against the middle, you're likely to get in trouble with both sides.*

play cat and mouse (with someone) to capture and release someone over and over; to treat a person in one's control in such a way that the person does not know what is going to happen next. □ *The police played cat and mouse with the suspect until they had sufficient evidence to make an arrest.* □ *Tom has been playing cat and mouse with Ann. Finally she got tired of it and broke up with him.*

play devil's advocate to put forward arguments against or objections to a proposition—which one may actually agree with—purely to test the validity of the proposition. (The devil's advocate was given the role of opposing the canonization of a saint in the mediaeval Church to prove that the grounds for canonization were sound.) □ *I agree with your plan. I'm just playing devil's advocate so you'll know what the opposition will say.* □ *Mary offered to play devil's advocate and argue against our case so that we would find out any flaws in it.*

played out no longer of interest or influence. (Informal.) □ *Jane's political ideas are all played out.* □ *That particular religious sect is played out now.*

play fair to do something by the rules or in a fair and just manner. □ *John won't do business with Bill any more because Bill doesn't play fair.* □ *You moved the golf ball with your foot! That's not playing fair!*

play fast and loose (with someone or something) to act carelessly, thoughtlessly, and irresponsibly. (Informal.) □ *I'm tired of your playing fast and loose with me. Leave me alone.* □ *Bob played fast and loose with Sally's affections.*

play gooseberry to be with two lovers who wish to be alone. (Informal.) □ *I'm not going to the cinema with Tom and Jean. I hate playing gooseberry.* □ *Come on! Let's go home! Bob and Mary don't want us playing gooseberry.*

play hard to get to be coy and excessively shy; to make it difficult for someone to talk to one or be friendly. □ *Why can't we go out? Why do you play hard to get?* □ *Sally annoys all the boys because she plays hard to get.*

play havoc with someone or something to cause a lot of damage to something; to ruin something; to create disorder in something. □ *The road-works played havoc with the traffic.* □ *A new baby can play havoc with one's household routine.*

play into someone's hands to do exactly what an opponent wants one to do, without one realizing it; to assist someone in a scheme without realizing it. □ *John is doing exactly what I hoped he would. He's playing into my hands.* □ *John played into my hands by taking the coins he found in my desk. I caught him and had him arrested.*

play one's cards close to one's chest AND **keep one's cards close to one's chest** to work or negotiate in a careful and private manner. □ *It's hard to figure out what John is up to because he plays his cards close to his chest.* □ *Don't let them know what you're up to. Keep your cards close to your chest.*

play one's cards right to work or negotiate correctly and skilfully. (Informal.) □ *If you play your cards right, you can get whatever you want.* □ *She didn't play her cards right, so she didn't get promotion.*

play one's trump card to use one's most powerful or effective strategy or device. □ *I won't play my trump card until I have tried everything else.* □ *I thought that the whole situation was hopeless until Mary played her trump card and told us her uncle would lend us the money.*

play on something to make use of something for one's own ends; to exploit something; to manage something for a desired effect. (The *on* can be replaced by *upon*.) □ *The shop assistant played on my sense of responsibility in trying to get me to buy the book.* □ *See if you can get her to confess by playing upon her sense of guilt.*

play politics to allow political concerns to dominate in matters where principles should prevail. □ *Look, I came here to discuss this* *trial, not play politics.* □ *They're not making reasonable decisions. They're playing politics.*

play possum to pretend to be inactive, unobserved, asleep, or dead. (Informal. The *possum* is an *opossum.*) □ *I knew that Bob wasn't asleep. He was just playing possum.* □ *I can't tell if this animal is dead or just playing possum.*

play safe not to take risks; to act in a safe manner. □ *You should play safe and take your umbrella.* □ *If you have a cold or the flu, play safe and go to bed.*

play second fiddle (to someone) to be in a subordinate position to someone. □ *I'm tired of playing second fiddle to John.* □ *I'm better trained than he is, and I have more experience. I shouldn't play second fiddle.*

play the field to date many different people rather than going steady with just one. (Informal.) □ *Tom wanted to play the field, so he said goodbye to Ann.* □ *He said he wanted to play the field rather than get married while he was still young.*

play the fool to act in a silly manner play safe to amuse other people. □ *The teacher told Tom to stop playing the fool and sit down.* □ *Fred likes playing the fool, but we didn't find him funny last night.*

play the game to behave or act in a fair and honest way. □ *You shouldn't try to disturb your opponent's concentration. That's not playing the game.* □ *Listening to other people's phone calls is certainly not playing the game.*

play the market to invest in the shares market. (As if it were a game or as if it were gambling.) □ *Would you rather put your money in the bank or play the market?* □ *I've learned my lesson playing the market. I lost a fortune.*

play to the gallery to perform in a manner that will get the strong approval of the audience; to perform in a manner that will get the approval of the less sophisticated members of the audience. □ *John is a competent actor, but he has a tendency to play to the gallery.* □ *When he made the rude remark, he was just playing to the gallery. He wanted others to find him amusing.*

play tricks (on someone) to trick or confuse someone. □ *I thought I saw a camel over there. I think that my eyes are playing tricks on me.* □ *Please don't play tricks on your little brother. It makes him cry.*

play up to cause trouble; to be a nuisance. (Informal.) □ *My leg is playing up. It really aches.* □ *Her arthritis always plays up in this cold, damp weather.* ALSO: **play someone up** to annoy someone. □ *That child played me up. He was naughty all day.* □ *The pupils played the substitute teacher up the entire day.*

play up to someone to try to gain someone's favour; to curry someone's favour; to flatter someone or to pretend to admire someone to gain favour. □ *Bill is always playing up to the teacher.* □ *Ann played up to Bill as if she wanted him to marry her.*

play with fire to do something very risky or dangerous. □ *The teacher was playing with fire by threatening a pupil.* □ *I wouldn't talk to Bob that way if I were you—unless you like playing with fire.*

pluck up (one's) courage to increase one's courage a bit; to become brave enough to do something. □ *Come on, Ann, make the dive. Pluck up your courage and do it.* □ *Fred plucked up courage and asked Jean for a date.*

poetic justice the appropriate but chance receiving of rewards or punishments by those deserving them. □ *It was poetic justice that Jane won the race after Mary tried to get her banned.* □ *The car robbers stole a car with no petrol. That's poetic justice.*

point the finger at someone to blame someone; to identify someone as the guilty person. □ *Don't point the finger at me! I didn't take the money.* □ *The manager refused to point the finger at anyone in particular and said the whole staff were sometimes guilty of being late.*

poke fun (at someone or something) to make fun of someone; to ridicule someone. (Informal.) □ *Stop poking fun at me! It's not nice.* □ *Bob is always poking fun.*

pot calling the kettle black [the instance of] someone with a fault accusing someone else of having the same fault. □ *Ann is always late, but she was rude enough to tell everyone when I was late. Now that's the pot calling the kettle black!* □ *You're calling me thoughtless? That's really a case of the pot calling the kettle black.*

pound for pound considering the amount of money involved; considering the cost. (Often seen in advertising.) □ *Pound for pound, you cannot buy a better car.* □ *Pound for pound, this detergent washes cleaner and brighter than any other product on the market.*

pound the streets to walk through the streets looking for a job. (Informal.) □ *I spent two months pounding the streets after the factory I worked for closed.* □ *Look, Bob. You'd better get on with your work unless you want to be out pounding the streets.*

pour cold water on something AND **throw cold water on something** to discourage doing something; to reduce enthusiasm for something. □ *When my father said I couldn't have the car, he poured cold water on my plans.* □ *John threw cold water on the whole project and refused to participate.*

pour money down the drain to waste money; to throw money away. □ *What a waste! You're just pouring money down the drain.* □ *Don't buy any more of that low-quality material. That's just pouring money down the drain.*

pour oil on troubled waters to calm things down. (If oil is poured on to rough seas during a storm, the water will become more calm.) □ *That was a good thing to say to John. It helped to pour oil on troubled waters. Now he looks happy.* □ *Bob is the kind of person who always pours oil on troubled waters.*

power behind the throne the person who controls the one who is apparently in charge. □ *Mr. Smith appears to run the shop, but his brother is the power behind the throne.* □ *They say that the mayor's husband is the power behind the throne.*

powers that be the people who are in authority. □ *The powers that be have decided to send back the immigrants.* □ *I have applied for a licence, and the powers that be are considering my application.*

practise what you preach to do what you advise other people to do. □ *If you'd practise what you preach, you'd be better off.* □ *You give good advice. Why not practise what you preach?*

praise someone or something to the skies to give someone much praise. □ *He wasn't very good, but his friends praised him to the skies.* □ *They liked your pie. Everyone praised it to the skies.*

preach to the converted to praise or recommend something to someone who is already in favour of it. □ *Mary was preaching to the converted when she tried to persuade Jean to become a feminist. She's been one for years.* □ *Bob found himself preaching to the converted when he was telling Jane the advantages of living in the country. She hates city life.*

presence of mind calmness and the ability to act sensibly in an emergency or difficult situation. □ *Jane had the presence of mind to phone the police when the child disappeared.* □ *The child had the presence of mind to take a note of the car's number-plate.*

press-gang someone into doing something to force someone into doing something. (From the noun *press-gang*, a group of sailors employed to seize men and force them to join the navy.) □ *Aunt Jane press-ganged me into helping with the church fête.* □ *The boss press-ganged us all into working late.*

pretty kettle of fish See fine kettle of fish.

prick up one's ears to listen more closely. □ *At the sound of my voice, my dog pricked up her ears.* □ *I pricked up my ears when I heard my name mentioned.*

pride of place the best or most important place or space. □ *Jack's parents gave pride of place in their living-room to his sports trophy.* □ *The art gallery promised to give pride of place to Mary's painting of the harbour.*

pride oneself on something to take special pride in something. □ *Ann prides herself on her apple pies.* □ *John prides himself on his ability to make people feel at ease.*

prime mover the force that sets something going; someone or something that starts something off. □ *The assistant manager was the prime mover in getting the manager sacked.* □ *Discontent with his job was the prime mover in John's deciding to emigrate.*

pull a face AND **make a face** to twist one's face into a strange expression, typically to show one's dislike, to express ridicule, or to make someone laugh. (Also plural: *pull faces, make faces.*) □ *The comedian pulled faces to amuse the children.* □ *Jane made a face when she was asked to work late.*

pull a fast one to succeed in an act of deception. (Informal.) □ *She was pulling a fast one when she said she had a headache and had to go home.* □ *Don't try to pull a fast one with me! I know what you're doing.*

pull oneself together to become calm or steady; to become emotionally stabilized; to regain one's composure. □ *Now, calm down. Pull yourself together.* □ *I'll be all right as soon as I can pull myself together. I just can't stop weeping.*

pull oneself up by one's bootstraps to achieve (something) through one's own efforts. (Informal.) □ *He's wealthy now, but he pulled himself up by his bootstraps.* □ *The orphan pulled himself up by his bootstraps to become a doctor.*

pull one's punches 1. [for a boxer] to strike with light blows to enable the other boxer to win. □ *Bill has been barred from the boxing ring for pulling his punches.* □ *"I never pulled my punches in my life!" cried Tom.* **2.** to hold back in one's criticism or attack. (Usually in the negative. The *one's* can be replaced with *any*.) □ *I didn't pull any punches. I told her just what I thought of her.* □ *The teacher doesn't pull any punches when it comes to discipline.*

pull one's socks up to make an effort to improve one's behaviour or performance. □ *If you don't want to be expelled from school, you'll have to pull your socks up.* □ *The firm will have to pull its socks up in order to stay in business.*

pull out all the stops to use all one's energy and effort in order to achieve something. (From the stops of a pipe-organ. The more that are pulled out, the louder it gets.) □ *You'll have to pull out all the stops if you're going to pass the exam.* □ *The doctors will pull out all the stops to save the child's life.*

pull someone's leg to kid, fool, or trick someone. (Informal.) □ *You don't mean that. You're just pulling my leg.* □ *Don't believe him. He's just pulling your leg.*

pull something out of a hat AND **pull something out of thin air** to produce something as if by magic. □ *This is a serious problem, and we just can't pull a solution out of a hat.* □ *I'm sorry, but I don't have a pen. What do you want me to do, pull one out of thin air?*

pull something out of thin air See pull something out of a hat.

pull strings to use influence (with someone to get something done or gain an advantage). □ *I can borrow the hall easily by pulling strings.* □ *Is it possible to get anything done around here without pulling strings?*

pull the rug out from under someone('s feet) to do something suddenly which leaves someone in a weak position; to make someone ineffective. □ *The news that his wife had left him pulled the rug out from under him.* □ *The boss certainly pulled the rug out from under Bob's feet when he lowered his salary.*

pull the wool over someone's eyes to deceive someone. □ *You can't pull the wool over my eyes. I know what's going on.* □ *Don't try to pull the wool over her eyes. She's too smart.*

push one's luck to expect continued good fortune; to expect to continue to escape bad luck. (Informal.) □ *You're okay so far, but don't push your luck.* □ *Bob pushed his luck once too often when he tried to flirt with the new secretary. She slapped him.*

put a brave face on it to try to appear happy or satisfied when faced with misfortune or danger. □ *We've lost all our money, but we must put a brave face on it for the sake of the children.* □ *Jim's lost his job and is worried, but he's putting a brave face on it.*

put all one's eggs in one basket to risk everything at once; to depend entirely on one plan, venture, etc. (Often negative.) □ *Don't put all your eggs in one basket. You shouldn't invest all your money in one business.* □ *John only applied to the one college he wanted to go to. He put all his eggs in one basket.*

put ideas into someone's head to suggest something—usually something that is bad or unfortunate for someone—to someone (who would not have thought of it otherwise). □ *Jack can't afford a holiday abroad. Please don't put ideas into his head.* □ *Bob would get along all right if his chums didn't put ideas into his head.*

put in a good word for someone to say something to someone in support of someone. □ *I hope you get the job. I'll put in a good word for you.* □ *You might get the part in the film if Mike puts in a good word for you.*

put it on to pretend; to act as if something were true. (Informal.) □ *Ann wasn't really angry. She was just putting it on.* □ *I can't believe she was just putting it on. She really looked mad.*

put on airs to act superior. (Informal.) □ Stop putting on airs. You're just human like the rest of us. □ Ann is always putting on airs. You'd think she was a queen.

put one across someone to deceive or trick someone. (Informal.) □ He tried to put one across the old lady by pretending to be her long-lost nephew. □ Meg thought she'd put one across her parents by claiming to spend the night at her friend's house.

put one in one's place to rebuke someone; to remind one of one's (lower) rank or station. □ My employer put me in my place for criticizing her. □ Lady Jane put the butler in his place when he grew too familiar.

put one's best foot forward to prepare to do one's best; to make the best attempt possible to make a good impression. □ When you apply for a position, you should always put your best foot forward. □ Since you failed last time, you must put your best foot forward now.

put one's foot down (about something) to be adamant about something. □ Ann put her foot down about what kind of car she wanted. □ She doesn't put her foot down very often, but when she does, she really means it.

put one's foot in it to say something which one regrets; to say something tactless, insulting, or hurtful. (Informal.) □ When I told Ann that her hair was more beautiful than I had ever seen it, I really put my foot in it. It was a wig. □ I put my foot in it by mistaking John's girlfriend for his wife.

put one's hand to the plough to begin to do a big and important task; to undertake a major effort. □ If John would only put his hand to the plough, he could do an excellent job of work. □ You'll never accomplish anything if you don't put your hand to the plough.

put one's house in order to put one's business or personal affairs into good order. □ There was some trouble at work and the manager was told to put his house in order. □ Every now and then, I have to put my house in order. Then life becomes more manageable.

put one's oar in AND **shove one's oar in; stick one's oar in** to interfere by giving unasked-for advice. (Informal.) □ You don't need to put your oar in. I don't need your advice. □ I'm sorry. I shouldn't have stuck my oar in when you were arguing with your wife.

put one's shoulder to the wheel to take up a task; to get busy. □ *You won't accomplish anything unless you put your shoulder to the wheel.* □ *I put my shoulder to the wheel and finished the task quickly.*

put one through one's paces to make one demonstrate what one can do; to test someone's abilities or capacity. □ *The teacher put the children through their paces before the exam.* □ *I auditioned for a part in the play, and the director really put me through my paces.*

put on one's thinking-cap to start thinking in a serious manner. □ *Let's put on our thinking-caps and decide where to go on holiday.* □ *It's time to put on our thinking-caps, children, and choose a name for the dog.*

put on weight to gain weight; to grow fatter. □ *I have to go on a diet because I've been putting on a little weight lately.* □ *The doctor says I need to put on some weight.*

put out (some) feelers to attempt to find out something without being too obvious. □ *I wanted to get a new position, so I put out some feelers.* □ *We'd like to move house and so we've put out feelers to see what's on the market.*

put paid to something to put an end to something; to prevent someone from doing something; to prevent something from happening. (From the practice of book-keepers of writing "paid" in the account book when a bill has been settled.) □ *Jean's father's objections put paid to John's thoughts of marrying her.* □ *Lack of money put paid to our holiday plans.*

put someone in mind of someone or something to remind someone of someone or something. □ *Mary puts me in mind of her mother when she was that age.* □ *This place puts me in mind of the village where I was brought up.*

put someone in the picture to give someone all the necessary facts about something. (Informal.) □ *They put the police in the picture about how the accident happened.* □ *Would someone put me in the picture about what went on in my absence?*

put someone on a pedestal to respect or admire someone too much; to worship someone. □ *He has put her on a pedestal and thinks she can do no wrong.* □ *Don't put me on a pedestal. I'm only human.*

put someone on the spot to ask someone embarrassing questions; to put someone in an uncomfortable or difficult position. □ *Don't put me on the spot. I can't give you an answer.* □ *We put Bob on the spot and demanded that he do everything he had promised.*

put someone or something out to pasture to retire someone or something. (Informal. Originally said of a horse which was too old to work.) □ *Please don't put me out to pasture. I have lots of good years left.* □ *This car is very old and keeps breaking down. It's time to put it out to pasture.*

put someone's nose out of joint to cause someone to feel slighted or insulted. (Informal.) □ *I'm afraid I put his nose out of joint by not inviting him to the picnic.* □ *Jane's nose was put out of joint when her baby brother was born.*

put someone through the wringer to give someone a difficult or exhausting time. (Informal.) □ *They are really putting me through the wringer at school.* □ *We all put Bob through the wringer over this contract.*

put someone to shame to show someone up; to embarrass someone; to make someone ashamed. □ *Your excellent efforts put us all to shame.* □ *I put him to shame by telling everyone about his bad behaviour.*

put someone to the test to test someone; to see what someone can achieve. □ *I think I can jump that far, but no one has ever put me to the test.* □ *I'm going to put you to the test now!*

put someone up to something to cause someone to do something; to bribe someone to do something; to give someone the idea of doing something. □ *Who put you up to it?* □ *Nobody put me up to it. I thought it up myself.*

put someone wise to someone or something to inform someone about someone or something. (Informal.) □ *I put her wise to the way we do things around here.* □ *I didn't know she was taking money. Mary put me wise to her.*

put something on ice AND **put something on the back burner** to delay or postpone something; to put something on hold. (Informal.) □ *I'm afraid that we'll have to put your project on ice for a while.* □ *Just put your idea on the back burner and keep it there until we get some money.*

put something on paper to write something down. □ *You have a great idea for a novel. Now put it on paper.* □ *I'm sorry, I can't discuss your offer until I see something in writing. Put it on paper, and then we'll talk.*

put something on the back burner See put something on ice.

put something over to accomplish something; to put something across. □ *This is a very hard thing to explain to a large audience. I hope I can put it over.* □ *This is a big request for money. I go before the board of directors this afternoon, and I hope I can put it over.*

put something plainly to state something firmly and explicitly. □ *To put it plainly, I want you out of this house immediately.* □ *Thank you. I think you've put your feelings quite plainly.*

put something right AND **set something right** to correct something; to alter a situation to make it more fair. □ *This is a very unfortunate situation. I'll ask the people responsible to set this matter right.* □ *I'm sorry that we overcharged you. We'll try to put it right.*

Put that in your pipe and smoke it! See how you like that!; It is final, and you have to live with it! (Informal.) □ *Well, I'm not going to do it, so put that in your pipe and smoke it!* □ *I'm sick of you, and I'm leaving. Put that in your pipe and smoke it!*

put the cart before the horse to have things in the wrong order; to have things confused and mixed up. □ *You're eating your dessert! You've put the cart before the horse.* □ *Slow down and get organized. Don't put the cart before the horse!* □ *John puts the cart before the horse in most of his projects.*

put the cat among the pigeons AND **set the cat among the pigeons** to cause trouble or a disturbance, especially by doing or saying something suddenly or unexpectedly. □ *Meg put the cat among the pigeons by announcing that she was leaving home.* □ *When Frank told of Bob's problems with the police, he really set the cat among the pigeons.*

put two and two together to find the answer to something from the information available; to reach an understanding of something. □ *Well, I put two and two together and came up with an idea of who did it.* □ *Don't worry. John won't figure it out. He can't put two and two together.*

putty in someone's hands [someone who is] easily influenced by someone else; [someone who is] excessively willing to do what someone else wishes. □ *Bob's wife is putty in his hands. She never thinks for herself.* □ *Jane is putty in her mother's hands. She always does exactly what her mother says.*

put up a (brave) front to appear to be brave (even if one is not). □ *Mary is frightened, but she's putting up a brave front.* □ *If she weren't putting up a front, I'd be more frightened than I am.*

put upon someone to make use of someone to an unreasonable degree; to take advantage of someone for one's own benefit. (Typically passive.) □ *My mother was always put upon by her neighbours. She was too nice to refuse their requests for help.* □ *Jane feels put upon by her husband's parents. They're always coming to stay with her.*

put words into someone's mouth to speak for another person without permission. □ *Stop putting words into my mouth. I can speak for myself.* □ *The solicitor was scolded for putting words into the witness's mouth.*

Put your money where your mouth is! a command to stop talking or boasting and make a bet, or to stop talking and provide money for something which one claims to support. □ *I'm tired of your bragging about your skill at betting. Put your money where your mouth is!* □ *You talk about betting, but you don't bet. Put your money where your mouth is!*

quake in one's shoes See *shake in one's shoes*.

queue up to get into a queue; to form a queue. □ *Will you all please queue up?* □ *It's time to go from here to the theatre. Please queue up.*

quick on the draw (Informal.) **1.** quick to draw a gun and shoot. □ *Some of the old cowboys were known to be quick on the draw.* □ *Wyatt Earp was particularly quick on the draw.* **2.** quick to respond to anything; quick to act. □ *John gets the right answer before anyone else. He's really quick on the draw.* □ *Sally will probably win the quiz game. She's really quick on the draw.*

quick on the uptake quick to understand (something). □ *Just because I'm not quick on the uptake, it doesn't mean I'm stupid.* □ *Mary understands jokes before anyone else because she's so quick on the uptake.*

quids in with someone in an advantageous or favourable position with someone. (Informal.) □ *You'll be quids in with Jean if you can charm her mother.* □ *Fred's quids in with the boss after his successful export deal.*

R

race against time 1. to hurry to beat a deadline; to hurry to achieve something by a certain time. □ *We had to race against time to finish the work before the deadline.* □ *You don't need to race against time. Take all the time you want.* **2.** a task which must be finished within a certain time; a situation in which one must hurry to complete something on time. □ *It was a race against time to finish before the deadline.* □ *The examination was a race against time, and Tom could not finish it.*

rack one's brains to try very hard to think of something. □ *I racked my brains all afternoon, but couldn't remember where I put the book.* □ *Don't waste any more time racking your brains. Go and borrow the book from the library.*

rain cats and dogs to rain very hard. (Informal.) □ *It's raining cats and dogs. Look at it pour!* □ *I'm not going out in that storm. It's raining cats and dogs.*

rained off cancelled or postponed because of rain. □ *Oh, the weather looks awful. I hope the picnic isn't rained off.* □ *It's starting to drizzle now. Do you think the game will be rained off?*

rain or shine See come rain or shine.

raise a few eyebrows to shock or surprise people mildly by doing or saying something. □ *What you just said may raise a few eyebrows, but it shouldn't make anyone really angry.* □ *John's sudden marriage to Ann raised a few eyebrows.*

raise one's sights to set higher goals for oneself. □ *When you're young, you tend to raise your sights too high.* □ *On the other hand, some people need to raise their sights higher.*

rally round someone or something to come together to support someone or something. □ *The family rallied round Jack when he lost* *his job.* □ *The former pupils rallied round their old school when it was in danger of being closed.*

rant and rave to shout angrily and wildly. □ *Bob rants and raves when anything displeases him.* □ *Father rants and raves if we arrive home late.*

rap someone's knuckles to rebuke or punish someone. □ *She rapped his knuckles for whispering too much.* □ *Don't rap my knuckles. I didn't do it.* ALSO: **get one's knuckles rapped; have one's knuckles rapped** to receive punishment. □ *I got my knuckles rapped for whispering too much.* □ *You should have your knuckles rapped for doing that!*

rarin' to go extremely keen to act or do something. (Informal.) □ *Jane can't wait to start her job. She's rarin' to go.* □ *Mary is rarin' to go and can't wait for her university term to start.*

rat race a fierce struggle for success, especially in one's career or business. □ *Bob's got tired of the rat race. He's retired and gone to live in the country.* □ *The money market is a rat race, and many people who work in it die of the stress.*

read between the lines to infer something (from something). (Usually figurative. Does not necessarily refer to written or printed information.) □ *After listening to what she said, if you read between the lines, you can begin to see what she really means.* □ *Don't believe everything you hear. Learn to read between the lines.*

read someone like a book to understand someone very well. □ *I've got John figured out. I can read him like a book.* □ *Of course I understand you. I read you like a book.*

read someone's mind to guess what someone is thinking. □ *You'll have to tell me what you want. I can't read your mind, you know.* □ *If I could read your mind, I'd know what you expect of me.*

read someone the Riot Act to give someone a severe scolding. (Under the Riot Act of 1715, an assembly of people could be dispersed by magistrates reading the act to them.) □ *The manager read me the Riot Act for coming in late.* □ *The teacher read the pupils the Riot Act for their failure to do their homework.*

read something into something to attach or attribute a new or different meaning to something; to find a meaning that is not intended in something. □ *This statement means exactly what it says. Don't try to read anything else into it.* □ *Am I reading too much into your comments?*

rear its ugly head [for something unpleasant] to appear or become obvious after lying hidden. □ *Jealousy reared its ugly head and destroyed their marriage.* □ *The question of money always rears its ugly head in matters of business.*

receive someone with open arms AND **welcome someone with open arms** to welcome someone eagerly. (Used literally or figuratively.) □ *I'm certain they wanted us to stay for dinner. They received us with open arms.* □ *When I came home from school, the whole family welcomed me with open arms.*

redbrick university one of the universities built in England in the late nineteenth century, contrasted with Oxford and Cambridge Universities. (Derogatory.) □ *John's tutor ridicules the redbrick universities.* □ *Alice is a snob. She refuses to go to a redbrick university.*

red herring a piece of information or suggestion introduced to draw attention away from the truth or real facts of a situation. (A red herring is a type of strong-smelling smoked fish that was once drawn across the trail of scent to mislead hunting dogs and put them off the scent. See also **draw a red herring**.) □ *The detectives were following a red herring, but they're on the right track now.* □ *Jack and Mary were hoping to confuse their parents with a series of red herrings so that the parents wouldn't realize that they had eloped.*

red tape over-strict attention to the wording and details of rules and regulations, especially by government or public departments. (From the colour of the tape used by government departments to tie up bundles of documents.) □ *Because of red tape, it took weeks for Frank to get a visa.* □ *Red tape prevented Jack's wife from joining him abroad.*

regain one's composure to become calm and composed. □ *I found it difficult to regain my composure after the argument.* □ *Here, sit down and relax so that you can regain your composure.*

rest on one's laurels to enjoy one's success and not try to achieve more. □ *Don't rest on your laurels. Try to continue to do great things!* □ *I think I'll rest on my laurels for a time before attempting anything new.*

return ticket a ticket (for a plane, train, bus, etc.) which allows one to go to a destination and return. □ *A return ticket will usually save you some money.* □ *How much is a return ticket to Harrogate?*

ride roughshod over someone or something to treat someone or something with disdain or scorn. □ *Tom seems to ride roughshod over his friends.* □ *You shouldn't have come into our country to ride roughshod over our laws and our traditions.*

riding for a fall risking failure or an accident, usually owing to overconfidence. □ *Tom drives too fast, and he seems too sure of himself. He's riding for a fall.* □ *Bill needs to stop borrowing money. He's riding for a fall.*

right up someone's street ideally suited to one's interests or abilities. (Informal.) □ *Skiing is right up my street. I love it.* □ *This kind of thing is right up John's street.*

ring a bell [for something] to cause someone to remember something or to seem familiar. (Informal.) □ *I've never met John Franklin, but his name rings a bell.* □ *The face in the photograph rang a bell. It was my cousin.*

ring down the curtain (on something) AND **bring down the curtain (on something)** to bring something to an end; to declare something to be at an end. □ *It's time to ring down the curtain on our relationship. We have nothing in common any more.* □ *We've tried our best to make this company a success, but it's time to ring down the curtain.* □ *After many years the old man brought down the curtain and closed the restaurant.*

ring in the New Year to celebrate the beginning of the New Year at midnight on December 31. □ *We are planning a big affair to ring in the New Year.* □ *How did you ring in the New Year?*

ring off to end a telephone call. □ *I must ring off now and get back to work.* □ *James rang off rather suddenly and rudely when Alice contradicted him.*

ring someone or something up AND **ring up someone or something 1.** [with *something*] to record the cost of an item on a cash register. □ *The cashier rang up each item and told me how much money I owed.* □ *Please ring this chewing-gum up first, and I'll put it in my handbag.* **2.** [with *someone*] to call someone on the telephone.

□ *Please ring up Ann and ask her if she wants to come over.* □ *Just ring me up any time.*

ring the changes to do or arrange things in different ways to achieve variety. (From bell-ringing.) □ *Jane doesn't have many clothes, but she rings the changes by adding different-coloured scarves to her basic outfits.* □ *Aunt Mary rings the changes in her small flat by rearranging the furniture.*

ring true to sound or seem true or likely. (From testing the quality of metal or glass by striking it and listening to the noise made.) □ *The pupil's excuse for being late doesn't ring true.* □ *Do you think that Mary's explanation for her absence rang true?*

ring up someone or something See ring someone or something up.

ripe old age a very old age. □ *Mr. Smith died last night, but he was a ripe old age—ninety-nine.* □ *All the Smiths seem to live to a ripe old age.*

rise and shine to get out of bed and be lively and energetic. (Informal. Often a command.) □ *Come on, children! Rise and shine! We're going to the seaside.* □ *Father always calls out "Rise and shine!" in the morning when we want to go on sleeping.*

rise to the occasion to meet the challenge of an event; to try extra hard to do a task. □ *John was able to rise to the occasion and make the conference a success.* □ *It was a big challenge, but he rose to the occasion.*

risk one's neck (to do something) to risk physical harm play safe to accomplish something. (Informal.) □ *Look at that traffic! I refuse to risk my neck just to cross the street to buy a paper.* □ *I refuse to risk my neck at all.*

road-hog someone who drives carelessly and selfishly. (Informal.) □ *Look at that road-hog driving in the middle of the road and stopping other drivers getting past him.* □ *That road-hog nearly knocked the children over. He was driving too fast.*

rob Peter to pay Paul to take from one person in order to give to another. □ *Why borrow money to pay your bills? That's just robbing Peter to pay Paul.* □ *There's no point in robbing Peter to pay Paul. You will still be in debt.*

rock the boat to cause trouble; to disturb a situation which is otherwise stable and satisfactory. (Often negative.) □ *Look, Tom, everything is going fine here. Don't rock the boat!* □ *You can depend on Tom to mess things up by rocking the boat.*

roll on something [for something, such as a time or a day] to approach rapidly. (Said by someone who wants the time or the day to arrive sooner than is possible. Usually a command.) □ *Roll on Saturday! I get the day off.* □ *Roll on spring! We hate the snow.*

romp home to win a race or competition easily. (Informal.) □ *Our team romped home in the relay race.* □ *Jack romped home in the election for president of the club.*

rooted to the spot unable to move because of fear or surprise. □ *Joan stood rooted to the spot when she saw the ghostly figure.* □ *Mary was rooted to the spot when the thief snatched her bag.*

rough it to live in discomfort; to live in uncomfortable conditions without the usual amenities. (Informal.) □ *The students are roughing it in a shack with no running water.* □ *Bob and Jack had nowhere to live, so they had to rough it in a tent until they found somewhere.*

round on someone to attack someone verbally. □ *Jane suddenly rounded on Tom for arriving late.* □ *Peter rounded on Meg, asking what she'd done with the money.*

rub along with someone to get along fairly well with someone. (Informal.) □ *Jack and Fred manage to rub along with each other, although they're not best friends.* □ *Jim just about rubs along with his in-laws.*

rub salt in the wound deliberately to make someone's unhappiness, shame, or misfortune worse. □ *Don't rub salt in the wound by telling me how enjoyable the party was.* □ *Jim is feeling miserable about losing his job, and Fred is rubbing salt in the wound by saying how good his replacement is.*

rub shoulders (with someone) to associate with someone; to work closely with someone. □ *I don't care to rub shoulders with someone who acts like that!* □ *I rub shoulders with John every day at work. We are good friends.*

rub someone's nose in it to remind one of something one has done wrong; to remind one of something bad or unfortunate that has happened. (From a method of house-training animals.) □ *When Bob failed his exam, his brother rubbed his nose in it.* □ *Mary knows she shouldn't have broken off her engagement. Don't rub her nose in it.*

rub someone up the wrong way to irritate someone. (Informal.) □ *I'm sorry I rubbed you up the wrong way. I didn't mean to upset you.* □ *Don't rub her up the wrong way!*

ruffle someone's feathers to upset or annoy someone. (A bird's feathers become ruffled if it is angry or afraid.) □ *You certainly ruffled Mrs. Smith's feathers by criticizing her garden.* □ *Try to be tactful and not ruffle people's feathers.*

rule the roost to be the boss or manager, especially at home. (Informal.) □ *Who rules the roost at your house?* □ *Our new office manager really rules the roost.*

run a fever AND **run a temperature** to have a body temperature higher than normal; to have a fever. □ *I ran a fever when I had the flu.* □ *The baby is running a temperature and is irritable.*

run against the clock to be in a race with time; to be in a great hurry to get something done before a particular time. □ *This morning, Bill set a new track record running against the clock. He lost the actual race this afternoon, however.* □ *The front runner was running against the clock. The others were a lap behind.*

run a temperature See **run a fever**.

run a tight ship to run a ship or an organization in an orderly, efficient, and disciplined manner. □ *The new office manager really runs a tight ship.* □ *The headmaster runs a tight ship.*

run for it to try and escape by running. (Informal.) □ *The guard's not looking. Let's run for it!* □ *The convict tried to run for it, but the warder caught him.*

run for one's life to run away to save one's life. □ *The dam has burst! Run for your life!* □ *The zoo-keeper told us all to run for our lives.*

run high [for feelings] to be in a state of excitement or anger. □ *Feelings were running high as the general election approached.* □ *The mood of the crowd was running high when they saw the man beat the child.*

run in the family for a characteristic to appear in all (or most) members of a family. □ *My grandparents lived well into their nineties, and longevity runs in the family.* □ *My brothers and I have red hair. It runs in the family.*

run of the mill common or average; typical. □ *The restaurant we went to was nothing special—just run of the mill.* □ *The service was good, but the food was run of the mill or worse.*

run riot AND **run wild** to get out of control. □ *The dandelions have run riot on our lawn.* □ *The children ran wild at the birthday party and had to be taken home.*

run someone or something to earth to find something after a search. (From a fox-hunt chasing a fox into its hole.) □ *Jean finally ran her long-lost cousin to earth in Paris.* □ *After months of searching, I ran a copy of Jim's book to earth.*

run someone ragged to keep someone very busy. (Informal.) □ *This busy season is running us all ragged at the shop.* □ *What a busy day. I ran myself ragged.*

run to seed AND **go to seed** to become worn-out and uncared for. □ *The estate has gone to seed since the old man's death.* □ *Pick things up around here. This place is going to seed. What a mess!*

run wild See run riot.

rush one's fences to act hurriedly without enough care or thought. (From horse-riding.) □ *Jack's always rushing his fences. He should think things out first.* □ *Think carefully before you buy that expensive house. Don't rush your fences.*

S

sacred cow something that is regarded by some people with such respect and veneration that they don't like being criticized by anyone in any way. (From the fact that the cow is regarded as sacred in India.) □ *University education is a sacred cow in the Smith family. Fred is regarded as a failure because he left school at sixteen.* □ *Don't talk about eating meat to Pam. Vegetarianism is one of her sacred cows.*

safe and sound safe and whole or healthy. □ *It was a rough trip, but we got there safe and sound.* □ *I'm glad to see you here safe and sound.*

sail through something to finish something quickly and easily. (Informal.) □ *The test was not difficult. I sailed through it.* □ *Bob sailed through his homework in a short amount of time.*

sail under false colours to pretend to be something that one is not. (Originally nautical, referring to a pirate ship disguised as a merchant ship.) □ *John has been sailing under false colours. He's really a spy.* □ *I thought you were wearing that uniform because you worked here. You are sailing under false colours.*

salt of the earth the most worthy of people; a very good or worthy person. (A biblical reference.) □ *Mrs. Jones is the salt of the earth. She is the first to help anyone in trouble.* □ *Frank's mother is the salt of the earth. She has five children of her own and yet fosters three others.*

same old story something that occurs or has occurred in the same way often. □ *Jim's got no money. It's the same old story. He's spent it all on clothing.* □ *The firm are getting rid of staff. It's the same old story—a shortage of orders.*

saved by the bell rescued from a difficult or dangerous situation just in time by something which brings the situation to a sudden end. (From the sounding of a bell marking the end of a round in a

169

boxing match.) □ *James didn't know the answer to the question, but he was saved by the bell when the teacher was called away from the room.* □ *I couldn't think of anything to say to the woman at the bus-stop, but I was saved by the bell by my bus arriving.*

save one's breath to refrain from talking, explaining, or arguing. (Informal.) □ *There is no sense in trying to convince her. Save your breath.* □ *Tell her to save her breath. He won't listen to her.*

save someone's skin to save someone from injury, embarrassment, or punishment. (Informal.) □ *I saved my skin by getting the job done on time.* □ *Thanks for saving my skin. If you hadn't given me an alibi, the police would have arrested me.*

save something for a rainy day to reserve something—usually money—for some future need. (*Save something* can be replaced with *put something aside, hold something back, keep something,* etc.) □ *I've saved a little money for a rainy day.* □ *Keep some sweets for a rainy day.*

say something under one's breath to say something so softly that hardly anyone can hear it. □ *John was saying something under his breath, and I don't think it was very pleasant.* □ *I'm glad he said it under his breath. If he had said it out loud, it would have caused an argument.*

say the word to give a signal to begin; to say yes or okay as a signal to begin. (Informal.) □ *I'm ready to start anytime you say the word.* □ *We'll all shout "Happy birthday!" when I say the word.*

scare someone stiff to scare someone severely; to make someone very frightened. □ *That loud noise scared me stiff.* □ *The robber jumped out and scared us stiff.*

scrape the bottom of the barrel to select from among the worst; to choose from what is left over. □ *You've bought a dreadful old car. You scraped the bottom of the barrel to get that one.* □ *The worker you sent over was the worst I've ever seen. Send me another—and don't scrape the bottom of the barrel.*

scratch someone's back to do a favour for someone in return for a favour done for you. (Informal.) □ *You scratch my back, and I'll scratch yours.* □ *We believe that the manager has been scratching the treasurer's back.*

scratch the surface just to begin to find out about something; to examine only the superficial aspects of something. □ *The investigation of the firm's books showed some inaccuracies. It is thought that the investigators have just scratched the surface.* □ *We don't know how bad the problem is. We've only scratched the surface.*

screw up one's courage to get one's courage together; to force oneself to be brave. □ *I suppose I have to screw up my courage and go to the dentist.* □ *I spent all morning screwing up my courage to take my driver's test.*

scrimp and save to be very thrifty; to live on very little money, often to save up for something. □ *We had to scrimp and save to send the children to college.* □ *The Smiths scrimp and save all year to go on a foreign holiday.*

search something with a fine-tooth comb See go over something with a fine-tooth comb.

second nature to someone easy and natural for someone. □ *Being polite is second nature to Jane.* □ *Driving is no problem for Bob. It's second nature to him.*

second to none better than anyone or anything else. □ *This is an excellent car—second to none.* □ *Mary is an excellent teacher—second to none.*

see double to see two of everything instead of one. □ *When I was driving, I saw two people on the road instead of one. I'm seeing double. There's something wrong with my eyes.* □ *Mike thought he was seeing double when he saw Mary with her sister. He didn't know she had a twin.*

see eye to eye (about something) AND **see eye to eye (on something)** to view something in the same way (as someone else). (Usually negative.) □ *John and Ann never see eye to eye about anything. They always disagree.* □ *James and Jean rarely see eye to eye either.*

see eye to eye (on something) See see eye to eye (about something).

seeing is believing one must believe something that one sees. □ *I never would have thought that a cow could swim, but seeing is* *believing.* □ *I can hardly believe we are in Paris, but there's the Eiffel Tower, and seeing is believing.*

see red to be angry. (Informal.) □ *Whenever I think of the needless destruction of trees, I see red.* □ *Bill really saw red when the tax bill arrived.*

see someone home to accompany someone home. □ *Bill agreed to see his aunt home after the film.* □ *You don't need to see me home. It's perfectly safe, and I can get there on my own.*

see something with half an eye to see or understand very easily. □ *You could see with half an eye that the children were very tired.* □ *Anyone could see with half an eye that the work was badly done.*

see stars to see flashing lights after receiving a blow to the head. □ *I saw stars when I bumped my head on the attic ceiling.* □ *The little boy saw stars when he fell head first on to the concrete.*

see the light to understand something clearly at last. □ *After a lot of studying and asking many questions, I finally saw the light.* □ *I know that geometry is difficult. Keep working at it. You'll see the light pretty soon.*

see the light at the end of the tunnel to foresee an end to one's problems after a long period of time. □ *I had been horribly ill for two months before I began to see the light at the end of the tunnel.* □ *We were in debt for years, but then we saw the light at the end of the tunnel.*

see the light of day [for something] to be finished or produced. (Often negative.) □ *The product will never see the light of day.* □ *His inventions will never see the light of day. They are too impractical.*

see the writing on the wall to know that something unpleasant or disastrous is certain to happen. (From a biblical reference.) □ *If you don't improve your performance, they'll sack you. Can't you see the writing on the wall?* □ *Jack saw the writing on the wall when the firm reduced his salary.*

sell someone a pup to cheat someone by selling the person something that is inferior or worthless. (Informal.) □ *Jack sold me a pup when I bought a bike from him. It broke down in two days.* □ *The salesman sold Jane a pup when he persuaded her to buy the second-hand washing-machine. Water pours out of it.*

sell someone or something short to underestimate someone or something; to fail to see the good qualities of someone or something. □ *This is a very good restaurant. Don't sell it short.* □ *When you say that John isn't interested in music, you're selling him short. Did you know he plays the violin quite well?*

send someone or something up to ridicule or make fun of someone or something; to satirize someone or something. (Informal.) □ *John is always sending Jane up by mocking the way she walks.* □ *The drama group sent their lecturers up.*

send someone packing to send someone away; to dismiss someone, possibly rudely. (Informal.) □ *I couldn't stand him any more, so I sent him packing.* □ *The maid proved to be so incompetent that I had to send her packing.*

send someone to Coventry to refuse to speak to or associate with someone or a group of people as a punishment. □ *The other children sent Tom to Coventry for telling tales to the teacher.* □ *Fred was sent to Coventry by his fellow workers for breaking the strike.*

separate the men from the boys AND **sort the men from the boys** to separate the competent ones from those who are less competent; to separate the brave or strong ones from those who are less brave or strong. □ *This is the kind of task that sorts the men from the boys.* □ *This project is very complex. It'll separate the men from the boys.*

separate the sheep from the goats to divide people into two groups in order to distinguish the good from the bad, etc. □ *Working in a place like this really separates the sheep from the goats.* □ *We can't go on with the game until we separate the sheep from the goats.*

separate the wheat from the chaff to separate what is of value from what is useless. □ *Could you have a look at this furniture and separate the wheat from the chaff?* □ *The difficult exam will separate the wheat from the chaff among the pupils.*

serve as a guinea pig [for someone or something] to be experimented on. □ *Try it on someone else! I don't want to serve as a guinea pig!* □ *Jane agreed to serve as a guinea pig. She'll be the one to try out the new flavour of icecream.*

serve notice to announce something. □ *John served notice that he was leaving the company.* □ *I'm serving notice that I'll resign as secretary next month.*

set foot somewhere to go or enter somewhere. (Often in the negative.) □ *If I were you, I wouldn't set foot in that town.* □ *I wouldn't set foot in her house! Not after the way she spoke to me.*

set great store by someone or something to have positive expectations for someone or something; to have high hopes for someone or something. □ *I set great store by my computer and its ability to help me in my work.* □ *We set great store by John because of his quick mind.*

set one back on one's heels to surprise, shock, or overwhelm someone. □ *Her sudden announcement set us all back on our heels.* □ *The manager scolded me, and that really set me back on my heels.*

set someone's teeth on edge **1.** [for a sour or bitter taste] to irritate one's mouth. □ *Have you ever eaten a lemon? It'll set your teeth on edge.* □ *Vinegar sets my teeth on edge.* **2.** [for a person or a noise] to be irritating or get on one's nerves. □ *Please don't scrape your finger-nails on the blackboard! It sets my teeth on edge!* □ *Here comes Bob. He's so annoying. He really sets my teeth on edge.*

set someone straight to explain something to someone. □ *I don't think you understand about taxation. Let me set you straight.* □ *Ann was confused, so I set her straight.*

set something right See put something right.

set the ball rolling See start the ball rolling.

set the cat among the pigeons See put the cat among the pigeons.

set the record straight to put right a mistake or misunderstanding; to make sure that an account, etc., is correct. □ *The manager thought Jean was to blame, but she soon set the record straight.* □ *Jane's mother heard that Tom is a married man, but he set the record straight. He's divorced.*

set the table AND **lay the table** to place plates, glasses, napkins, etc., on the table before a meal. □ *Jane, would you please lay the table?* □ *I'm tired of setting the table. Ask someone else to do it.*

set the world on fire to do exciting things that bring fame and glory. (Frequently negative.) □ *I'm not very ambitious. I don't want* *to set the world on fire.* □ *You don't have to set the world on fire. Just do a good job.*

set upon someone or something to attack someone or something violently. □ *The dogs set upon the bear and chased it up a tree.* □ *Bill set upon Tom and struck him hard in the face.*

set up shop somewhere to establish one's place of work somewhere. (Informal.) □ *Mary set up shop in a small office building in Oak Street.* □ *The police officer said, "You can't set up shop right here on the pavement!"*

shades of someone or something reminders of someone or something; reminiscent of someone or something. □ *When I met Jim's mother, I thought "shades of Aunt Mary."* □ *"Shades of school," said Jack as the university lecturer rebuked him for being late.*

shaggy-dog story a kind of funny story which relies for its humour on its length and its sudden ridiculous ending. □ *Don't let John tell a shaggy-dog story. It'll go on for hours.* □ *Mary didn't get the point of Fred's shaggy-dog story.*

shake in one's shoes AND **quake in one's shoes** to be afraid; to shake from fear. □ *I was shaking in my shoes because I had to go and see the manager.* □ *Stop quaking in your shoes, Bob. I'm not going to sack you.*

share and share alike with equal shares. □ *I kept five and gave the other five to Mary—share and share alike.* □ *The two room-mates agreed that they would divide expenses—share and share alike.*

sharp practice dishonest or illegal methods or behaviour. □ *I'm sure that Jim's firm was guilty of sharp practice in getting that export order.* □ *The Smith brothers accused their competitors of sharp practice, but they couldn't prove it.*

shift one's ground to change one's opinions or arguments, often without being challenged or opposed. □ *At first Jack and I were on opposite sides, but he suddenly shifted his ground and started agreeing with me.* □ *Jim has very fixed views. You won't find him shifting his ground.*

shipshape (and Bristol fashion) in good order; neat and tidy. (A nautical term. Bristol was a major British port.) □ *You had better get* *this room shipshape before your mother gets home.* □ *Mr. Jones always keeps his garden shipshape and Bristol fashion.*

ships that pass in the night people who meet each other briefly by chance and are unlikely to meet again. □ *Mary would have liked to see Jim again, but to him, they were ships that passed in the night.* □ *When you travel a lot on business, your encounters are just so many ships that pass in the night.*

shirk one's duty to neglect one's job or task. □ *The guard was sacked for shirking his duty.* □ *You cannot expect to continue shirking your duty without someone noticing.*

short and sweet brief (and pleasant because of briefness). □ *That was a good sermon—short and sweet.* □ *I don't care what you say, as long as you keep it short and sweet.*

shot across the bows something acting as a warning. (A naval term.) □ *The student was sent a letter warning him to attend lectures, but he ignored the shot across the bows.* □ *Fred's solicitor sent Bob a letter as a shot across the bows to get him to pay the money he owed Fred.*

shot-gun wedding a forced wedding. (Informal. From the bride's father having threatened the bridegroom with a shot-gun to force him to marry.) □ *Mary was six months pregnant when she married Bill. It was a real shot-gun wedding.* □ *Bob would never have married Jane if she hadn't been pregnant. Jane's father saw to it that there was a shot-gun wedding.*

shot in the arm a boost; something that gives someone energy. (Informal.) □ *Thank you for cheering me up. Your visit was a real shot in the arm.* □ *Your friendly greeting card was just what I needed—a real shot in the arm.*

shot in the dark a random or wild guess or try. (Informal.) □ *I don't know how I guessed the right answer. It was just a shot in the dark.* □ *I was lucky to take on such a good worker as Sally. When I employed her, it was just a shot in the dark.*

shove one's oar in See put one's oar in.

show of hands a vote expressed by people raising their hands. □ *We were asked to vote for the candidates for captain by a show of hands.*

□ *Jack wanted us to vote on paper, not by a show of hands, so that we could have a secret ballot.*

show oneself in one's true colours to show what one is really like or what one is really thinking. □ *Jane always pretends to be sweet and gentle, but she showed herself in her true colours when she lost the match.* □ *Mary's drunken husband didn't show himself in his true colours until after they were married.*

show one's hand to reveal one's intentions to someone. (From card-games.) □ *I don't know whether Jim's intending to marry Jane or not. He's not one to show his hand.* □ *If you want to get a rise, don't show the boss your hand too soon.*

show one's paces to show what one can do; to demonstrate one's abilities. (From horses demonstrating their skill and speed.) □ *The runners had to show their paces for a place in the relay team.* □ *All the singers had to show their paces to be selected for the choir.*

show one's teeth to act in an angry or threatening manner. □ *We thought Bob was meek and mild, but he really showed his teeth when Jack insulted his girlfriend.* □ *The enemy forces didn't expect the country they invaded to show its teeth.*

show the flag to be present at a gathering just so that the organization to which one belongs will be represented, or just to show others that one has attended. (From a ship flying its country's flag.) □ *The firm wants all the salesmen to attend the international conference in order to show the flag.* □ *As many as possible of the family should attend the wedding. We must show the flag.*

show the white feather to reveal fear or cowardice. (From the fact that a white tail-feather was a sign of inferior breeding in a fighting cock.) □ *Jim showed the white feather by refusing to fight with Jack.* □ *The enemy army showed the white feather by running away.*

shut up shop to stop working or operating, for the day or forever. (Informal.) □ *It's five o'clock. Time to shut up shop.* □ *I can't make any money in this town. The time has come to shut up shop and move to another town.*

signed, sealed, and delivered formally and officially signed; [for a formal document to be] executed. (Informal.) □ *Here is the deed to the property—signed, sealed, and delivered.* □ *I can't begin work on this project until I have the contract signed, sealed, and delivered.*

sign one's own death-warrant to do something that will lead to one's ruin, downfall, or death. (As if one were signing a paper which called for one's own death.) □ *I wouldn't ever gamble a large sum of money. That would be signing my own death-warrant.* □ *The killer signed his own death-warrant when he walked into the police station and gave himself up.*

silly season the time of year, usually in the summer, when there is a lack of important news, and newspapers contain articles about unimportant or trivial things instead. □ *It must be the silly season. There's a story here about peculiarly shaped potatoes.* □ *There's a piece on the front page about people with big feet. Talk about the silly season.*

since the year dot See from the year dot.

sing someone's praises to praise someone highly and enthusiastically. □ *The boss is singing the praises of his new secretary.* □ *The theatre critics are singing the praises of the young actor.*

sink or swim fail or succeed. □ *After I've studied and learned all I can, I have to take the test and sink or swim.* □ *It's too late to help John now. It's sink or swim for him.*

sink our differences to forget or to agree to set aside disagreements of opinion, attitude, etc. (Also with *their* or *your*, as in the examples.) □ *We decided to sink our differences and try to be friends for Mary's sake.* □ *Individual members of the team must sink their differences and work for the success of the team.* □ *You two must sink your differences, or your marriage will fail.*

sit at someone's feet to admire someone greatly; to be influenced by someone's teaching; to be taught by someone. □ *Jack sat at the feet of Picasso when he was studying in Europe.* □ *Tom would love to sit at the feet of the musician Yehudi Menuhin.*

sit (idly) by to remain inactive when other people are doing something; to ignore a situation which calls for help. □ *Bob sat idly by even though everyone else was hard at work.* □ *I can't sit by while all those people need food.*

sit on one's hands to do nothing; to fail to help. □ *When we needed help from Mary, she just sat on her hands.* □ *We need the co-operation of everyone. You can't sit on your hands!*

sitting on a powder keg in a risky or explosive situation; in a situation where something serious or dangerous may happen at any time. □ *Things are very tense at work. The whole office is sitting on a powder keg.* □ *The fire at the oilfield seems to be under control for now, but all the workers there are sitting on a powder keg.*

(sitting) on top of the world feeling wonderful; glorious; ecstatic. □ *Wow, I feel on top of the world.* □ *Since he got a new job, he's on top of the world.* □ *I've been sitting on top of the world all week because I passed my exams.*

sitting pretty living in comfort or luxury; in a good situation. (Informal.) □ *My uncle died and left enough money for me to be sitting pretty for the rest of my life.* □ *Now that I have a good job, I'm sitting pretty.*

six of one and half a dozen of the other about the same one way or another. □ *It doesn't matter to me which way you do it. It's six of one and half a dozen of the other.* □ *What difference does it make? They're both the same—six of one and half a dozen of the other.*

sixth sense a supposed power to know or feel things that are not perceptible by the five senses of sight, hearing, smell, taste, and touch. □ *My sixth sense told me to avoid going home by my usual route. Later I discovered there had been a fatal accident on it.* □ *Meg's sixth sense told her not to trust Tom, even though he seemed honest enough.*

skate over something to pass lightly over something, trying to avoid drawing attention or avoid taking something into consideration. □ *Sally prefers to skate over her reasons for leaving her job.* □ *Meg skated over the reason for her quarrel with Dick.*

(skating) on thin ice in a risky situation. □ *If you try that you'll really be on thin ice. That's too risky.* □ *You're skating on thin ice if you criticize the lecturer. He has a hot temper.*

skeleton in the cupboard a hidden and shocking secret. (Often in the plural.) □ *You can ask anyone about how reliable I am. I don't mind. I don't have any skeletons in the cupboard.* □ *My uncle was in jail for a day once. That's our family's only skeleton in the cupboard.*

slate something to criticize something severely. □ *The critics slated the place.* □ *The teacher slated the pupil's performance.*

slice of the cake a share of something. □ *There's not much work around and so everyone must get a slice of the cake.* □ *The firm makes huge profits, and the workers want a slice of the cake.*

slip of the tongue an error in speaking where a word is pronounced incorrectly, or where something is said which the speaker did not mean to say. □ *I didn't mean to tell her that. It was a slip of the tongue.* □ *I failed to understand the instructions because the speaker made a slip of the tongue at an important point.*

small hours the hours immediately after midnight. □ *The dance went on to the small hours.* □ *Jim goes to bed in the small hours and gets up at lunch-time.*

smell of the lamp [for a book] to show signs of being revised and researched carefully and to lack spontaneity. □ *I preferred her earlier spontaneous novels. The later ones smell of the lamp.* □ *The student has done a lot of research, but has few original ideas. His essay smells of the lamp.*

snake in the grass a low and deceitful person. □ *Sally said that Bob couldn't be trusted because he was a snake in the grass.* □ *"You snake in the grass!" cried Sally. "You cheated me."*

something sticks in one's craw something bothers one. □ *Her criticism stuck in my craw.* □ *I knew that everything I said would stick in his craw and upset him.*

sort the men from the boys See separate the men from the boys.

speak of the devil said when someone whose name has just been mentioned appears or is heard from. □ *Well, speak of the devil! Hello, Tom. We were just talking about you.* □ *I had just mentioned Sally when—speak of the devil—she walked in the door.*

speak one's mind to say frankly what one thinks (about something). □ *Please let me speak my mind, and then you can do whatever you wish.* □ *You can always depend on John to speak his mind. He'll let you know what he really thinks.*

speak out of turn to say something unwise or imprudent; to say something at the wrong time. □ *Excuse me if I'm speaking out of turn, but what you are proposing is quite wrong.* □ *What Bob said about the boss was true, even though he was speaking out of turn.*

speak the same language [for people] to have similar ideas, tastes, etc. □ *Jane and Jack get along very well. They really speak the same language about almost everything.* □ *Bob and his father don't speak the same language when it comes to politics.*

spend a penny to urinate. (Informal. From the former cost of admission to the cubicles in public lavatories.) □ *Stop the car. The little girl needs to spend a penny.* □ *The station toilets are closed and I have to spend a penny.*

spick and span very clean. (Informal.) □ *I have to clean up the house and get it spick and span for the party on Friday night.* □ *I love to have everything around me spick and span.*

spike someone's guns to spoil someone's plans; to make it impossible for someone to carry out a course of action. (From driving a metal spike into the touch-hole of an enemy gun to render it useless.) □ *The boss was going to sack Sally publicly, but she spiked his guns by resigning.* □ *Jack intended borrowing his father's car when he was away, but his father spiked his guns by locking it in the garage.*

spill the beans See let the cat out of the bag.

splash out on something to spend a lot of money on something in an extravagant way. (Informal.) □ *Jack splashed out on a new car that he couldn't afford.* □ *Let's splash out on a really good meal out.*

split hairs to quibble; to try to make petty distinctions. □ *They don't have any serious differences. They are just splitting hairs.* □ *Don't waste time splitting hairs. Accept it the way it is.*

split the difference to divide the difference (with someone else). □ *You want to sell for £120, and I want to buy for £100. Let's split the difference and close the deal at £110.* □ *I don't want to split the difference. I want £120.*

spoil the ship for a ha'porth of tar to risk ruining something valuable by not buying something relatively inexpensive but essential for it. (Ha'porth is a halfpenny's worth. From the use of tar to make boats watertight.) □ *Meg spent a lot of money on a new dress but refused to buy shoes. She certainly spoilt the ship for a ha'porth of tar.* □ *Bob bought a new car but doesn't get it serviced because it's too expensive. He'll spoil the ship for a ha'porth of tar.*

spoon-feed to treat someone with too much care or help; to teach someone with methods that are too easy and do not stimulate the learner to independent thinking. □ *The teacher spoon-feeds the pupils by dictation notes on the novel instead of getting the children to read the books themselves.* □ *You mustn't spoon-feed the new recruits by telling them what to do all the time. They must use their initiative.*

sporting chance a reasonably good chance. □ *If you hurry, you have a sporting chance of catching the bus.* □ *The firm has only a sporting chance of getting the export order.*

spot on exactly right or accurate. (Informal.) □ *Jack's assessment of the state of the firm was spot on.* □ *Mary's description of the stolen car was spot on.*

spread oneself too thin to do too many things, so that one can do none of them well. □ *It's a good idea to get involved in a lot of activities, but don't spread yourself too thin.* □ *I'm too busy these days. I'm afraid I've spread myself too thin.*

square deal a fair and honest transaction; fair treatment. (Informal.) □ *All the workers want is a square deal, but their boss under-pays them.* □ *You always get a square deal with that travel firm.*

square meal a nourishing, filling meal. (Informal.) □ *All you've eaten today is junk food. You should sit down to a square meal.* □ *The tramp hadn't had a square meal in weeks.*

square peg in a round hole a misfit; one who is poorly adapted to one's surroundings. □ *John just can't seem to get along with the people he works with. He's just a square peg in a round hole.* □ *I'm not a square peg in a round hole. It's just that no one understands me.*

stack the cards (against someone or something) to arrange things against someone or something; to make it difficult for some-one to succeed. (Informal. Originally from card-playing. Usually in the passive.) □ *I can't make any progress at my office. The cards are stacked against me.* □ *The cards seem to be stacked against me. I am having very bad luck.*

stand a chance to have a chance. □ *Do you think I stand a chance of winning first place?* □ *Everyone stands a chance of catching the disease.*

stand corrected to admit that one has been wrong. □ *I realize that I accused him wrongly. I stand corrected.* □ *We appreciate now that our conclusions were wrong. We stand corrected.*

stand down to withdraw from a competition or a position. □ *John has stood down from the election for president of the club.* □ *It is time our chairman stood down and made room for a younger person.*

standing joke a subject that regularly and over a period of time causes amusement whenever it is mentioned. □ *Uncle Jim's driving was a standing joke. He used to drive incredibly slowly.* □ *Their mother's inability to make a decision was a standing joke in the Smith family all their lives.*

stand on ceremony to hold rigidly to formal manners. (Often in the negative.) □ *Please help yourself to more. Don't stand on ceremony.* □ *We are very informal around here. Hardly anyone stands on ceremony.*

stand someone in good stead to be useful or beneficial to someone. □ *This is a fine overcoat. I'm sure it'll stand you in good stead for many years.* □ *I did the managing director a favour which I'm sure will stand me in good stead.*

stand to reason to seem reasonable; [for a fact or conclusion] to survive careful or logical evaluation. □ *It stands to reason that it'll be colder in January than it is in June.* □ *It stands to reason that Bill left in a hurry, because he didn't pack his clothes.*

start (off) with a clean slate to start out again afresh; to ignore the past and start over again. □ *James started off with a clean slate when he went to a new school.* □ *When Bob got out of jail, he started off with a clean slate.*

start the ball rolling AND **get the ball rolling; set the ball rolling** to start something; to get some process going; to get a discussion started. □ *If I could just get the ball rolling, then other people would help.* □ *Jack started the ball rolling by asking for volunteers.* ALSO: **keep the ball rolling** □ *Tom started the project, and we kept the ball rolling.*

stay the distance See go the distance.

steal a march on someone to get some sort of an advantage over someone without being noticed. □ *I got the contract because I was able to steal a march on my competitor.* □ *You have to be clever and fast to steal a march on anyone.*

steal someone's thunder to prevent someone from receiving the public recognition expected upon the announcement of an achievement, by making the announcement in public before the intended receiver of the recognition can do so. □ *I stole Mary's thunder by telling her friends about Mary's engagement to Tom before she could do* *so herself.* □ *Someone stole my thunder by leaking my announcement to the press.*

steal the show to give the best or most popular performance in a show, play, or some other event; to get attention for oneself. □ *The lead in the play was very good, but the butler stole the show.* □ *Ann always tries to steal the show when she and I make a presentation.*

step into dead men's shoes AND **fill dead men's shoes** to take over the job or position of someone who has died; to gain an advantage by someone's death. □ *The only hope of promotion in that firm is to step into dead men's shoes.* □ *Jack and Ben are both going out with rich widows. They hope to fill dead men's shoes.*

step in(to the breach) to move into a space or vacancy; to fulfil a needed role or function that has been left vacant. □ *When Ann resigned as president, I stepped into the breach.* □ *A number of people asked me to step into the breach and take her place.*

step on someone's toes AND **tread on someone's toes** to interfere with or offend someone. (Also used literally. Note example with *anyone*.) □ *When you're in public office, you have to avoid stepping on anyone's toes.* □ *Ann trod on someone's toes during the last campaign and lost the election.*

stew in one's own juice to be left alone to suffer one's anger or disappointment. (Informal.) □ *John has such a terrible temper. When he got angry with us, we just let him go away and stew in his own juice.* □ *After John stewed in his own juice for a while, he decided to come back and apologize to us.*

stick it out to put up with or endure a situation, however difficult. (Informal.) □ *This job's boring, but we're sticking it out until we find something more interesting.* □ *I know the children are being annoying, but can you stick it out until their mother returns?*

stick one's neck out to take a risk. (Informal.) □ *Why should I stick my neck out to do something for her? What's she ever done for me?* □ *He made a risky investment. He stuck his neck out because he thought he could make some money.*

stick one's oar in See *put one's oar in.*

stick out like a sore thumb to be very prominent or unsightly; to be very obvious. (Informal.) □ *Bob is so tall that he sticks out like* *a sore thumb in a crowd.* □ *The house next door needs painting. It sticks out like a sore thumb.*

stick to one's guns to remain firm in one's opinions and convictions; to stand up for one's rights. (Informal.) □ *I'll stick to my guns on this matter. I'm sure I'm right.* □ *Bob can be persuaded to do it our way. He probably won't stick to his guns on this point.*

stir up a hornets' nest to create trouble or difficulties. □ *By finding pupils copying from each other, you've really stirred up a hornets' nest.* □ *Bill stirred up a hornets' nest when he discovered the theft.*

storm in a teacup an uproar about something trivial or unimportant. □ *This isn't a serious problem—just a storm in a teacup.* □ *Even a storm in a teacup can take a lot of time to get settled.*

straight away right away; immediately, without thinking or considering. □ *We'll have to go straight away.* □ *Straight away I knew something was wrong.*

straight from the shoulder sincerely; frankly; holding nothing back. □ *Sally always speaks straight from the shoulder. You never have to guess what she really means.* □ *Bill told the staff the financial facts— straight from the shoulder and brief.*

straw in the wind an indication or sign of what might happen in the future. □ *The student's argument with the lecturer was a straw in the wind in terms of student-teacher relations. The students are planning a strike.* □ *Two or three people getting the sack represents just a straw in the wind. I think the whole work-force will have to go.*

stretch one's legs to walk around after sitting down or lying down for a time. (Informal.) □ *We wanted to stretch our legs during the theatre interval.* □ *After sitting in the car all day, the travellers decided to stretch their legs.*

strike a bargain to reach an agreement on a price (for something). □ *They argued for a while and finally struck a bargain.* □ *They were unable to strike a bargain, so they left.*

strike a chord to cause someone to remember [someone or something]; to remind someone of [someone or something]; to be familiar. □ *The woman in the portrait struck a chord, and I realized that she was my grandmother.* □ *His name strikes a chord, but I don't know why.*

strike a happy medium to find a compromise position; to arrive at a position half-way between two unacceptable extremes. □ *Ann likes very spicy food, but Bob doesn't care for spicy food at all. We are trying to find a restaurant which strikes a happy medium.* □ *Tom is either very happy or very sad. He can't seem to strike a happy medium.*

strike the right note to achieve the desired effect; to do something suitable or pleasing. (A musical reference.) □ *Meg struck the right note when she wore a dark suit to the interview.* □ *The politician's speech failed to strike the right note with the crowd.*

strike while the iron is hot to do something at the best possible time; to do something when the time is ripe. □ *He was in a good mood, so I asked for a loan of £200. I thought I'd better strike while the iron was hot.* □ *Please go to the bank and settle this matter now! They are willing to be reasonable. You've got to strike while the iron is hot.*

stuff and nonsense nonsense. (Informal.) □ *Come on! Don't give me all that stuff and nonsense!* □ *I don't understand this book. It's all stuff and nonsense as far as I am concerned.*

stumbling-block something that prevents or obstructs progress. □ *We'd like to buy that house, but the high price is the stumbling-block.* □ *Jim's age is a stumbling-block to getting another job. He's over sixty.*

sugar the pill AND **sweeten the pill** to make something unpleasant more pleasant. (From the sugar coating on some pills to disguise the bitter taste of the medicine.) □ *Mary's parents wouldn't let her go out and tried to sugar the pill by inviting some of her friends around.* □ *Tom hated boarding-school and his parents tried to sweeten the pill by giving him a lot of pocket-money.*

suit someone down to the ground See suit someone to a T.

suit someone to a T AND **suit someone down to the ground** to be very appropriate for someone. □ *This kind of employment suits me to a T.* □ *This is Sally's kind of house. It suits her down to the ground.*

survival of the fittest the idea that the most able or fit will survive (while the less able and less fit will perish). (This is used literally as a part of the theory of evolution.) □ *In college, it's the survival of the fittest. You have to keep working in order to survive and graduate.*

☐ *I don't look after my house-plants very well, but the ones I have are really flourishing. It's the survival of the fittest, I suppose.*

swallow one's pride to forget one's pride and accept something humiliating. ☐ *I had to swallow my pride and admit that I was wrong.* ☐ *When you're a pupil, you find yourself swallowing your pride quite often.*

swallow something hook, line, and sinker to believe something completely. (Informal. These terms refer to fishing and fooling a fish into being caught.) ☐ *I made up a story about why I was so late. They all swallowed it hook, line, and sinker.* ☐ *I feel like a fool. I swallowed the trick hook, line, and sinker.*

swan around to go around in an idle and irresponsible way. (Informal.) ☐ *Mrs. Smith's swanning around abroad while her husband's in hospital here.* ☐ *Mary's not looking for a job. She's just swanning around visiting all her friends.*

swan-song the last work or performance of a playwright, musician, actor, etc., before death or retirement. ☐ *His portrayal of Lear was the actor's swan-song.* ☐ *We didn't know that her performance last night was the singer's swan-song.*

sweep something under the carpet AND **brush something under the carpet** to try to hide something unpleasant, shameful, etc., from the attention of others. ☐ *The boss said he couldn't sweep the theft under the carpet, that he'd have to call in the police.* ☐ *The headmaster tried to brush the children's truancy under the carpet, but the inspector wanted to investigate it.*

sweeten the pill See sugar the pill.

swim against the tide to do the opposite of what everyone else does; to go against the trend. ☐ *Bob tends to do what everybody else does. He isn't likely to swim against the tide.* ☐ *Mary always swims against the tide. She's a very contrary person.*

T

tail wagging the dog a situation where a small or minor part is controlling the whole thing. □ *John was just employed yesterday, and today he's bossing everyone around. It's a case of the tail wagging the dog.* □ *Why is this minor matter being given so much importance? It's the tail wagging the dog!*

take a leaf out of someone's book to behave or to do something in the way that someone else would; to use someone as an example. □ *Take a leaf out of your brother's book and work hard.* □ *Eventually June took a leaf out of her friend's book and started dressing smartly.*

take a stab at something to make a try at something, sometimes without much hope of success. (Informal. Also with have.) □ *I don't know if I can do it, but I'll take a stab at it.* □ *Come on, Mary. Take a stab at catching a fish. You might end up liking fishing.* □ *Would you like to have a stab at this problem?*

take leave of one's senses to become irrational. □ *What are you doing? Have you taken leave of your senses?* □ *What a terrible situation! It's enough to make one take leave of one's senses.*

take one's medicine to accept the punishment or the bad fortune which one deserves. □ *I know I did wrong, and I know I have to take my medicine.* □ *Billy knew he was going to be punished, and he didn't want to take his medicine.*

take someone down a peg (or two) to reprimand someone who is acting in too arrogant a way. (Informal.) □ *The teacher's scolding took Bob down a peg or two.* □ *He was so rude that someone was bound to take him down a peg.*

take someone to task to scold or reprimand someone. □ *The teacher took John to task for his bad behaviour.* □ *I lost a big contract, and the managing director took me to task in front of everyone.*

take someone under one's wing to take over and care for a person. □ *John wasn't doing well at school until an older pupil took him under her wing.* □ *I took the new workers under my wing, and they learned the job in no time.*

take something as read to assume something or regard something as being understood and accepted without reading it out, stating it, or checking it. □ *Can we take the minutes of the meeting as read, or should I read them?* □ *I think we can take their agreement as read, but I'll check with them if you like.*

take something in one's stride to accept something as natural or expected. □ *The argument surprised him, but he took it in his stride.* □ *It was a very rude remark, but Mary took it in her stride.*

take something lying down to endure something unpleasant without fighting back. □ *He insulted me publicly. You don't expect me to take that lying down, do you?* □ *I'm not the kind of person who'll take something like that lying down.*

take something on the chin to experience and endure a blow stoically. (Informal.) □ *The bad news was a real shock, but John took it on the chin.* □ *The worst luck comes my way, but I always end up taking it on the chin.*

take something to heart to take something very seriously. □ *John took the criticism to heart and made an honest effort to improve.* □ *I know Bob said a lot of cruel things to you, but he was angry. You shouldn't take those things to heart.*

take the rough with the smooth to accept the bad things along with the good things. □ *We all have disappointments. You have to learn to take the rough with the smooth.* □ *There are good days and bad days, but every day you take the rough with the smooth. That's life.*

take the wind out of someone's sails to put an end to someone's boasting or arrogance and make the person feel embarrassed; to take an advantage away from someone. (Informal.) □ *John was bragging about how much money he earned until he learned that most of us make more. That took the wind out of his sails.* □ *Learning that one has been totally wrong about something can really take the wind out of one's sails.*

take the words (right) out of one's mouth [for someone else] to say what you were going to say. □ *John said exactly what I was* *going to say. He took the words out of my mouth.* □ *I agree with you. You took the words right out of my mouth.*

take up the cudgels on behalf of someone or something to support or defend someone or something. □ *We'll have to take up the cudgels on behalf of Jim or he'll lose the debate.* □ *Meg has taken up the cudgels on behalf of an environmental movement.*

talking-shop a place or meeting where things are discussed, but action may or may not be taken. (Informal.) □ *Many people think the City Chambers is just a talking-shop.* □ *The firm's board meeting is always just a talking-shop. The chairman makes all the decisions himself.*

talk nineteen to the dozen to talk a lot, usually quickly. (Informal.) □ *The old friends talk nineteen to the dozen when they meet once a year.* □ *You won't get Jean to stop chattering. She always talks nineteen to the dozen.*

talk of the town the subject of gossip; someone or something that everyone is talking about. □ *Joan's argument with the town council is the talk of the town.* □ *Fred's father is the talk of the town since the police arrested him.*

talk through one's hat to talk nonsense. (Informal.) □ *John doesn't know anything about gardening. He's just talking through his hat.* □ *Jean said that the Smiths are emigrating, but she's talking through her hat.*

talk until one is blue in the face to talk until one is exhausted. (Informal.) □ *I talked until I was blue in the face, but I couldn't change her mind.* □ *She had to talk until she was blue in the face to convince him.*

tarred with the same brush having the same faults or bad points as someone else. □ *Jack and his brother are tarred with the same brush. They're both crooks.* □ *The Smith children are tarred with the same brush. They're all lazy.*

teach one's grandmother to suck eggs to try to tell or show someone more knowledgeable or experienced than oneself how to do something. □ *Don't suggest showing Mary how to knit. It will be teaching your grandmother to suck eggs. She's an expert.* □ *Don't teach your grandmother to suck eggs. Jack has been playing tennis for years.*

Tell it to the marines. AND **Tell that to the marines.** I do not believe you (maybe the marines will). (Informal.) □ *That's silly. Tell it to the marines.* □ *I don't care how good you think your reason is. Tell that to the marines!*

tell tales out of school to tell secrets or spread rumours. (Does not refer only to schoolchildren.) □ *I wish that John would keep quiet. He's telling tales out of school again.* □ *If you tell tales out of school a lot, people won't know when to believe you.*

ten a penny See two a penny.

thank one's lucky stars to be thankful for one's luck. (Informal.) □ *You can thank your lucky stars that I was there to help you.* □ *I thank my lucky stars that I studied the right things for the test.*

thick and fast in large numbers or amounts and at a rapid rate. □ *The enemy soldiers came thick and fast.* □ *New problems seem to come thick and fast.*

thick-skinned not easily upset or hurt; insensitive. □ *Tom won't worry about your insults. He's completely thick-skinned.* □ *Jane's so thick-skinned she didn't realize Fred was being rude to her.*

thin end of the wedge a minor or unimportant event or act that is the first stage in something more serious or unfortunate. □ *If you let Pam stay for a few days, it will be the thin end of the wedge. She'll stay for ages.* □ *The boss thinks that if he gives his secretary a rise, it will be the thin end of the wedge and all the staff will demand the same.*

thin on the ground few in number; rare. □ *Jobs in that area are thin on the ground.* □ *Butterflies are thin on the ground here now.*

thin-skinned easily upset or hurt; sensitive. □ *You'll have to handle Mary's mother carefully. She's very thin-skinned.* □ *Jane weeps easily when people tease her. She's too thin-skinned.*

through hell and high water through all sorts of severe difficulties. (Informal.) □ *I came through hell and high water to get to this meeting. Why don't you start on time?* □ *You'll have to go through hell and high water to accomplish your goal, but it'll be worth it.*

through thick and thin through good times and bad times. (Informal.) □ *We've been together through thick and thin and we won't desert* *each other now.* □ *Over the years, we went through thick and thin and enjoyed every minute of it.*

throw a fit to become very angry; to put on a display of anger. □ *Sally threw a fit when I showed up without the things she asked me to buy.* □ *My dad threw a fit when I got home three hours late.*

throw a party (for someone) to give or hold a party for someone. □ *Mary was leaving town, so we threw a party for her.* □ *Do you know a place where we could throw a party?*

throw a spanner in the works to cause problems for someone's plans. (Informal.) □ *I don't want to throw a spanner in the works, but have you checked your plans with a solicitor?* □ *When John refused to help us, he really threw a spanner in the works.*

throw caution to the winds to become very careless. □ *Jane, who is usually quite cautious, threw caution to the winds and went windsurfing.* □ *I don't mind taking a little chance now and then, but I'm not the type of person who throws caution to the winds.*

throw cold water on something See pour cold water on something.

throw down the gauntlet to challenge (someone) to an argument or (figurative) combat. □ *When Bob challenged my conclusions, he threw down the gauntlet. I was ready for an argument.* □ *Frowning at Bob is the same as throwing down the gauntlet. He loves to get into a fight about anything.*

throw good money after bad to waste additional money after wasting money once. □ *I bought a used car and then had to spend £300 on repairs. That was throwing good money after bad.* □ *The Browns are always throwing good money after bad. They bought a plot of land which turned out to be swamp, and then had to pay to have it filled in.*

throw in one's hand to give up or abandon a course of action. (From a player giving up in a card-game.) □ *I got tired of the tennis competition and threw in my hand.* □ *John spent only one year at university and then threw in his hand.*

throw the book at someone to charge someone with, or convict someone of, as many crimes as possible; to reprimand or punish someone severely. □ *I made the police officer angry, so he took me to* *the station and threw the book at me.* □ *The judge threatened to throw the book at me if I didn't stop insulting the police officer.*

thumb a lift AND **hitch a lift** to get a lift from a passing motorist; to make a sign with one's thumb that indicates to passing drivers that one is asking for a lift. □ *My car broke down on the motorway, and I had to thumb a lift to get back to town.* □ *Sometimes it's dangerous to hitch a lift with a stranger.*

thumb one's nose at someone or something to make a rude gesture of disgust—touching the end of one's nose with one's thumb—at someone or something. (Both literal and figurative uses.) □ *The tramp thumbed his nose at the lady and walked away.* □ *You can't just thumb your nose at people who give you trouble. You've got to learn to get along with them.*

tickle someone's fancy to interest someone; to attract someone. (Informal.) □ *I have an interesting proposal here which I think will tickle your fancy.* □ *The idea of dancing doesn't exactly tickle my fancy.*

tick over to move along at a quiet, even pace, without either stopping or going quickly. (Informal. From an engine ticking over.) □ *The firm didn't make large profits, but it's ticking over.* □ *We must try to keep our finances ticking over until the recession ends.*

tied to one's mother's apron-strings dominated by one's mother; dependent on one's mother. □ *Tom is still tied to his mother's apron-strings.* □ *Isn't he a little old to be tied to his mother's apron-strings?*

tie someone in knots to make someone confused or upset. (Informal.) □ *The speaker tied herself in knots trying to explain her difficult subject in simple language.* □ *I was trying to be tactful, but I just tied myself in knots.*

tie the knot to get married. (Informal.) □ *Well, I hear that you and John are going to tie the knot.* □ *My parents tied the knot almost forty years ago.*

tighten one's belt to manage to spend less money. (Informal.) □ *Things are beginning to cost more and more. It looks as though we'll all have to tighten our belts.* □ *Times are hard, and prices are high. I can tighten my belt for only so long.*

till the cows come home for a very long time. (Cows are returned to the barn at the end of the day. Informal.) □ *We could discuss this* *until the cows come home and still reach no decisions.* □ *He could drink beer until the cows come home.*

time out of mind for a very long time; longer than anyone can remember. □ *There has been a church in the village time out of mind.* □ *The Smith family have lived in that house time out of mind.*

tip someone the wink to give someone privileged or useful information in a secret or private manner. (Informal.) □ *John tipped Mary the wink that there was a vacancy in his department.* □ *Jack got his new house at a good price. A friend tipped him the wink that it was going on the market.*

tip the scales at something to weigh some amount. □ *Tom tips the scales at nearly 14 stone.* □ *I'll be glad when I tip the scales at a few pounds less.*

toe the line to do what one is expected or required to do; to follow the rules. (Informal.) □ *You'll get ahead, Sally. Don't worry. Just toe the line, and everything will be okay.* □ *John finally got the sack. He just couldn't learn to toe the line.*

tongue-in-cheek insincere; joking. □ *Ann made a tongue-in-cheek remark to John, and he got angry because he thought she was serious.* □ *The play seemed very serious at first, but then everyone saw that it was tongue-in-cheek, and the audience began laughing.*

to the bitter end to the very end. (Originally nautical. This originally had nothing to do with bitterness.) □ *I kept trying to the bitter end.* □ *It took me a long time to get through college, but I worked hard at it all the way to the bitter end.*

to the letter exactly as instructed; exactly as written. □ *I didn't make an error. I followed your instructions to the letter.* □ *We didn't prepare the recipe to the letter, but the cake still turned out very well.*

touch-and-go very uncertain or critical. □ *Things were touch-and-go at the office until a new manager was employed.* □ *Jane had a serious operation, and everything was touch-and-go for several hours.*

touch a sore point See touch a sore spot.

touch a sore spot AND **touch a sore point** to refer to a sensitive matter which will upset someone. (Also used literally.) □ *I seem to have touched a sore spot. I'm sorry. I didn't mean to upset you.* □ *When* *you talk to him, avoid talking about money. It's best not to touch a sore point if possible.*

touch wood a phrase said to cancel out imaginary bad luck. □ *My stereo has never given me any trouble—touch wood.* □ *We plan to be in London by tomorrow evening—touch wood.*

trade on something to use a fact or a situation to one's advantage. □ *Tom was able to trade on the fact that he had once been in the army.* □ *John traded on his poor eyesight to get a seat closer to the stage.*

tread on someone's toes See step on someone's toes.

true to one's word keeping one's promise. □ *True to his word, Tom appeared at exactly eight o'clock.* □ *We'll soon know if Jane is true to her word. We'll see if she does what she promised.*

try it on to behave in a bold, disobedient, or unlawful manner to discover whether such behaviour will be allowed. (Informal.) □ *Tony knew he wouldn't get away with working only four days a week. He was just trying it on by asking the boss.* □ *The children really try it on when their mother's out.*

try one's wings to try to do something one has recently become qualified to do. (Like a young bird uses its wings to try to fly.) □ *John just got his driver's licence and wants to borrow the car to try his wings.* □ *I learned to skin-dive, and I want to go to the seaside to try my wings.*

try someone's patience to do something annoying which may cause someone to lose patience; to cause someone to be annoyed. □ *Stop whistling. You're trying my patience. Very soon I'm going to lose my temper.* □ *Some pupils think it's fun to try the teacher's patience.*

tuck into something to eat something with hunger and enjoyment. (Informal.) □ *The children really tucked into the icecream.* □ *Jean would like to have tucked into the cream cakes, but she's on a strict diet.*

tumble to something suddenly to understand or realize something. (Informal.) □ *I suddenly tumbled to the reason for his behaviour.* □ *When will Meg tumble to the fact that her husband is dishonest?*

turn a blind eye to someone or something to ignore something and pretend you do not see it. □ *The usherette turned a blind eye to* *the little boy who sneaked into the theatre.* □ *How can you turn a blind eye to all those starving children?*

turn someone's head to make someone conceited. □ *John's compliments really turned Sally's head.* □ *Victory in the competition is bound to turn Tom's head. He'll think he's too good for us.*

turn something to good account to use something in such a way that it is to one's advantage; to make good use of a situation, experience, etc. □ *Pam turned her illness to good account and did a lot of reading.* □ *Many people turn their retirement to good account and take up interesting hobbies.*

turn something to one's advantage to make an advantage for oneself out of something (which might otherwise be a disadvantage). □ *Sally found a way to turn the problem to her advantage.* □ *The icecream shop manager was able to turn the hot weather to her advantage.*

turn the other cheek to choose not to respond to abuse or to an insult. □ *When Bob got angry with Mary and shouted at her, she just turned the other cheek.* □ *Usually I turn the other cheek when someone is rude to me.*

turn the tables (on someone) to cause a reversal in someone's plans; to reverse a situation and put someone in a different position, especially in a less advantageous position. □ *I went to Jane's house to help get ready for a surprise party for Bob. It turned out that the surprise party was for me! Jane really turned the tables on me!* □ *Turning the tables like that requires a lot of planning and a lot of secrecy.*

turn the tide to cause a reversal in the direction of events; to cause a reversal in public opinion. □ *It looked as though the team was going to lose, but near the end of the game, our star player turned the tide by scoring a goal.* □ *At first, people were opposed to our plan. After a lot of discussion, we were able to turn the tide and get them to agree with us.*

turn turtle to turn upside down. □ *The boat turned turtle, and everyone got soaked.* □ *The car ran off the road and turned turtle in the ditch.*

turn up trumps to do the right or required thing, often unexpectedly or at the last minute. (Informal.) □ *I thought our team would let us down, but they turned up trumps in the second half of the match.*

☐ *We always thought the boss was mean, but he turned up trumps and made a large contribution to Mary's leaving present.*

two a penny AND **ten a penny** very common; easily obtained and therefore cheap. ☐ *People with qualifications like yours are two a penny. You should take another training course.* ☐ *Flats to rent here are no longer two a penny.*

two can play at that game See under game at which two can play.

up a blind alley at a dead end; on a route that leads nowhere. (Informal.) □ *I have been trying to find out something about my ancestors, but I'm up a blind alley. I can't find anything.* □ *The police are up a blind alley in their investigation of the crime.*

up and doing active and lively. □ *The children are always up and doing early in the morning.* □ *If Jean wants to be at work early, it's time she was up and doing.*

up in arms rising up in anger. □ *The citizens were up in arms, pounding on the gates of the palace, demanding justice.* □ *My father was really up in arms when he got his rates bill this year.*

up in the air undecided; uncertain. □ *I don't know what Sally plans to do. Things were sort of up in the air the last time we talked.* □ *Let's leave this question up in the air until next week. Then we will make a decision.*

upper crust the higher levels of society; the upper class. (Informal. Refers to the top, as opposed to the bottom, crust of a pie.) □ *Jane speaks like that because she pretends to be from the upper crust, but her father was a miner.* □ *James is from the upper crust, but he is penniless.* ALSO **upper-crust** of the upper class; belonging to or typical of the upper class. (Informal.) □ *Pam has a grating upper-crust voice.* □ *Many people dislike Bob because of his snobbish, upper-crust attitude.*

upset the applecart to spoil or ruin something. □ *Tom really upset the applecart by telling Mary the truth about Jane. Now the two women are no longer friends.* □ *We were going abroad, but the children upset the applecart by getting the mumps.*

up to no good doing something bad or criminal. (Informal.) □ *I could tell from the look on Tom's face that he was up to no good.* □

There are three boys in the front garden. I don't know what they are doing, but I think they are up to no good.

use every trick in the book to use every method possible. (Informal.) □ *I used every trick in the book, but I still couldn't manage to get a ticket to the game on Saturday.* □ *Bob used every trick in the book to get Mary to go out with him, but he still failed. She simply refuses to go out with him.*

vanish into thin air to disappear without leaving a trace. □ *My money gets spent so fast. It seems to vanish into thin air.* □ *When I came back, my car was gone. I had locked it, and it couldn't have vanished into thin air!*

vent one's spleen to get rid of one's feelings of anger caused by someone or something by attacking someone or something else. □ *Because Jack didn't get the job, he was angry, and he vented his spleen by shouting at his wife.* □ *Peter kicked his car to vent his spleen for losing the race.*

vexed question a difficult problem about which there is a lot of discussion without a solution being found. □ *The two brothers quarrelled over the vexed question of which of them should take charge of their father's firm.* □ *We've seen a house that we like, but there's the vexed question of where we'll get the money from.*

villain of the piece someone or something that is responsible for something bad or wrong. □ *I wondered who told the newspapers about the local scandal. I discovered that Joan was the villain of the piece.* □ *We couldn't think who had stolen the meat. The dog next door turned out to be the villain of the piece.*

waiting in the wings ready or prepared to do something, especially to take over someone else's job or position. (From waiting at the side of the stage to go on.) □ *Mr. Smith retires as manager next year, and Mr. Jones is just waiting in the wings.* □ *Jane was waiting in the wings, hoping that a member of the hockey team would drop out and she would get a place on the team.*

walk a tightrope to be in a situation where one must be very cautious. □ *I've been walking a tightrope all day trying to please both bosses. I need to relax.* □ *Our business is about to fail. We've been walking a tightrope for three months, trying to control our cash flow.*

walk on air to be very happy; to be euphoric. □ *Ann was walking on air when she got the job.* □ *On the last day of school, all the children are walking on air.*

walk on eggs to be very cautious. (Informal. Never used literally.) □ *The manager is very hard to deal with. You really have to walk on eggs.* □ *I've been walking on eggs ever since I started working here. There's a very large staff turnover.*

walls have ears we may be overheard. □ *Let's not discuss this matter here. Walls have ears, you know.* □ *Shhh. Walls have ears. Someone may be listening.*

want it both ways to want to have both of two seemingly incompatible things; to want to have it both ways. □ *John wants it both ways. He can't have it both ways.* □ *You like marriage and you like freedom. You want it both ways.*

warm the cockles of someone's heart to make someone feel pleased and happy. □ *It warms the cockles of my heart to hear you say that.* □ *Hearing that old song again warmed the cockles of her heart.*

warts and all including all the faults and disadvantages. □ *Jim has many faults, but Jean loves him, warts and all.* □ *The place where we* *went on holiday had some very run-down parts, but we liked it, warts and all.*

water under the bridge [something] past and forgotten. □ *Please don't worry about it any more. It's all water under the bridge.* □ *I can't change the past. It's water under the bridge.*

wear more than one hat to have more than one set of responsibilities; to hold more than one office. □ *The mayor is also the police chief. She wears more than one hat.* □ *I have too much to do to wear more than one hat.*

wear out one's welcome to stay too long (at an event to which one has been invited); to visit somewhere too often. □ *Tom visited the Smiths so often that he wore out his welcome.* □ *At about midnight, I decided that I had worn out my welcome, so I went home.*

weep buckets to weep a great many tears. (Informal.) □ *The girls wept buckets at the sad film.* □ *Mary wept buckets when her dog died.*

weigh one's words to consider one's own words carefully when speaking. □ *I always weigh my words when I speak in public.* □ *John was weighing his words carefully because he didn't want to be misunderstood.*

weigh on someone's mind [for a worrying matter] to be constantly in a person's thoughts; [for something] to be bothering someone's thinking. □ *This problem has been weighing on my mind for many days now.* □ *I hate to have things weighing on my mind. I can't sleep when I'm worried.*

welcome someone with open arms See receive someone with open arms.

well up in something having a great deal of knowledge about something. □ *Jane's husband is well up in computers.* □ *Joan's well up in car maintenance. She took lessons at night-school.*

wheeling and dealing taking part in clever but sometimes dishonest or immoral business deals. □ *John loves wheeling and dealing in the money markets.* □ *Jack's got tired of all the wheeling and dealing of big business and retired to run a pub in the country.*

wheels within wheels circumstances, often secret or personal, which all have an effect on each other and lead to a complicated, confusing situation. □ *This is not a staightforward matter of choos-*

ing the best person for the job. There are wheels within wheels and one of the applicants is the boss's son-in-law. □ *I don't know why Jane was accepted by the college and Mary wasn't. There must have been wheels within wheels, because Mary had better qualifications.*

when the time is ripe at exactly the right time. □ *I'll tell her the good news when the time is ripe.* □ *When the time is ripe, I'll bring up the subject again.*

whip something into shape See lick something into shape.

whistle for something to expect or look for something with no hope of getting it. (Informal.) □ *I'm afraid you'll have to whistle for it if you want to borrow money. I don't have any.* □ *Jane's father told her to whistle for it when she asked him to buy her a car.*

white elephant something which is useless and which is either a nuisance or expensive to keep up. (From the gift of a white elephant by the Kings of Siam to courtiers who displeased them, knowing the cost of the upkeep would ruin them.) □ *Bob's father-in-law has given him an old Rolls-Royce, but it's a real white elephant. He has no place to park it and can't afford the petrol for it.* □ *Those antique vases Aunt Mary gave me are white elephants. They're ugly and take ages to clean.*

whole (bang) shooting match the whole lot. (Informal.) □ *They didn't even sort through the books. They just threw out the whole shooting match.* □ *All these tables are damaged. Take the whole bang shooting match away and replace them.*

win the day AND **carry the day** to be successful; to win a competition, argument, etc. (Originally meaning to win a battle.) □ *Our team didn't play well at first, but we won the day in the end.* □ *Hard work carried the day, and James passed his exams.*

win through to succeed. □ *After many setbacks, we won through in the end.* □ *The rescuers had difficulty reaching the injured climber, but they won through.*

wise after the event knowledgeable of how a situation should have been dealt with only after it has passed. □ *I know now I should have agreed to help him, but that's being wise after the event. At the time I thought he was just being lazy.* □ *Jack now realizes that he shouldn't have married Mary when they had nothing in common, but he didn't see it at the time. He's now wise after the event.*

wish someone joy of something to express the hope that someone will enjoy having or doing something, usually while being glad that one does not have to have it or do it. □ *I wish you joy of that old car. I had one just like it and spent a fortune on repairs for it.* □ *Mary wished us joy of going to Nepal on holiday. She preferred somewhere more comfortable.*

with all one's heart and soul very sincerely. □ *Oh Bill, I love you with all my heart and soul, and I always will!* □ *She thanked us with all her heart and soul for the gift.*

wither on the vine [for something] to decline or fade away at an early stage of development. (Also used literally in reference to grapes or other fruit.) □ *You have a great plan, Tom. Let's keep it alive. Don't let it wither on the vine.* □ *The whole project withered on the vine when the contract was cancelled.*

with every other breath [saying something] repeatedly or continually. □ *Bob was out in the garden raking leaves and cursing with every other breath.* □ *The child was so grateful that she was thanking me with every other breath.*

with flying colours easily and excellently. □ *John passed his geometry test with flying colours.* □ *Sally qualified for the race with flying colours.*

within an inch of doing something very close to doing something. □ *I came within an inch of losing my job.* □ *Bob came within an inch of hitting Mike across the face.*

within an inch of one's life very close to death. □ *When Mary was seriously ill in the hospital, she came within an inch of her life.* □ *The thug beat up the old man to within an inch of his life.*

within hailing distance close enough to hear someone call out. □ *When the boat came within hailing distance, I asked if I could borrow some petrol.* □ *We weren't within hailing distance, so I couldn't hear what you said to me.*

without batting an eye without showing surprise or emotion; without blinking an eye. □ *I knew I had insulted her, and she turned to me and asked me to leave without batting an eye.* □ *The child can tell lies without batting an eye.*

without rhyme or reason without purpose, order, or reason. (See variations in the examples.) □ *The teacher said my report was disorganized. My paragraphs seemed to be without rhyme or reason.* □ *Everything you do seems to be without rhyme or reason.* □ *This procedure seems to have no rhyme or reason.*

with the best will in the world however much one wishes to do something, or however hard one tries to do something. □ *With the best will in the world, Jack won't be able to help Mary get the job.* □ *With the best will in the world, they won't finish the job in time.*

woe betide someone someone will regret something very much. □ *Woe betide John if he's late. Mary will be angry.* □ *Woe betide the students if they don't work harder. They will be asked to leave college.*

won't hold water to be inadequate, insubstantial, or ill-conceived. (Informal.) □ *Sorry, your ideas won't hold water. Nice try, though.* □ *The solicitor's case wouldn't hold water, so the defendant was released.*

work one's fingers to the bone to work very hard. □ *I worked my fingers to the bone so you children could have everything you needed. Now look at the way you treat me!* □ *I spent the day working my fingers to the bone, and now I want to relax.*

worn to a shadow exhausted and thin, often from overwork. □ *Working all day and looking after the children in the evening has left Pam worn to a shadow.* □ *Ruth's worn to a shadow worrying about her son, who's very ill.*

Worse luck! Unfortunately!; The worst thing has happened! □ *I have an exam tomorrow, worse luck!* □ *We ran out of money on holiday, worse luck!*

wrongfoot someone to take someone by surprise, placing the person in a difficult situation. □ *The chairman of the committee wrongfooted his opponents by calling a meeting when most of them were on holiday and had no time to prepare for it.* □ *The teacher wrongfooted the class by giving the test a day early.*

Z

zero hour the time at which something is due to begin; a crucial moment. □ *We'll know whether the new computer system works effectively at zero hour, when we switch over to it.* □ *The runners are getting nervous as zero hour approaches. The starter's gun will soon go off.*

Phrase-Finder Index

Use this index to find the form of a phrase that you want to look up in the dictionary. First, pick out any major word in the phrase you are seeking. Second, look that word up in this index to find the form of the phrase used in the dictionary. Third, look up the phrase in the dictionary.

Some of the words occurring in the dictionary entries do not occur as entries in this index. Some words are omitted because they occur so frequently that their lists would cover many pages. Some of the grammar or function words, such as the articles *a*, *an*, and *the*, are not indexed. In these instances, you should look up the phrase under some other word.

account give a good account of
oneself
account turn something to good
account
across put one across someone
across shot across the bows
act act the goat
act read someone the Riot Act
active on active duty
Adam not know someone from
Adam
ado much ado about nothing
advanced advanced in years
advantage turn something to
one's advantage
advocate play devil's advocate
affair fine state of affairs
afraid afraid of one's own
shadow
after much sought after
after throw good money after bad
after wise after the event
again never darken my door again
against dead set against someone
or something
against go against the grain
against have a case (against
someone)
against hope against hope
against pit someone or
something against someone or
something
against play both ends (against
the middle)
against race against time
against run against the clock
against stack the cards (against
someone or something)
against swim against the tide
age come of age
age donkey's ages
age in this day and age
age ripe old age
ahead full steam ahead
aid aid and abet someone
air air of sanctity
air airs and graces
air clear the air
air give oneself airs

air have one's nose in the air
air in the air
air keep one's nose in the air
air on the air
air out of thin air
air pull something out of thin air
air put on airs
air up in the air
air vanish into thin air
air walk on air
alert on the alert (for someone or
something)
alike share and share alike
all (all) at sea (about something)
all all ears (and eyes)
all (all) Greek to me
all all hours (of the day and night)
all all over bar the shouting
all all skin and bones
all all thumbs
all all to the good
all carry all before one
all get away (from it all)
all in all one's born days
all in all probability
all jack-of-all-trades
all know all the tricks of the trade
all on all fours
all once and for all
all pull out all the stops
all put all one's eggs in one
basket
all warts and all
all with all one's heart and soul
alley up a blind alley
alone go it alone
alone leave well alone
alone let well alone
along inch along (something)
along jolly someone along
along rub along with someone
altogether in the altogether
among put the cat among the
pigeons
among set the cat among the
pigeons
and all ears (and eyes)
and (as) large as life (and twice
as ugly)

at at half-mast
at at large
at at liberty
at at loggerheads (with someone)
at at one's wits' end
at at sixes and sevens
at at someone's beck and call
at at the bottom of the ladder
at at the drop of a hat
at at the eleventh hour
at at the end of one's tether
at at the expense of someone or something
at at the top of one's voice
at burn the candle at both ends
at champ at the bit
at clutch at straws
at cock a snook at someone
at down at heel
at fall apart at the seams
at foam at the mouth
at game at which two can play
at go off at a tangent
at go off at half cock
at have a go (at something)
at have something at one's fingertips
at ill at ease
at in at the kill
at jump at the chance (to do something)
at jump at the opportunity (to do something)
at leap at the chance (to do something)
at leap at the opportunity (to do something)
at look daggers at someone
at love at first sight
at make eyes at someone
at make oneself at home
at old hand at doing something
at pipped at the post
at point the finger at someone
at poke fun (at someone or something)
at see the light at the end of the tunnel
at sit at someone's feet

at take a stab at something
at throw the book at someone
at thumb one's nose at someone or something
at tip the scales at something
at two can play at that game
attendance dance attendance on someone
average on average
avoid avoid someone or something like the plague
away come away empty-handed
away get away (from it all)
away get carried away
away give the game away
away straight away
axe have an axe to grind
babe babe in arms
baby leave someone holding the baby
back back of beyond
back back to the drawing-board
back drop back
back get back on one's feet
back give someone the shirt off one's back
back go back on one's word
back hark(en) back to something
back have eyes in the back of one's head
back have one's back to the wall
back like water off a duck's back
back pay someone a back-handed compliment
back put something on the back burner
back scratch someone's back
back set one back on one's heels
backyard in one's (own) backyard
bacon bring home the bacon
bad come to a bad end
bad go from bad to worse
bad good riddance (to bad rubbish)
bad in a bad mood
bad in a bad way
bad leave a bad taste in someone's mouth

211

berth give someone or something a wide berth
best best bib and tucker
best come off second-best
best give something one's best shot
best in the best of health
best past someone's or something's best
best put one's best foot forward
best with the best will in the world
betide woe betide someone
better have seen better days
between draw a line between something and something else
between fall between two stools
between hit someone (right) between the eyes
between no love lost between someone and someone else
between read between the lines
beyond back of beyond
beyond beyond one's ken
beyond beyond the pale
beyond beyond the shadow of a doubt
beyond beyond words
beyond can't see beyond the end of one's nose
bib best bib and tucker
bide bide one's time
big have a big mouth
big one's eyes are bigger than one's stomach
bill fill the bill
bill foot the bill
bill get a clean bill of health
bird early bird
bird eat like a bird
birthday in one's birthday suit
bit champ at the bit
bit do one's bit
bit hair of the dog (that bit one)
bit Not a bit (of it).
bite bite someone's head off
bite bite the hand that feeds one
bitter bitter pill to swallow
bitter to the bitter end

black as black as one is painted
black (as) black as pitch
black black sheep (of the family)
black get a black eye
black in black and white
black pot calling the kettle black
blanche carte blanche
blank blank cheque
blank draw a blank
blind turn a blind eye to someone or something
blind up a blind alley
block chip off the old block
block stumbling-block
blood blue blood
blood draw blood
blood flesh and blood
blood in one's blood
blood in the blood
blood make someone's blood boil
blood make someone's blood run cold
blow blow hot and cold
blow blow off steam
blow blow one's own trumpet
blow blow the lid off (something)
blow blow up in someone's face
blow land a blow (somewhere)
blue blue blood
blue like a bolt out of the blue
blue once in a blue moon
blue out of the blue
blue talk until one is blue in the face
board back to the drawing-board
board go by the board
boat burn one's boats
boat in the same boat
boat rock the boat
body keep body and soul together
body over my dead body
boil have a low boiling-point
boil make someone's blood boil
bold (as) bold as brass
bolt like a bolt out of the blue
bolt nuts and bolts (of something)
bombshell drop a bombshell
bone all skin and bones
bone bone of contention

breathe not breathe a word (about someone or something)

breathe not breathe a word (of something)

bridge burn one's bridges (behind one)

bridge cross a bridge before one comes to it

bridge water under the bridge

brief hold no brief for someone or something

bright (as) bright as a button

bring bring down the curtain (on something)

bring bring home the bacon

bring bring something home to someone

bring bring something to a head

bring bring something to light

Bristol shipshape (and Bristol fashion)

broad in broad daylight

broke go broke

broken die of a broken heart

brow by the sweat of one's brow

brow knit one's brow

brush brush something under the carpet

brush get the brush-off

brush have a brush with something

brush tarred with the same brush

buck pass the buck

bucket weep buckets

bud nip something in the bud

buff in the buff

bull bull in a china shop

bull cock-and-bull story

bull hit the bull's-eye

burn burn one's boats

burn burn one's bridges (behind one)

burn burn the candle at both ends

burn burn the midnight oil

burn fiddle while Rome burns

burn get one's fingers burned

burn have money to burn

burn keep the home fires burning

burner put something on the back burner

bury bury the hatchet

bury dead and buried

bush beat about the bush

bush bush telegraph

bushel hide one's light under a bushel

business business end of something

business get down to business

business get one's nose out of someone's business

business have no business doing something

business mind one's own business

business monkey business

busman busman's holiday

but everything but the kitchen sink

but last but not least

but no ifs or buts about it

but nothing but skin and bones

butter look as if butter wouldn't melt in one's mouth

butterfly get butterflies in one's stomach

button (as) bright as a button

buy buy a pig in a poke

buy buy something for a song

by by fits and starts

by by leaps and bounds

by by no means

by by return post

by by the same token

by by the seat of one's pants

by by the skin of one's teeth

by by the sweat of one's brow

by by virtue of something

by by word of mouth

by cheek by jowl

by conspicuous by one's absence

by fall by the wayside

by fly-by-night

by get by (on a shoe-string)

by go by the board

by hang by a hair

by hang by a thread

by hang on by an eyebrow
by hang on by one's eyebrows
by lead someone by the nose
by learn something by heart
by learn something by rote
by let the chance slip by
by live by one's wits
by not by a long shot
by past someone's or something's sell-by date
by pull oneself up by one's bootstraps
by saved by the bell
by set great store by someone or something
by sit (idly) by
cake piece of cake
cake slice of the cake
calf kill the fatted calf
call at someone's beck and call
call call a spade a spade
call call it a day
call call of nature
call not able to call one's time one's own
call pot calling the kettle black
calm (as) calm as a millpond
camp have a foot in both camps
can before you can say Jack Robinson
can can't hold a candle to someone
can can't make head nor tail of someone or something
can can't see beyond the end of one's nose
can can't see one's hand in front of one's face
can game at which two can play
can open a can of worms
can two can play at that game
canary look like the cat that swallowed the canary
candle burn the candle at both ends
candle can't hold a candle to someone
candle not worth a candle

cannot can't hold a candle to someone
cannot can't make head nor tail of someone or something
cannot can't see beyond the end of one's nose
cannot can't see one's hand in front of one's face
canoe paddle one's own canoe
cap feather in one's cap
cap put on one's thinking-cap
card keep one's cards close to one's chest
card on the cards
card play one's cards close to one's chest
card play one's cards right
card play one's trump card
card stack the cards (against someone or something)
care not have a care in the world
carpet brush something under the carpet
carpet sweep something under the carpet
carry carry a torch for someone
carry carry all before one
carry carry the day
carry carry the weight of the world on one's shoulders
carry get carried away
cart put the cart before the horse
carte carte blanche
case have a case (against someone)
case open-and-shut case
cash hard cash
cast cast in the same mould
cat Cat got your tongue?
cat let the cat out of the bag
cat look like the cat that swallowed the canary
cat look like the cat that swallowed the cream
cat play cat and mouse (with someone)
cat put the cat among the pigeons
cat rain cats and dogs
cat set the cat among the pigeons

catch catch one's breath
catch catch someone on the hop
catch catch someone's eye
catch catch the sun
catch find time to catch one's breath
catch get time to catch one's breath
caught caught over a barrel
cause cause tongues to wag
caution throw caution to the winds
centre dead centre
centre left, right, and centre
centre off-centre
ceremony stand on ceremony
chaff separate the wheat from the chaff
champ champ at the bit
chance chance one's arm
chance fancy someone's chances
chance fighting chance
chance have a snowball's chance in hell
chance jump at the chance (to do something)
chance leap at the chance (to do something)
chance let the chance slip by
chance on the off-chance
chance once-in-a-lifetime chance
chance sporting chance
chance stand a chance
change change hands
change change horses in mid-stream
change change someone's tune
change chop and change
change ring the changes
channel go through the proper channels
chapter chapter and verse
chapter chapter of accidents
charity (as) cold as charity
chase lead someone (on) a merry chase
cheap dirt cheap
cheek cheek by jowl
cheek tongue-in-cheek

cheek turn the other cheek
cheese cheese-paring
cheese cheesed off
cheque blank cheque
chest get something off one's chest
chest keep one's cards close to one's chest
chest play one's cards close to one's chest
chew chew the cud
chicken no spring chicken
child expecting (a child)
childhood in one's second childhood
chill chilled to the bone
chill chilled to the marrow
chin keep one's chin up
chin take something on the chin
china bull in a china shop
chink chink in one's armour
chip chip off the old block
chip have a chip on one's shoulder
choice Hobson's choice
choose pick and choose
chop chop and change
chord strike a chord
circle come full circle
circle go round in circles
civil keep a civil tongue (in one's head)
clap clap eyes on someone or something
clay have feet of clay
clean get a clean bill of health
clean have clean hands
clean make a clean breast of something
clean make a clean sweep
clean start (off) with a clean slate
clear clear the air
climb climb down
clip clip someone's wings
cloak cloak-and-dagger
clock run against the clock
clockwork go like clockwork
close close one's eyes to something

compliment pay someone a back-handed compliment

compliment pay someone a compliment

composure regain one's composure

condition in mint condition

condition in the peak of condition

condition in the pink (of condition)

conspicuous conspicuous by one's absence

contention bone of contention

contradiction contradiction in terms

convert preach to the converted

conviction have the courage of one's convictions

cook cook someone's goose

cook cook the books

cool cool one's heels

corner cut corners

corner have turned the corner

corner hole-and-corner

corner hole-in-the-corner

corner out of the corner of one's eye

correct stand corrected

cost cost a pretty penny

cost cost the earth

counsel keep one's own counsel

count count heads

courage have the courage of one's convictions

courage pluck up (one's) courage

courage screw up one's courage

course par for the course

court laugh something out of court

Coventry send someone to Coventry

cow sacred cow

cow till the cows come home

Cox Box and Cox

crack crack a bottle

crack fair crack of the whip

crack make cracks (about someone or something)

crack paper over the cracks (in something)

cramp cramp someone's style

craw something sticks in one's craw

cream look like the cat that swallowed the cream

credit get credit (for something)

credit give credit where credit is due

cropper come a cropper

cross cross a bridge before one comes to it

cross cross one's heart (and hope to die)

cross cross swords (with someone)

cross cross the Rubicon

crust upper crust

crux crux of the matter

cry cry one's eyes out

cry cry over spilled milk

cry cry wolf

cry far cry from something

cry hue and cry

cuckoo cloud-cuckoo-land

cud chew the cud

cudgel take up the cudgels on behalf of someone or something

culture culture vulture

cup in one's cups

cup not someone's cup of tea

cupboard cupboard love

cupboard skeleton in the cupboard

curl curl up (and die)

curry curry favour (with someone)

curtain bring down the curtain (on something)

curtain ring down the curtain (on something)

cut cut a fine figure

cut cut a long story short

cut cut and dried

cut cut and thrust

cut cut both ways

cut cut corners

cut cut it (too) fine

cut cut no ice
cut cut one's coat according to one's cloth
cut cut one's coat to suit one's cloth
cut cut one's eye-teeth on something
cut cut one's teeth on something
cut cut someone dead
cut cut someone down to size
cut cut someone to the quick
cut cut teeth
cut have one's work cut out (for one)
dagger cloak-and-dagger
dagger look daggers at someone
daily daily dozen
daily daily grind
dammit (as) near as dammit
damn damn someone or something with faint praise
damp damp squib
dance dance attendance on someone
dance lead someone (on) a merry dance
Darby Darby and Joan
dark dark horse
dark in the dark (about someone or something)
dark shot in the dark
darken never darken my door again
darken not to darken someone's door
date past someone's or something's sell-by date
Davy Davy Jones's locker
Davy go to Davy Jones's locker
day all hours (of the day and night)
day (as) happy as the day is long
day call it a day
day carry the day
day for days on end
day have seen better days
day in all one's born days
day in this day and age
day late in the day

day nine days' wonder
day not give someone the time of day
day one's days are numbered
day order of the day
day pass the time of day (with someone)
day save something for a rainy day
day see the light of day
day win the day
daylight daylight robbery
daylight in broad daylight
dead cut someone dead
dead dead and buried
dead dead centre
dead dead on one's or its feet
dead dead set against someone or something
dead dead to the world
dead fill dead men's shoes
dead flog a dead horse
dead in a dead heat
dead knock someone dead
dead over my dead body
dead step into dead men's shoes
deal square deal
deal wheeling and dealing
death at death's door
death death to something
death die a natural death
death kiss of death
death matter of life and death
death sign one's own death-warrant
debt pay one's debt to society
decision eleventh-hour decision
deep go off the deep end
deep in deep water
deliver signed, sealed, and delivered
den beard the lion in his den
description beggar description
desert get one's just deserts
devil full of the devil
devil give the devil her due
devil give the devil his due
devil go to the devil
devil play devil's advocate
devil speak of the devil

Dick (every) Tom, Dick, and Harry
die cross one's heart (and hope to die)
die curl up (and die)
die die a natural death
die die laughing
die die of a broken heart
die die of boredom
difference sink our differences
difference split the difference
different horse of a different colour
dig dig one's own grave
dilemma on the horns of a dilemma
dine dine out on something
dip lucky dip
dirt dirt cheap
dirty dirty look
distance go the distance
distance keep one's distance (from someone or something)
distance stay the distance
distance within hailing distance
ditch last-ditch effort
do do a double take
do do an about-face
do do justice to something
do do one's bit
do do someone down
do do someone good
do do someone proud
do do someone's heart good
do do the trick
do fair do's
do feel it beneath one (to do something)
do find it in one's heart to do something
do have a penchant for doing something
do have half a mind to do something
do have no business doing something
do have the wherewithal (to do something)
do in no mood to do something
do in thing (to do)

do instrumental in doing something
do jump at the chance (to do something)
do jump at the opportunity (to do something)
do kick oneself (for doing something)
do lead someone to do something
do leap at the chance (to do something)
do leap at the opportunity (to do something)
do make a point of (doing) something
do make do (with someone or something)
do move heaven and earth to do something
do old hand at doing something
do press-gang someone into doing something
do risk one's neck (to do something)
do up and doing
do within an inch of doing something
doctor just what the doctor ordered
dog dog in the manger
dog hair of the dog (that bit one)
dog lead a dog's life
dog rain cats and dogs
dog shaggy-dog story
dog tail wagging the dog
doghouse in the doghouse
doldrums in the doldrums
dollar feel like a million dollars
dollar look like a million dollars
done done to a turn
done no sooner said than done
done over and done with
donkey donkey's ages
donkey donkey's years
donkey donkey-work
door at death's door
door get one's foot in the door
door keep the wolf from the door
door never darken my door again

due give credit where credit is due
due give the devil her due
due give the devil his due
dues pay one's dues
Dutch double Dutch
Dutch go Dutch
duty in the line of duty
duty on active duty
duty shirk one's duty
eager eager beaver
eagle eagle eye
ear all ears (and eyes)
ear bend someone's ear
ear flea in one's ear
ear go in one ear and out the other
ear have one's ear to the ground
ear in one ear and out the other
ear keep one's ear to the ground
ear prick up one's ears
ear walls have ears
early early bird
earth come down to earth
earth cost the earth
earth down to earth
earth move heaven and earth to do something
earth pay the earth
earth run someone or something to earth
earth salt of the earth
ease ill at ease
easy free and easy
eat eat humble pie
eat eat like a bird
eat eat like a horse
eat eat one's hat
eat eat one's heart out
eat eat one's words
eat eat out of someone's hands
eat eat someone out of house and home
edge set someone's teeth on edge
edgeways get a word in (edgeways)
effort last-ditch effort
egg have egg on one's face
egg put all one's eggs in one basket

egg teach one's grandmother to suck eggs
egg walk on eggs
either either feast or famine
elbow elbow-grease
elephant white elephant
eleven at the eleventh hour
eleven eleventh-hour decision
else draw a line between something and something else
else no love lost between someone and someone else
empty come away empty-handed
end at a loose end
end at one's wits' end
end at the end of one's tether
end burn the candle at both ends
end business end of something
end can't see beyond the end of one's nose
end come to a bad end
end come to an untimely end
end for days on end
end go off the deep end
end make (both) ends meet
end make someone's hair stand on end
end meet one's end
end not see further than the end of one's nose
end play both ends (against the middle)
end see the light at the end of the tunnel
end thin end of the wedge
end to the bitter end
English in plain English
enough enough is as good as a feast
enough good enough for someone or something
enough old enough to be someone's father
enough old enough to be someone's mother
enter enter the lists
envy green with envy
errand on a fool's errand
escape escape someone's notice

fall fall apart at the seams
fall fall between two stools
fall fall by the wayside
fall fall down on the job
fall fall foul of someone or something
fall fall from grace
fall fall into line
fall riding for a fall
false sail under false colours
familiar have a familiar ring
family black sheep (of the family)
family in the family
family in the family way
family like one of the family
family run in the family
famine either feast or famine
fancy fancy someone's chances
fancy flight of fancy
fancy tickle someone's fancy
far come from far and wide
far far cry from something
far go so far as to say something
fashion parrot-fashion
fashion shipshape (and Bristol fashion)
fast get nowhere fast
fast hard-and-fast rule
fast play fast and loose (with someone or something)
fast pull a fast one
fast thick and fast
fat kill the fatted calf
fat live off the fat of the land
father old enough to be someone's father
fault generous to a fault
favour curry favour (with someone)
fear fools rush in (where angels fear to tread)
fear in fear and trembling
fear never fear
feast either feast or famine
feast enough is as good as a feast
feast feast one's eyes (on someone or something)
feather feather in one's cap
feather feather one's (own) nest

feather in fine feather
feather knock someone down with a feather
feather make the feathers fly
feather ruffle someone's feathers
feather show the white feather
feed bite the hand that feeds one
feed spoon-feed
feel feel fit
feel feel it beneath one (to do something)
feel feel like a million dollars
feel feel like a new person
feel feel something in one's bones
feeler put out (some) feelers
feelings no hard feelings
feet dead on one's or its feet
feet drag one's feet
feet find one's feet
feet get back on one's feet
feet get cold feet
feet get to one's feet
feet have feet of clay
feet have one's feet on the ground
feet keep one's feet on the ground
feet land on both feet
feet land on one's feet
feet let the grass grow under one's feet
feet on one's feet
feet pull the rug out from under someone('s feet)
feet sit at someone's feet
fellow hail-fellow-well-met
fence mend (one's) fences
fence rush one's fences
fever run a fever
few raise a few eyebrows
fiddle (as) fit as a fiddle
fiddle fiddle while Rome burns
fiddle play second fiddle (to someone)
field (fresh fields and) pastures new
field play the field
fight fight shy of something
fight fighting chance
fight go down fighting

food food for thought
fool fool's paradise
fool fools rush in (where angels fear to tread)
fool More fool you!
fool nobody's fool
fool on a fool's errand
fool play the fool
foot dead on one's or its feet
foot drag one's feet
foot find one's feet
foot foot the bill
foot get back on one's feet
foot get cold feet
foot get one's foot in the door
foot get to one's feet
foot have a foot in both camps
foot have feet of clay
foot have one's feet on the ground
foot keep one's feet on the ground
foot land on both feet
foot land on one's feet
foot let the grass grow under one's feet
foot not set foot somewhere
foot on one's feet
foot pull the rug out from under someone('s feet)
foot put one's best foot forward
foot put one's foot down (about something)
foot put one's foot in it
foot set foot somewhere
foot sit at someone's feet
for be getting on for something
for be thankful for small mercies
for buy something for a song
for carry a torch for someone
for come in for something
for fish for compliments
for fit for a king
for food for thought
for for days on end
for for sale
for for the record
for get a good run for one's money

for get credit (for something)
for give one's right arm (for someone or something)
for give someone pause for thought
for give someone tit for tat
for glutton for punishment
for go for someone or something
for go in for something
for good enough for someone or something
for good-for-nothing
for have a lot going for one
for have a penchant for doing something
for have a soft spot for someone or something
for have one's work cut out (for one)
for have something in store (for someone)
for hell for leather
for hold no brief for someone or something
for in the market (for something)
for jockey for position
for keep an eye out (for someone or something)
for kick oneself (for doing something)
for leave oneself wide open for something
for like looking for a needle in a haystack
for lovely weather for ducks
for make a beeline for someone or something
for make a name for oneself
for make a pitch for someone or something
for make up for lost time
for money for jam
for money for old rope
for none the worse for wear
for not able to see the wood for the trees
for not for anything in the world
for not for love nor money
for not for the world

future in the near future
gain ill-gotten gains
gallery play to the gallery
game fair game
game fun and games
game game at which two can play
game give the game away
game name of the game
game play the game
game two can play at that game
gang press-gang someone into doing something
garden lead someone up the garden path
gauntlet throw down the gauntlet
gear in high gear
generous generous to a fault
get be getting on for something
get get a black eye
get get a clean bill of health
get get a good run for one's money
get get a lucky break
get get a lump in one's throat
get get a slap on the wrist
get get a start
get get a tongue-lashing
get get a word in (edgeways)
get get above oneself
get get away (from it all)
get get back on one's feet
get get butterflies in one's stomach
get get by (on a shoe-string)
get get carried away
get get cold feet
get get credit (for something)
get get down to brass tacks
get get down to business
get get in someone's hair
get get into full swing
get get into the swing of things
get get nowhere fast
get get off lightly
get get off to a flying start
get get on the good side of someone
get get one's come-uppance

get get one's fill of someone or something
get get one's fingers burned
get get one's foot in the door
get get one's just deserts
get get one's money's worth
get get one's nose out of someone's business
get get one's second wind
get get one's teeth into something
get get out of the wrong side of the bed
get get someone off the hook
get get someone's number
get get something off one's chest
get get something out of one's system
get get something under one's belt
get get the ball rolling
get get the brush-off
get get the hang of something
get get the last laugh
get get the runaround
get get the shock of one's life
get get the show on the road
get get time to catch one's breath
get get to one's feet
get get to the bottom of something
get get under someone's skin
get get what is coming to one
get get wind of something
get getting on (in years)
get give as good as one gets
get play hard to get
ghost give up the ghost
gild gild the lily
gill green about the gills
gill green around the gills
gill pale around the gills
give give a good account of oneself
give give as good as one gets
give give credit where credit is due
give give ground
give give it to someone straight
give give of oneself

good get on the good side of someone

good give a good account of oneself

good give as good as one gets

good good enough for someone or something

good good-for-nothing

good good riddance (to bad rubbish)

good have a good command of something

good have a good head on one's shoulders

good make good as something

good make good money

good make good time

good make someone look good

good never had it so good

good put in a good word for someone

good stand someone in good stead

good throw good money after bad

good turn something to good account

good up to no good

goose cook someone's goose

gooseberry play gooseberry

got Cat got your tongue?

gotten ill-gotten gains

grace airs and graces

grace fall from grace

grade make the grade

grain go against the grain

grandmother teach one's grandmother to suck eggs

grasp grasp the nettle

grass let the grass grow under one's feet

grass snake in the grass

grave (as) quiet as the grave

grave dig one's own grave

grease elbow-grease

great going great guns

great make a great show of something

great set great store by someone or something

Greek (all) Greek to me

Greek Greek to me

green green about the gills

green green around the gills

green green with envy

green have green fingers

grief come to grief

grin grin and bear it

grind daily grind

grind grind to a halt

grind have an axe to grind

grindstone keep one's nose to the grindstone

grip lose one's grip

grist grist to the mill

grit grit one's teeth

ground break new ground

ground give ground

ground have one's ear to the ground

ground have one's feet on the ground

ground keep one's ear to the ground

ground keep one's feet on the ground

ground one's old stamping-ground

ground shift one's ground

ground suit someone down to the ground

ground thin on the ground

grow grow on someone

grow let the grass grow under one's feet

guard on one's guard

guinea serve as a guinea pig

gun going great guns

gun jump the gun

gun shot-gun wedding

gun spike someone's guns

gun stick to one's guns

gut hate someone's guts

ha'porth spoil the ship for a ha'porth of tar

had never had it so good

hail hail-fellow-well-met

hat at the drop of a hat
hat be old hat
hat eat one's hat
hat Hang on to your hat!
hat hang one's hat up somewhere
hat Hold on to your hat!
hat keep something under one's hat
hat pass the hat round
hat pull something out of a hat
hat talk through one's hat
hat wear more than one hat
hatchet bury the hatchet
hate hate someone's guts
haul haul someone over the coals
have hardly have time to breathe
have have (high) hopes of something
have have a bee in one's bonnet
have have a big mouth
have have a bone to pick (with someone)
have have a brush with something
have have a case (against someone)
have have a chip on one's shoulder
have have a down on someone
have have a familiar ring
have have a foot in both camps
have have a go (at something)
have have a good command of something
have have a good head on one's shoulders
have have a heart
have have a heart of gold
have have a heart of stone
have have a heart-to-heart (talk)
have have a lot going for one
have have a low boiling-point
have have a near miss
have have a penchant for doing something
have have a price on one's head
have have a say (in something)
have have a snowball's chance in hell

have have a soft spot for someone or something
have have a sweet tooth
have have a thin time (of it)
have have a voice (in something)
have have a word with someone
have have an axe to grind
have have an itching palm
have have an itchy palm
have have an out
have have another think coming
have have ants in one's pants
have have bats in one's belfry
have have been through the mill
have have clean hands
have have egg on one's face
have have eyes in the back of one's head
have have feet of clay
have have green fingers
have have half a mind to do something
have have it both ways
have have money to burn
have have no business doing something
have have no staying-power
have have none of something
have have one's back to the wall
have have one's ear to the ground
have have one's feet on the ground
have have one's finger in the pie
have have one's hand in the till
have have one's head in the clouds
have have one's heart in one's boots
have have one's nose in a book
have have one's nose in the air
have have one's wits about one
have have one's work cut out (for one)
have have other fish to fry
have have seen better days
have have someone in one's pocket
have have someone on a string

heart have a heart-to-heart (talk)
heart have one's heart in one's boots
heart learn something by heart
heart lose heart
heart open one's heart (to someone)
heart take something to heart
heart warm the cockles of someone's heart
heart with all one's heart and soul
hearty hale and hearty
heat in a dead heat
heaven in seventh heaven
heaven move heaven and earth to do something
heavy heavy going
heel cool one's heels
heel down at heel
heel hard on someone's heels
heel hard on the heels of something
heel head over heels in love (with someone)
heel kick one's heels
heel kick up one's heels
heel set one back on one's heels
hell go to hell
hell have a snowball's chance in hell
hell hell for leather
hell through hell and high water
help help oneself
help not lift a finger (to help someone)
help pitch in (and help)
hem hem and haw
her give the devil her due
here here's to someone or something
herring draw a red herring
herring red herring
hide have someone's hide
hide hide one's face in shame
hide hide one's light under a bushel
hide neither hide nor hair
high go sky-high

high have (high) hopes of something
high high and mighty
high high-flyer
high in high gear
high run high
high through hell and high water
hill over the hill
his beard the lion in his den
his give the devil his due
history go down in history
hit hit (someone) below the belt
hit hit a snag
hit hit it off (with someone)
hit hit rock bottom
hit hit (right) between the eyes
hit hit the bull's-eye
hitch hitch a lift
Hobson Hobson's choice
hog go the whole hog
hog road-hog
hold can't hold a candle to someone
hold hold forth
hold hold no brief for someone or something
hold Hold on to your hat!
hold hold one's fire
hold hold one's own
hold hold one's peace
hold hold one's tongue
hold hold out the olive branch
hold hold true
hold hold water
hold leave someone holding the baby
hold no holds barred
hold not hold water
hold won't hold water
hole hole-and-corner
hole hole-in-the-corner
hole pick holes in something
hole square peg in a round hole
holiday busman's holiday
holiday on holiday
holier holier-than-thou
home bring home the bacon

in come out in the wash
in contradiction in terms
in dog in the manger
in down in the mouth
in drop in one's tracks
in feather in one's cap
in feel something in one's bones
in find it in one's heart to do something
in fish in troubled waters
in flash in the pan
in flea in one's ear
in fly in the face of someone or something
in fly in the ointment
in fools rush in (where angels fear to tread)
in get a lump in one's throat
in get a word in (edgeways)
in get butterflies in one's stomach
in get in someone's hair
in get one's foot in the door
in getting on (in years)
in go down in history
in go in for something
in go in one ear and out the other
in go round in circles
in hand in glove (with someone)
in hang in the balance
in have a bee in one's bonnet
in have a foot in both camps
in have a say (in something)
in have a snowball's chance in hell
in have a voice (in something)
in have ants in one's pants
in have bats in one's belfry
in have eyes in the back of one's head
in have one's finger in the pie
in have one's hand in the till
in have one's head in the clouds
in have one's heart in one's boots
in have one's nose in a book
in have one's nose in the air
in have someone in one's pocket
in have something in hand
in have something in mind
in have something in stock

in have something in store (for someone)
in have too many irons in the fire
in head over heels in love (with someone)
in hide one's face in shame
in hole-in-the-corner
in in (just) a second
in in a (pretty) pickle
in in a (tight) spot
in in a bad mood
in in a bad way
in in a dead heat
in in a fix
in in a flash
in in a huff
in in a jam
in in a jiffy
in in a mad rush
in in a nutshell
in in a quandary
in in a sense
in in a split second
in in a stage whisper
in in a stew (about someone or something)
in in all one's born days
in in all probability
in in arrears
in in at the kill
in in black and white
in in broad daylight
in in clover
in in deep water
in in dribs and drabs
in in fear and trembling
in in fine feather
in in force
in in full swing
in in high gear
in in league (with someone)
in in leaps and bounds
in in less than no time
in in lieu of something
in in luck
in in mint condition
in in name only
in in no mood to do something
in in one ear and out the other

in pack them in
in pain in the neck
in paper over the cracks (in something)
in pick holes in something
in pie in the sky
in pig(gy)-in-the-middle
in pitch in (and help)
in put all one's eggs in one basket
in put in a good word for someone
in put one in one's place
in put one's foot in it
in put one's house in order
in put one's oar in
in put someone in mind of someone or something
in put someone in the picture
in Put that in your pipe and smoke it!
in putty in someone's hands
in quake in one's shoes
in quids in with someone
in ring in the New Year
in rub salt in the wound
in rub someone's nose in it
in run in the family
in shake in one's shoes
in ships that pass in the night
in shot in the arm
in shot in the dark
in shove one's oar in
in show oneself in one's true colours
in skeleton in the cupboard
in snake in the grass
in something sticks in one's craw
in square peg in a round hole
in stand someone in good stead
in stew in one's own juice
in stick one's oar in
in storm in a teacup
in straw in the wind
in take something in one's stride
in talk until one is blue in the face
in throw a spanner in the works
in throw in one's hand
in tie someone in knots
in tongue-in-cheek

in up in arms
in up in the air
in use every trick in the book
in waiting in the wings
in well up in something
in with the best will in the world
inch inch along (something)
inch within an inch of doing something
inch within an inch of one's life
information mine of information
instrumental instrumental in doing something
into come into something
into fall into line
into fit someone in(to something)
into get into full swing
into get into the swing of things
into get one's teeth into something
into into the bargain
into lick something into shape
into out of the frying-pan into the fire
into pile in(to something)
into play into someone's hands
into press-gang someone into doing something
into put ideas into someone's head
into put words into someone's mouth
into read something into something
into step in(to the breach)
into step into dead men's shoes
into tuck into something
into vanish into thin air
into whip something into shape
iron have too many irons in the fire
iron iron hand in a velvet glove
iron strike while the iron is hot
is as black as one is painted
is (as) happy as the day is long
is enough is as good as a feast
is expense is no object
is get what is coming to one
is give credit where credit is due

is money is no object
is Put your money where your mouth is!
is seeing is believing
is strike while the iron is hot
is talk until one is blue in the face
is when the time is ripe
it believe it or not
it call it a day
it cross a bridge before one comes to it
it cut it (too) fine
it dead on one's or its feet
it feel it beneath one (to do something)
it find it in one's heart to do something
it get away (from it all)
it give it to someone straight
it go it alone
it grin and bear it
it hand it to someone
it have a thin time (of it)
it have it both ways
it have what it takes
it hit it off (with someone)
it let someone have it
it lord it over someone
it make a go of it
it make it worth someone's while
it make nothing of it
it never had it so good
it no ifs or buts about it
it no two ways about it
it Not a bit (of it).
it nothing to it
it on one's (own) head be it
it on the face of it
it past it
it put a brave face on it
it put it on
it put one's foot in it
it Put that in your pipe and smoke it!
it rear its ugly head
it rough it
it rub someone's nose in it
it run for it
it stick it out

it Tell it to the marines.
it try it on
it want it both ways
itch have an itching palm
itchy have an itchy palm
ivory live in an ivory tower
Jack before you can say Jack Robinson
jack jack-of-all-trades
jam in a jam
jam jam tomorrow
jam money for jam
Jekyll Jekyll and Hyde
jiffy in a jiffy
Joan Darby and Joan
job fall down on the job
job job lot
Job Job's comforter
job just the job
job lie down on the job
job nine-to-five job
jockey jockey for position
johnny johnny-come-lately
joint put someone's nose out of joint
joke joking apart
joke standing joke
jolly jolly someone along
Jones Davy Jones's locker
Jones go to Davy Jones's locker
jowl cheek by jowl
joy wish someone joy of something
juice stew in one's own juice
jump jump at the chance (to do something)
jump jump at the opportunity (to do something)
jump jump down someone's throat
jump jump on someone
jump jump out of one's skin
jump jump the gun
jump jumping-off point
just get one's just deserts
just in (just) a second
just just the job
just just what the doctor ordered
justice do justice to something

justice poetic justice
keen keen on someone or something
keep keep a civil tongue (in one's head)
keep keep a stiff upper lip
keep keep a straight face
keep keep a weather eye open
keep keep an eye out (for someone or something)
keep keep body and soul together
keep keep house
keep keep in with someone
keep keep late hours
keep keep one's cards close to one's chest
keep keep one's chin up
keep keep one's distance (from someone or something)
keep keep one's ear to the ground
keep keep one's eye on the ball
keep keep one's feet on the ground
keep keep one's hand in (something)
keep keep one's head above water
keep keep one's mouth shut (about someone or something)
keep keep one's nose in the air
keep keep one's nose to the grindstone
keep keep one's own counsel
keep keep one's side of the bargain
keep keep one's wits about one
keep keep one's word
keep keep oneself to oneself
keep keep someone in line
keep keep someone in stitches
keep keep someone on a string
keep keep someone on tenterhooks
keep keep someone posted
keep keep something under one's hat
keep keep something under wraps
keep keep the ball rolling
keep keep the home fires burning

keep keep the lid on something
keep keep the wolf from the door
keg sitting on a powder keg
ken beyond one's ken
kettle fine kettle of fish
kettle pot calling the kettle black
kettle pretty kettle of fish
kick kick one's heels
kick kick oneself (for doing something)
kick kick up a fuss
kick kick up a row
kick kick up one's heels
kid handle someone with kid gloves
kid kids' stuff
kill in at the kill
kill kill the fatted calf
kill kill time
killer lady-killer
kilter out of kilter
kind nothing of the kind
kindness milk of human kindness
king fit for a king
kiss kiss of death
kitchen everything but the kitchen sink
kite fly a kite
knit knit one's brow
knock knock about (somewhere)
knock knock around (somewhere)
knock knock people's heads together
knock knock someone cold
knock knock someone dead
knock knock someone down with a feather
knot at a rate of knots
knot tie someone in knots
knot tie the knot
know know a thing or two (about someone or something)
know know all the tricks of the trade
know know one's ABC
know know one's place
know know the ropes

leg stretch one's legs
lend lend (someone) a hand
less in less than no time
less less than pleased
let let down one's hair
let let off steam
let let one's hair down
let let someone have it
let let someone off (the hook)
let let something ride
let let something slide
let let something slip (out)
let let the cat out of the bag
let let the chance slip by
let let the grass grow under one's feet
let let well alone
let live and let live
letter to the letter
level find one's own level
liberty at liberty
lick give something a lick and a promise
lick lick one's lips
lick lick something into shape
lid blow the lid off (something)
lid keep the lid on something
lie lie down on the job
lie lie through one's teeth
lie take something lying down
lieu in lieu of something
life (as) large as life (and twice as ugly)
life get the shock of one's life
life have the time of one's life
life late in life
life lead a dog's life
life life (and soul) of the party
life matter of life and death
life never in one's life
life new lease of life
life one's way of life
life run for one's life
life within an inch of one's life
lifetime once-in-a-lifetime chance
lift hitch a lift
lift not lift a finger (to help someone)
lift thumb a lift

light according to one's (own) lights
light bring something to light
light come to light
light hide one's light under a bushel
light in the light of something
light make light of something
light see the light
light see the light at the end of the tunnel
light see the light of day
lightly get off lightly
like avoid someone or something like the plague
like eat like a bird
like eat like a horse
like feel like a million dollars
like feel like a new person
like go down like a lead balloon
like go like clockwork
like like a bolt out of the blue
like like a fish out of water
like like a sitting duck
like like looking for a needle in a haystack
like like one of the family
like like sitting ducks
like like water off a duck's back
like likes of someone
like look like a million dollars
like look like the cat that swallowed the canary
like look like the cat that swallowed the cream
like read someone like a book
like stick out like a sore thumb
lily gild the lily
limb out on a limb
limelight in the limelight
limit go to the limit
line draw a line between something and something else
line fall into line
line in the line of duty
line keep someone in line
line lay something on the line
line out of line
line out of line (with something)

make make (both) ends meet
make make a beeline for someone or something
make make a clean breast of something
make make a clean sweep
make make a comeback
make make a face
make make a go of it
make make a great show of something
make make a mountain out of a molehill
make make a name for oneself
make make a pitch for someone or something
make make a point of (doing) something
make make an example of someone
make make cracks (about someone or something)
make make do (with someone or something)
make make eyes at someone
make make fun of someone or something
make make good as something
make make good money
make make good time
make make it worth someone's while
make make light of something
make make merry
make make mischief
make make no bones about something
make make nothing of it
make make oneself at home
make make or break someone
make make someone look good
make make someone's blood boil
make make someone's blood run cold
make make someone's hair stand on end
make make someone's head spin
make make someone's head swim

make make someone's mouth water
make make something from scratch
make make something to order
make make the feathers fly
make make the fur fly
make make the grade
make make up for lost time
man odd man out
manger dog in the manger
many have too many irons in the fire
march give one one's marching orders
march steal a march on someone
marine Tell it to the marines.
mark mark my word(s)
market glut on the market
market in the market (for something)
market play the market
marrow chilled to the marrow
mast at half-mast
mast nail one's colours to the mast
match meet one's match
match whole (bang) shooting match
matter crux of the matter
matter matter-of-fact
matter matter of life and death
matter matter of opinion
me (all) Greek to me
me Greek to me
me hand-me-down
meal square meal
mealy mealy-mouthed
mean by no means
medicine dose of one's own medicine
medicine take one's medicine
medium strike a happy medium
meet hail-fellow-well-met
meet make (both) ends meet
meet meet one's end
meet meet one's match
meet meet one's Waterloo
meet meet someone half-way

more More fool you!
more more's the pity
more wear more than one hat
mother old enough to be someone's mother
mother tied to one's mother's apron-strings
motion go through the motions
mould cast in the same mould
mountain make a mountain out of a molehill
mouse play cat and mouse (with someone)
mouth born with a silver spoon in one's mouth
mouth by word of mouth
mouth down in the mouth
mouth foam at the mouth
mouth have a big mouth
mouth keep one's mouth shut (about someone or something)
mouth leave a bad taste in someone's mouth
mouth live from hand to mouth
mouth look as if butter wouldn't melt in one's mouth
mouth make someone's mouth water
mouth mealy-mouthed
mouth melt in one's mouth
mouth not open one's mouth
mouth put words into someone's mouth
mouth Put your money where your mouth is!
mouth take the words (right) out of one's mouth
move move heaven and earth to do something
move not move a muscle
move prime mover
much much ado about nothing
much much of a muchness
much much sought after
muchness much of a muchness
mum mum's the word
muscle not move a muscle
music face the music
must needs must

muster pass muster
my mark my word(s)
my never darken my door again
my over my dead body
nail nail in someone's or something's coffin
nail nail one's colours to the mast
naked naked eye
name in name only
name make a name for oneself
name name of the game
name on a first-name basis (with someone)
name on first-name terms (with someone)
natural die a natural death
nature call of nature
nature second nature to someone
near (as) near as dammit
near have a near miss
near in the near future
near near the bone
near near the knuckle
necessity out of necessity
neck breathe down someone's neck
neck millstone around one's neck
neck neck and neck
neck pain in the neck
neck risk one's neck (to do something)
neck stick one's neck out
need needs must
needle like looking for a needle in a haystack
needle pins and needles
neither neither fish nor fowl
neither neither hide nor hair
nest feather one's (own) nest
nest foul one's own nest
nest stir up a hornets' nest
nettle grasp the nettle
never never darken my door again
never never fear
never never had it so good
never never in one's life
never never mind
new break new ground
new feel like a new person

not not for the world
not not give someone the time of day
not not half bad
not not have a care in the world
not not hold water
not not in the same league as someone or something
not not know someone from Adam
not not lift a finger (to help someone)
not not long for this world
not not move a muscle
not not open one's mouth
not not see further than the end of one's nose
not not set foot somewhere
not not show one's face
not not sleep a wink
not not someone's cup of tea
not not take no for an answer
not not to darken someone's door
not not up to scratch
not not utter a word
not not worth a candle
not not worth a penny
note strike the right note
nothing good-for-nothing
nothing make nothing of it
nothing much ado about nothing
nothing nothing but skin and bones
nothing nothing of the kind
nothing nothing short of something
nothing nothing to it
nothing nothing to write home about
notice escape someone's notice
notice serve notice
nowhere come out of nowhere
nowhere get nowhere fast
nowhere in the middle of nowhere
null null and void
number get someone's number
number one's days are numbered
nut nuts and bolts (of something)

nutshell in a nutshell
oar put one's oar in
oar shove one's oar in
oar stick one's oar in
object expense is no object
object money is no object
occasion rise to the occasion
odd odd man out
odd over the odds
odour odour of sanctity
of afraid of one's own shadow
of air of sanctity
of all hours (of the day and night)
of apple of someone's eye
of at a rate of knots
of at the bottom of the ladder
of at the drop of a hat
of at the end of one's tether
of at the expense of someone or something
of at the top of one's voice
of back of beyond
of baptism of fire
of bed of roses
of beyond the shadow of a doubt
of black sheep (of the family)
of bone of contention
of business end of something
of by the seat of one's pants
of by the skin of one's teeth
of by the sweat of one's brow
of by virtue of something
of by word of mouth
of call of nature
of can't make head nor tail of someone or something
of can't see beyond the end of one's nose
of can't see one's hand in front of one's face
of carry the weight of the world on one's shoulders
of chapter of accidents
of cock of the walk
of come of age
of come out of nowhere
of come out of one's shell
of crux of the matter
of die of a broken heart

of matter of life and death
of matter of opinion
of middle-of-the-road
of milk of human kindness
of mine of information
of moment of truth
of much of a muchness
of name of the game
of new lease of life
of Not a bit (of it).
of not breathe a word (of something)
of not give someone the time of day
of not see further than the end of one's nose
of not someone's cup of tea
of nothing of the kind
of nothing short of something
of nuts and bolts (of something)
of odour of sanctity
of of the first water
of of the old school
of on behalf of someone
of on the eve of something
of on the face of it
of on the horns of a dilemma
of on the spur of the moment
of on the strength of something
of on the tip of one's tongue
of on top of the world
of one's way of life
of open a can of worms
of order of the day
of out of kilter
of out of line
of out of line (with something)
of out of luck
of out of necessity
of out of one's mind
of out of order
of out of place
of out-of-pocket expenses
of out of practice
of out of print
of out of season
of out of service
of out of sorts
of out of stock

of out of the blue
of out of the corner of one's eye
of out of the frying-pan into the fire
of out of the question
of out of the running
of out of the swim of things
of out of the woods
of out of thin air
of out of this world
of out of turn
of out of work
of part and parcel of something
of parting of the ways
of pass the time of day (with someone)
of piece of cake
of presence of mind
of pretty kettle of fish
of pride of place
of pull something out of a hat
of pull something out of thin air
of put someone in mind of someone or something
of put someone's nose out of joint
of run of the mill
of salt of the earth
of scrape the bottom of the barrel
of see the light at the end of the tunnel
of see the light of day
of shades of someone or something
of show of hands
of (sitting) on top of the world
of six of one and half a dozen of the other
of slice of the cake
of slip of the tongue
of smell of the lamp
of speak of the devil
of speak out of turn
of spoil the ship for a ha'porth of tar
of survival of the fittest
of take a leaf out of someone's book
of take leave of one's senses

on hang on by one's eyebrows
on hang on someone's every word
on hang on to someone's coat-tails
on Hang on to your hat!
on hard on someone's heels
on hard on the heels of something
on have a chip on one's shoulder
on have a down on someone
on have a good head on one's shoulders
on have a price on one's head
on have egg on one's face
on have one's feet on the ground
on have someone on a string
on have someone or something on
on have something on file
on have something on one's hands
on have something on the brain
on Hold on to your hat!
on hot on something
on jump on someone
on keen on someone or something
on keep one's eye on the ball
on keep one's feet on the ground
on keep someone on a string
on keep someone on tenterhooks
on keep the lid on something
on land on both feet
on land on one's feet
on lay something on the line
on lead someone (on) a merry chase
on lead someone (on) a merry dance
on lie down on the job
on live on borrowed time
on lost on someone
on make someone's hair stand on end
on new one on someone
on night on the town
on on a first-name basis (with someone)
on on a fool's errand
on on a par with someone or something
on on active duty
on on all fours

on on average
on on behalf of someone
on on cloud nine
on on first-name terms (with someone)
on on holiday
on on one's (own) head be it
on on one's feet
on on one's guard
on on one's honour
on on one's mind
on on one's toes
on on order
on on record
on on sale
on on second thoughts
on on someone's behalf
on on the air
on on the alert (for someone or something)
on on the cards
on on the dot
on on the eve of something
on on the face of it
on on the horns of a dilemma
on on the loose
on on the mend
on on the off-chance
on on the sly
on on the spot
on on the spur of the moment
on on the strength of something
on on the tip of one's tongue
on on thin ice
on on tiptoe
on on top of the world
on one-up (on someone)
on open fire (on someone)
on out on a limb
on out on parole
on pick on someone
on pin one's faith on someone or something
on play on something
on play tricks (on someone)
on pour cold water on something
on pour oil on troubled waters
on pride oneself on something
on put a brave face on it

open leave oneself wide open for something

open leave oneself wide open to something

open not open one's mouth

open open a can of worms

open open-and-shut case

open open book

open open fire (on someone)

open open one's heart (to someone)

open open Pandora's box

open open season for something

open open secret

open open the door to something

open receive someone with open arms

open welcome someone with open arms

opinion in one's opinion

opinion matter of opinion

opportunity jump at the opportunity (to do something)

opportunity leap at the opportunity (to do something)

or believe it or not

or (come) rain or shine

or either feast or famine

or make or break someone

or no ifs or buts about it

or rain or shine

or sink or swim

or take someone down a peg (or two)

or without rhyme or reason

order give one one's marching orders

order just what the doctor ordered

order make something to order

order on order

order order of the day

order out of order

order put one's house in order

other go in one ear and out the other

other have other fish to fry

other in one ear and out the other

other in other words

other look the other way

other other way round

other six of one and half a dozen of the other

other turn the other cheek

other with every other breath

our sink our differences

out come out in the wash

out come out of nowhere

out come out of one's shell

out cry one's eyes out

out dine out on something

out eat one's heart out

out eat out of someone's hands

out eat someone out of house and home

out get one's nose out of someone's business

out get out of the wrong side of the bed

out get something out of one's system

out go in one ear and out the other

out have an out

out have one's work cut out (for one)

out have something out (with someone)

out hold out the olive branch

out in one ear and out the other

out jump out of one's skin

out keep an eye out (for someone or something)

out laugh something out of court

out let something slip (out)

out let the cat out of the bag

out like a bolt out of the blue

out like a fish out of water

out make a mountain out of a molehill

out odd man out

out out of kilter

out out of line

out out of line (with something)

out out of luck

out out of necessity

out out of one's mind

own sign one's own death-warrant
own stew in one's own juice
P's mind one's P's and Q's
pace put one through one's paces
pace show one's paces
pack pack someone off (to somewhere)
pack pack them in
pack packed out
pack send someone packing
paddle paddle one's own canoe
paid put paid to something
pain pain in the neck
paint as black as one is painted
pale beyond the pale
pale pale around the gills
palm have an itching palm
palm have an itchy palm
pan flash in the pan
pan out of the frying-pan into the fire
Pandora open Pandora's box
pants by the seat of one's pants
pants have ants in one's pants
paper paper over the cracks (in something)
paper put something on paper
par on a par with someone or something
par par for the course
paradise fool's paradise
parcel part and parcel of something
pare cheese-paring
paring cheese-paring
parole out on parole
parrot parrot-fashion
part in part
part part and parcel of something
part parting of the ways
party life (and soul) of the party
party party line
party throw a party (for someone)
pass come to a pretty pass
pass pass as someone or something
pass pass muster
pass pass the buck

pass pass the hat round
pass pass the time of day (with someone)
pass ships that pass in the night
past past it
past past someone's or something's best
past past someone's or something's sell-by date
pasture (fresh fields and) pastures new
pasture put someone or something out to pasture
path lead someone up the garden path
patience try someone's patience
Paul rob Peter to pay Paul
pause give someone pause for thought
pay pay an arm and a leg (for something)
pay pay lip-service (to something)
pay pay one's debt to society
pay pay one's dues
pay pay someone a back-handed compliment
pay pay someone a compliment
pay pay the earth
pay pay the piper
pay pay through the nose (for something)
pay rob Peter to pay Paul
peace hold one's peace
peak in the peak of condition
pedestal put someone on a pedestal
peg square peg in a round hole
peg take someone down a peg (or two)
penchant have a penchant for doing something
penny cost a pretty penny
penny not worth a penny
penny spend a penny
penny ten a penny
penny two a penny
people knock people's heads together
person feel like a new person

play play up
play play up to someone
play play with fire
play played out
play two can play at that game
please (as) pleased as Punch
please less than pleased
plough put one's hand to the plough
pluck pluck up (one's) courage
pocket have someone in one's pocket
pocket out-of-pocket expenses
poetic poetic justice
point have a low boiling-point
point jumping-off point
point make a point of (doing) something
point miss the point
point point the finger at someone
point touch a sore point
poke buy a pig in a poke
poke poke fun (at someone or something)
pole be poles apart
politics play politics
port any port in a storm
position jockey for position
possum play possum
post by return post
post from pillar to post
post keep someone posted
post pipped at the post
pot pot calling the kettle black
pound pound for pound
pound pound the streets
pour pour cold water on something
pour pour money down the drain
pour pour oil on troubled waters
powder sitting on a powder keg
power have no staying-power
power power behind the throne
power powers that be
practice out of practice
practice sharp practice
practise practise what you preach
praise damn someone or something with faint praise

praise praise someone or something to the skies
praise sing someone's praises
preach practise what you preach
preach preach to the converted
presence presence of mind
press press-gang someone into doing something
pretty come to a pretty pass
pretty cost a pretty penny
pretty in a (pretty) pickle
pretty pretty kettle of fish
pretty sitting pretty
price have a price on one's head
prick prick up one's ears
pride pride of place
pride pride oneself on something
pride swallow one's pride
prime prime mover
print out of print
probability in all probability
progress in progress
promise give something a lick and a promise
proper go through the proper channels
proud do someone proud
proud house-proud
public in the public eye
pull pull a face
pull pull a fast one
pull pull one's punches
pull pull one's socks up
pull pull oneself together
pull pull oneself up by one's bootstraps
pull pull out all the stops
pull pull someone's leg
pull pull something out of a hat
pull pull something out of thin air
pull pull strings
pull pull the rug out from under someone('s feet)
pull pull the wool over someone's eyes
Punch (as) pleased as Punch
punch pull one's punches
punishment glutton for punishment

raring rarin' to go
rat rat race
rate at a rate of knots
rave rant and rave
raw in the raw
read read between the lines
read read someone like a book
read read someone the Riot Act
read read someone's mind
read read something into something
read take something as read
rear rear its ugly head
reason listen to reason
reason lose one's reason
reason stand to reason
reason without rhyme or reason
receive receive someone with open arms
record for the record
record on record
record one for the record (books)
record set the record straight
red draw a red herring
red red herring
red red tape
red see red
redbrick redbrick university
regain regain one's composure
rest rest on one's laurels
retreat beat a (hasty) retreat
return by return post
return return ticket
rhyme without rhyme or reason
riches from rags to riches
riddance good riddance (to bad rubbish)
ride let something ride
ride ride roughshod over someone or something
ride riding for a fall
right give one's right arm (for someone or something)
right have the right of way
right hit someone (right) between the eyes
right in one's right mind
right left, right, and centre
right play one's cards right

right put something right
right right up someone's street
right set something right
right strike the right note
right take the words (right) out of one's mouth
ring have a familiar ring
ring ring a bell
ring ring down the curtain (on something)
ring ring in the New Year
ring ring off
ring ring someone or something up
ring ring the changes
ring ring true
ring ring up someone or something
riot read someone the Riot Act
riot run riot
ripe ripe old age
ripe when the time is ripe
rise rise and shine
rise rise to the occasion
risk risk one's neck (to do something)
road get the show on the road
road middle-of-the-road
road road-hog
rob rob Peter to pay Paul
robbery daylight robbery
Robinson before you can say Jack Robinson
rock hit rock bottom
rock rock the boat
roll get the ball rolling
roll heads will roll
roll keep the ball rolling
roll roll on something
roll set the ball rolling
roll start the ball rolling
Rome fiddle while Rome burns
romp romp home
roost come home to roost
roost rule the roost
root rooted to the spot
rope know the ropes
rope learn the ropes
rope money for old rope

say say the word
scale tip the scales at something
scare scare someone stiff
school of the old school
school tell tales out of school
scrape bow and scrape
scrape pinch and scrape
scrape scrape the bottom of the barrel
scratch make something from scratch
scratch not up to scratch
scratch scratch someone's back
scratch scratch the surface
screw screw up one's courage
scrimp scrimp and save
sea (all) at sea (about something)
seal signed, sealed, and delivered
seam fall apart at the seams
search search something with a fine-tooth comb
season open season for something
season out of season
season silly season
seat by the seat of one's pants
second come off second-best
second get one's second wind
second in (just) a second
second in a split second
second in one's second childhood
second on second thoughts
second play second fiddle (to someone)
second second nature to someone
second second to none
secret open secret
see can't see beyond the end of one's nose
see can't see one's hand in front of one's face
see not able to see the wood for the trees
see not see further than the end of one's nose
see see double
see see eye to eye (about something)
see see eye to eye (on something)

see see red
see see someone home
see see something with half an eye
see see stars
see see the light
see see the light at the end of the tunnel
see see the light of day
see see the writing on the wall
see seeing is believing
seed go to seed
seed run to seed
seen have seen better days
sell past someone's or something's sell-by date
sell sell someone a pup
sell sell someone or something short
send send someone or something up
send send someone packing
send send someone to Coventry
sense horse sense
sense in a sense
sense sixth sense
sense take leave of one's senses
separate separate the men from the boys
separate separate the sheep from the goats
separate separate the wheat from the chaff
serve serve as a guinea pig
serve serve notice
service out of service
service pay lip-service (to something)
set dead set against someone or something
set not set foot somewhere
set set foot somewhere
set set great store by someone or something
set set one back on one's heels
set set someone straight
set set someone's teeth on edge
set set something right
set set the ball rolling

show show the white feather
show steal the show
shut keep one's mouth shut (about someone or something)
shut open-and-shut case
shut shut up shop
shy fight shy of something
side be a thorn in someone's side
side get on the good side of someone
side get out of the wrong side of the bed
side keep one's side of the bargain
sight love at first sight
sight lower one's sights
sight raise one's sights
sign sign one's own death-warrant
sign signed, sealed, and delivered
silly silly season
silver born with a silver spoon in one's mouth
since since the year dot
sing sing someone's praises
single (in) single file
sink everything but the kitchen sink
sink sink or swim
sink sink our differences
sinker swallow something hook, line, and sinker
sit like a sitting duck
sit like sitting ducks
sit sit (idly) by
sit sit at someone's feet
sit sit on one's hands
sit sitting on a powder keg
sit (sitting) on top of the world
sit sitting pretty
six at sixes and sevens
six six of one and half a dozen of the other
six sixth sense
size cut someone down to size
skate skate over something
skate (skating) on thin ice
skeleton skeleton in the cupboard
skin all skin and bones
skin by the skin of one's teeth

skin get under someone's skin
skin jump out of one's skin
skin no skin off someone's nose
skin nothing but skin and bones
skin save someone's skin
skin thick-skinned
skin thin-skinned
sky go sky-high
sky pie in the sky
sky praise someone or something to the skies
slap get a slap on the wrist
slate slate something
slate start (off) with a clean slate
sleep not sleep a wink
sleeve have something up one's sleeve
sleeve laugh up one's sleeve
slice slice of the cake
slide let something slide
slip let something slip (out)
slip let the chance slip by
slip slip of the tongue
sly on the sly
small be thankful for small mercies
small small hours
smell smell of the lamp
smoke Put that in your pipe and smoke it!
smooth take the rough with the smooth
snag hit a snag
snake snake in the grass
snook cock a snook at someone
snowball have a snowball's chance in hell
so go so far as to say something
so never had it so good
society pay one's debt to society
socks pull one's socks up
soft have a soft spot for someone or something
some put out (some) feelers
song buy something for a song
song swan-song
soon no sooner said than done
sore stick out like a sore thumb
sore touch a sore point

stick something sticks in one's craw
stick stick it out
stick stick one's neck out
stick stick one's oar in
stick stick out like a sore thumb
stick stick to one's guns
stiff keep a stiff upper lip
stiff scare someone stiff
stir stir up a hornets' nest
stitch keep someone in stitches
stock have something in stock
stock in stock
stock lock, stock, and barrel
stock out of stock
stomach get butterflies in one's stomach
stomach one's eyes are bigger than one's stomach
stone have a heart of stone
stone leave no stone unturned
stool fall between two stools
stop pull out all the stops
store have something in store (for someone)
store set great store by someone or something
storm any port in a storm
storm storm in a teacup
story cock-and-bull story
story cut a long story short
story same old story
story shaggy-dog story
straight give it to someone straight
straight keep a straight face
straight set someone straight
straight set the record straight
straight straight away
straight straight from the shoulder
straw clutch at straws
straw straw in the wind
stream change horses in mid-stream
Street in Queer Street
street pound the streets
street right up someone's street

strength on the strength of something
stretch at full stretch
stretch stretch one's legs
stride take something in one's stride
strike strike a bargain
strike strike a chord
strike strike a happy medium
strike strike the right note
strike strike while the iron is hot
string get by (on a shoe-string)
string have someone on a string
string keep someone on a string
string pull strings
string tied to one's mother's apron-strings
stuff kids' stuff
stuff stuff and nonsense
stumble stumbling-block
style cramp someone's style
suck teach one's grandmother to suck eggs
sugar sugar the pill
suit cut one's coat to suit one's cloth
suit follow suit
suit in one's birthday suit
suit suit someone down to the ground
suit suit someone to a T
sun catch the sun
surface scratch the surface
survival survival of the fittest
swallow bitter pill to swallow
swallow look like the cat that swallowed the canary
swallow look like the cat that swallowed the cream
swallow swallow one's pride
swallow swallow something hook, line, and sinker
swan swan around
swan swan-song
sweat by the sweat of one's brow
sweep make a clean sweep
sweep sweep something under the carpet
sweet have a sweet tooth

sweet short and sweet
sweet sweeten the pill
swim in the swim (of things)
swim make someone's head swim
swim out of the swim of things
swim sink or swim
swim swim against the tide
swing get into full swing
swing get into the swing of things
swing in full swing
sword cross swords (with someone)
sympathy extend one's sympathy (to someone)
system get something out of one's system
T suit someone to a T
table lay the table
table set the table
table turn the tables (on someone)
tack get down to brass tacks
tail can't make head nor tail of someone or something
tail hang on to someone's coat-tails
tail in two shakes of a lamb's tail
tail tail wagging the dog
take as a duck takes to water
take do a double take
take have what it takes
take not take no for an answer
take take a leaf out of someone's book
take take a stab at something
take take leave of one's senses
take take one's medicine
take take someone down a peg (or two)
take take someone to task
take take someone under one's wing
take take something as read
take take something in one's stride
take take something lying down
take take something on the chin
take take something to heart

take take the rough with the smooth
take take the wind out of someone's sails
take take the words (right) out of one's mouth
take take up the cudgels on behalf of someone or something
tale tell tales out of school
talk have a heart-to-heart (talk)
talk money talks
talk talk nineteen to the dozen
talk talk of the town
talk talk through one's hat
talk talk until one is blue in the face
talk talking-shop
tangent go off at a tangent
tape red tape
tar spoil the ship for a ha'porth of tar
tar tarred with the same brush
task take someone to task
taste leave a bad taste in someone's mouth
tat give someone tit for tat
tea not someone's cup of tea
teach teach one's grandmother to suck eggs
teacup storm in a teacup
teeth armed to the teeth
teeth by the skin of one's teeth
teeth cut one's eye-teeth on something
teeth cut one's teeth on something
teeth cut teeth
teeth get one's teeth into something
teeth grit one's teeth
teeth lie through one's teeth
teeth set someone's teeth on edge
teeth show one's teeth
telegraph bush telegraph
tell Tell it to the marines.
tell tell tales out of school
temper lose one's temper
temperature run a temperature

ten ten a penny
tenterhook keep someone on tenterhooks
term contradiction in terms
term on first-name terms (with someone)
test put someone to the test
tether at the end of one's tether
than holier-than-thou
than in less than no time
than less than pleased
than no sooner said than done
than not see further than the end of one's nose
than one's eyes are bigger than one's stomach
than wear more than one hat
thank thank one's lucky stars
thankful be thankful for small mercies
that bite the hand that feeds one
that hair of the dog (that bit one)
that look like the cat that swallowed the canary
that look like the cat that swallowed the cream
that powers that be
that Put that in your pipe and smoke it!
that ships that pass in the night
that two can play at that game
them pack them in
thick (as) thick as thieves
thick (as) thick as two short planks
thick thick and fast
thick thick-skinned
thick through thick and thin
thief (as) thick as thieves
thieves (as) thick as thieves
thin (as) thin as a rake
thin have a thin time (of it)
thin on thin ice
thin out of thin air
thin pull something out of thin air
thin (skating) on thin ice
thin spread oneself too thin
thin thin end of the wedge
thin thin on the ground

thin thin-skinned
thin through thick and thin
thin vanish into thin air
thing get into the swing of things
thing in the swim (of things)
thing in thing (to do)
thing know a thing or two (about someone or something)
thing out of the swim of things
think have another think coming
think put on one's thinking-cap
this in this day and age
this not long for this world
this out of this world
Thomas doubting Thomas
thorn be a thorn in someone's side
thou holier-than-thou
thought food for thought
thought give someone pause for thought
thought lose one's train of thought
thought lost in thought
thought on second thoughts
thousand one in a thousand
thread hang by a thread
throat get a lump in one's throat
throat jump down someone's throat
throat one's words stick in one's throat
throne power behind the throne
through go through something with a fine-tooth comb
through go through the motions
through go through the proper channels
through have been through the mill
through lie through one's teeth
through pay through the nose (for something)
through put one through one's paces
through put someone through the wringer
through sail through something
through talk through one's hat

to come to grief
to come to light
to come to the fore
to cross a bridge before one comes to it
to cross one's heart (and hope to die)
to cut one's coat according to one's cloth
to cut one's coat to suit one's cloth
to cut someone down to size
to cut someone to the quick
to dead to the world
to death to something
to do justice to something
to done to a turn
to down to earth
to dressed (up) to the nines
to everything from A to Z
to extend one's sympathy (to someone)
to eyeball to eyeball
to feel it beneath one (to do something)
to find it in one's heart to do something
to find time to catch one's breath
to fools rush in (where angels fear to tread)
to from pillar to post
to from rags to riches
to from stem to stern
to generous to a fault
to get down to brass tacks
to get down to business
to get off to a flying start
to get time to catch one's breath
to get to one's feet
to get to the bottom of something
to get what is coming to one
to give it to someone straight
to give voice to something
to go from bad to worse
to go so far as to say something
to go to Davy Jones's locker
to go to hell
to go to rack and ruin
to go to seed

to go to someone's head
to go to the devil
to go to the limit
to go to the loo
to go to the toilet
to go to the wall
to go to town
to go to waste
to good riddance (to bad rubbish)
to Greek to me
to grind to a halt
to grist to the mill
to hand it to someone
to hang on to someone's coat-tails
to Hang on to your hat!
to hardly have time to breathe
to hark(en) back to something
to have a bone to pick (with someone)
to have a heart-to-heart (talk)
to have an axe to grind
to have half a mind to do something
to have money to burn
to have one's back to the wall
to have one's ear to the ground
to have other fish to fry
to have something coming to one
to have the wherewithal (to do something)
to have to live with something
to here's to someone or something
to Hold on to your hat!
to in no mood to do something
to in thing (to do)
to jump at the chance (to do something)
to jump at the opportunity (to do something)
to keep one's cards close to one's chest
to keep one's ear to the ground
to keep one's nose to the grindstone
to keep oneself to oneself
to lead someone to believe something
to lead someone to do something

toe on one's toes
toe step on someone's toes
toe toe the line
toe tread on someone's toes
together keep body and soul together
together knock people's heads together
together pull oneself together
together put two and two together
toilet go to the toilet
token by the same token
Tom (every) Tom, Dick, and Harry
tomorrow jam tomorrow
tongue Cat got your tongue?
tongue cause tongues to wag
tongue find one's tongue
tongue get a tongue-lashing
tongue hold one's tongue
tongue keep a civil tongue (in one's head)
tongue on the tip of one's tongue
tongue slip of the tongue
tongue tongue-in-cheek
too cut it (too) fine
too have too many irons in the fire
too none too something
too spread oneself too thin
tooth armed to the teeth
tooth by the skin of one's teeth
tooth cut one's eye-teeth on something
tooth cut one's teeth on something
tooth cut teeth
tooth get one's teeth into something
tooth go over something with a fine-tooth comb
tooth go through something with a fine-tooth comb
tooth grit one's teeth
tooth have a sweet tooth
tooth lie through one's teeth
tooth search something with a fine-tooth comb

tooth set someone's teeth on edge
tooth show one's teeth
top at the top of one's voice
top on top of the world
top over the top
top (sitting) on top of the world
torch carry a torch for someone
touch have the Midas touch
touch touch a sore point
touch touch a sore spot
touch touch-and-go
touch touch wood
tower live in an ivory tower
town go to town
town night on the town
town talk of the town
track drop in one's tracks
track off the beaten track
trade jack-of-all-trades
trade know all the tricks of the trade
trade trade on something
train lose one's train of thought
tread fools rush in (where angels fear to tread)
tread tread on someone's toes
tree not able to see the wood for the trees
tremble in fear and trembling
trespass no trespassing
trick do the trick
trick know all the tricks of the trade
trick play tricks (on someone)
trick use every trick in the book
trouble fish in troubled waters
trouble pour oil on troubled waters
true dream come true
true hold true
true moment of truth
true ring true
true show oneself in one's true colours
true true to one's word
trump play one's trump card
trump turn up trumps
trumpet blow one's own trumpet

up look up to someone
up make up for lost time
up not up to scratch
up one-up (on someone)
up play up
up play up to someone
up pluck up (one's) courage
up prick up one's ears
up pull one's socks up
up pull oneself up by one's bootstraps
up put someone up to something
up put up a (brave) front
up queue up
up right up someone's street
up ring someone or something up
up ring up someone or something
up rub someone up the wrong way
up screw up one's courage
up send someone or something up
up set up shop somewhere
up shut up shop
up stir up a hornets' nest
up take up the cudgels on behalf of someone or something
up turn up trumps
up up a blind alley
up up and doing
up up in arms
up up in the air
up up to no good
up well up in something
upon once upon a time
upon put upon someone
upon set upon someone or something
uppance get one's come-uppance
upper keep a stiff upper lip
upper upper crust
upset upset the applecart
uptake quick on the uptake
use use every trick in the book
utter not utter a word
vain in vain
value face value
vanish vanish into thin air
velvet iron hand in a velvet glove

vent vent one's spleen
verse chapter and verse
vex vexed question
villain villain of the piece
vine wither on the vine
virtue by virtue of something
visit flying visit
voice at the top of one's voice
voice give voice to something
voice have a voice (in something)
voice lower one's voice
void null and void
voyage maiden voyage
vulture culture vulture
wag cause tongues to wag
wag tail wagging the dog
wait not able to wait
wait waiting in the wings
walk cock of the walk
walk walk a tightrope
walk walk on air
walk walk on eggs
wall drive someone up the wall
wall go to the wall
wall have one's back to the wall
wall see the writing on the wall
wall walls have ears
want want it both ways
warm warm the cockles of someone's heart
warrant sign one's own death-warrant
wart warts and all
wash come out in the wash
waste go to waste
water as a duck takes to water
water fish in troubled waters
water hold water
water in deep water
water keep one's head above water
water like a fish out of water
water like water off a duck's back
water make someone's mouth water
water not hold water
water of the first water
water pour cold water on something

wind in the wind
wind straw in the wind
wind take the wind out of someone's sails
wind throw caution to the winds
wing clip someone's wings
wing take someone under one's wing
wing try one's wings
wing waiting in the wings
wink not sleep a wink
wink tip someone the wink
wise put someone wise to someone or something
wise wise after the event
wiser none the wiser
wish wish someone joy of something
wit at one's wits' end
wit have one's wits about one
wit keep one's wits about one
wit live by one's wits
with at loggerheads (with someone)
with born with a silver spoon in one's mouth
with come down with something
with cross swords (with someone)
with curry favour (with someone)
with damn someone or something with faint praise
with fix someone up (with something)
with go over something with a fine-tooth comb
with go through something with a fine-tooth comb
with green with envy
with hand in glove (with someone)
with handle someone with kid gloves
with have a bone to pick (with someone)
with have a brush with something
with have a word with someone
with have something out (with someone)

with have to live with something
with head over heels in love (with someone)
with hit it off (with someone)
with in league (with someone)
with keep in with someone
with knock someone down with a feather
with leave word (with someone)
with lock horns (with someone)
with make do (with someone or something)
with on a first-name basis (with someone)
with on a par with someone or something
with on first-name terms (with someone)
with out of line (with something)
with over and done with
with pass the time of day (with someone)
with pick a quarrel (with someone)
with play cat and mouse (with someone)
with play fast and loose (with someone or something)
with play havoc with someone or something
with play with fire
with quids in with someone
with receive someone with open arms
with rub along with someone
with rub shoulders (with someone)
with search something with a fine-tooth comb
with see something with half an eye
with start (off) with a clean slate
with take the rough with the smooth
with tarred with the same brush
with welcome someone with open arms
with with all one's heart and soul
with with every other breath

write nothing to write home about

write see the writing on the wall

wrong get out of the wrong side of the bed

wrong rub someone up the wrong way

wrongfoot wrongfoot someone

year advanced in years

year donkey's years

year from the year dot

year getting on (in years)

year ring in the New Year

year since the year dot

yesterday not born yesterday

you before you can say Jack Robinson

you mind you

you More fool you!

you practise what you preach

your Cat got your tongue?

your Hang on to your hat!

your Hold on to your hat!

your Put that in your pipe and smoke it!

your Put your money where your mouth is!

Z everything from A to Z

zero zero hour